S0-BOD-888

"Running Down Your Dreams"

By
Joseph W. Sharp

For more resources on putting your dreams into action, visit:
www.runningdownyourdreams.com

Running Down Your Dreams

Published by:
Live With Purpose Publishing
Lancaster, PA 17603
www.livewithpurposecoaching.com

ISBN# 978-1470044848

Copyright © 2011 by Joseph W. Sharp

Printed in the United States of America

No part of this publication may be reproduced, stored in a retrieval system, or transmitted in any form by any means—electronic, mechanical, digital photocopy, recording, or any other without the prior permission of the author.

All rights reserved solely by the author. The author guarantees all contents are original and do not infringe upon the legal rights of any other person or work. No part of this book may be reproduced in any form without the permission of the author.

Scripture quotations taken from the Holy Bible, New International Version®. Copyright © 1973, 1978, 1984 Biblica. Used by permission of Zondervan. All rights reserved. All Scripture quotations unless indicated otherwise are taken from the New International Version® of the Holy Bible.

Prelude:

I never saw myself as a writer. I might have been writing poetry for several decades but I only I saw it as a hobby. I began my successful entrepreneurial career at the age of twenty. After many twists and turns that come with creating and launching a wide range of businesses, traveling the world and facing a multitude of unique life adversities, the dream of writing this book began to take shape. It took patience and perseverance. My desire is to help you leverage the lessons, dreams, and wisdom found within each chapter so you can be propelled with greater velocity towards each of your dreams!

I am challenging you to walk with me through a 40-day journey. I encourage you to read one chapter per day and reflect on the reading, your dreams, and your life at large. This book is a compilation of short stories within ten main areas of life that we all face at some level. Some are interviews conducted with a wide variety of personalities, and others are taken from my own life. They will all help you as you pursue running down your dreams and striving to live a life of deep purpose and meaning.

I recognize that you might not connect with every story personally; however, what I believe will happen as we go through this 40-day journey together is that your dreams will become clearer. Maybe some new dreams to pursue will take form. Perhaps you will gain the confidence you need to finally take action on the dreams that have been close to your heart for many years. If you feel stuck in a rut, maybe your eyes will be open to a whole new way to live life that is full of passion and purpose. The only three ground rules I'd like to outline for you before you begin this journey are:

1. All of your dreams are possible. Nothing is too silly, and nothing is impossible. You need to go through this journey with that mindset.

2. Open your mind to new ideas. If you remain open and truly listen to the core messages behind each chapter, I believe you will be best prepared to take from the journey what is uniquely there for you so you can apply to it the pursuit of your dreams.

3. Read one chapter each day, and take time daily to reflect on what you read in each story before you continue on to the next chapter. You will get the most out of this book if you walk with me through the journey side by side, and don't rush ahead.

Through forty powerful, real life stories I believe I can encourage and impart wisdom if you are searching for...

- Your purpose in life
- The strength and courage to run down your dreams in life
- How to channel your passion in life
- Greater understanding of your unique abilities and spiritual gifts in life
- How to transform your life to be one full of deep meaning and purpose

I pray that when you are done reading this book, you will not only have practical insights to apply to your life but also concrete plans that will help you realize your dreams. A dream is nothing more than a thought in your mind until you truly have the courage to take action. I desire to give you greater clarity and confidence as you pursue your current dreams, and I equally desire to help spur you on towards new dreams yet to be realized in your life. I believe my deepest purpose in life is to serve God by passionately helping others to learn just how to "run down their dreams," and go places I will personally never go. Your dreams are truly unique. You are the only one on this planet who is uniquely qualified to complete them for the betterment of the world and God's glory. Will you join me now on this 40-day journey as you walk towards running down your dreams?

Dedications:

I would have never been in a place to write this book if it wouldn't be for the amazing relationships in my life. I certainly grew up in a non-traditional way with a childhood full of unique challenges that many children never have to face. I am thankful to God though for the strength in character that was fashioned in me through my early years. I have for a long time said that my father, and my grandmother symbolize a lot of who I am. Today, I wear a cross on my neck that symbolizes the most special relationships in life. I'll tell you more about that as you read this book. Woven through engraving on the back is both of their names: "Robert" and "Esther" in honor of them. My father was a man of strong work ethic, drive, determination, and loyalty. All characteristics he helped instill in me that I believe gave fuel to my entrepreneurial career that fully launched at age twenty. He taught me the value of a dollar and I believe that appreciation today grounds me to not live for the accumulation of money. My grandmother on the other hand is alive today in her 90s and full of passion. She lives outward focused and constantly cares about others before herself, many times to a fault. I see the blessing in her gift though and I believe she taught and encouraged me to live in a similar way. I pray I spend the rest of my life on this Earth honoring her by applying the gifts she shared and growing in a like-minded way to make a beautiful contribution to the world. I am devoted to serving others through that passionate calling.

I have been blessed with some great friends that have seen me through much and have spurred me on to become a better man. God has taught me so much through my long-term relationships with Andy, Steve, Mike, and others. I have also been blessed with friends that have helped me build and maintain my businesses over the years. One of my college roommates, Nick, was the first to join me in pursuing the story of Sharp Innovations, Inc. that has been a successful business for well over a decade. Late in the first year of operation, I was fortunate to have Tom Hopta enter into my life. He has been my right-hand man, and CFO since then. I would never be where I am today without him. Tom has been a true rock of Gibraltar for me. We all need people of great commitment, dedication, and support in our lives and for that I remain eternally grateful. I have had friends/co-workers of faith which have been creative resources and back-bones for me like Paul Mindemann has. I have also been greatly blessed by some friends that have been sources of spiritual encouragement and accountability over the years. My life was ever-changed after I met my great friend Steve Charman from Sydney, Australia. A couple years later, another amazing friend and mentor, Michael Gilchrist crossed my path. They both asked me the tough questions, supported me, and have spurred me on to greater heights as I pursue my dreams in life. For that I am eternally grateful.

This book truly has been a life project that would have not been realized in the full beauty that it is today if it wasn't for my editorial team, led by Becky Shaw and Diane Moore. I am deeply thankful for everyone who dedicated their time to help me complete this life project. They took my vision and content and helped it become molded into a work that was more meaningful and impactful for you as the reader today. I'm very grateful to Peter Stevenson and Chris Divyak, who helped with the design process of the book. Also, all of the photography was shot by a special person in my life: Jeremy Hess. He is gifted in capturing the light of life and God's heart/character within people and situations like no other I have experienced. He actually was also led to me as my first coaching client which will forever remain sentimental to me because he was the first brick in the path that has become my coaching career through Live With Purpose Coaching.

Furthermore, how could I ever forget my coaches? They inspire me, teach me, and challenge me to always grow which I value so much. Even though I am a business and life coach, I believe the best coaches are coachable themselves. To Ed Staub, Gina Pelligrini, Adrienne Duffy, Dan Sullivan, Dan Fichtner, Dave Weidmann, Judd Buckwalter, and Pastor Steve Cornell I salute you all with deep love and appreciation and look forward to continuing this journey we call life with you by my side.

Lastly, I dedicate this book to my future bride and children, Lord willing. I look forward to reading this with you all and pouring out everything in my heart to show you the deepest love that is possible. You drive me to continue to grow as a man and leader, so one day I can be the best husband and father possible.

Endorsements:

" Joe is a passionate entrepreneur with a heart for equipping others to pursue their dreams for God's glory. Not only is this commitment evident on each page of Running Down Your Dreams, but Joe has further demonstrated his passion through his support of HOPE International, which empowers entrepreneurs living in poverty around the world."

- Jeff Rutt, Founder, HOPE International.

" I have been working with Joe in a coaching relationship for almost 2 years now, and it has changed my life. Not just my job but my life. I am a better father, husband, brother and son than I have ever been before. Joe has helped me see my dreams. This book should help many people, as Joe has helped me."

-Kyle Ingham, President, Ingham's Powder Coating

" Joe Sharp is dedicated to helping others transform their lives and business in a positive direction. Joe's help with my dreams and direction in life have been priceless, one of the best investments I have ever made thus far."

- Frank L. Tunis, Owner of Frank Tunis Photography

" Author Joe Sharp does an admirable job of helping the reader explore their own path to greater purpose while running down their dreams by sharing his own stories of learning life's lessons the hard way. He mixes both funny and heartbreaking personal stories with valuable insight from the mentors who helped him with his personal journey. Joe shows amazing courage by sharing the "good, bad, and the ugly" of his own life, not hesitating to give the reader an open window to his own personal faults and weaknesses."

- Bob Garvey, Coach/Sales Trainer at Sandler Training

" Joe, has been a valuable asset to our company. He has gone over and above to help us pursue our dreams both personally and for our business."

- Bill Leachman, Owner of Gemini 5 Designs

Table of Contents

Journey 1:

Dreams Found Through Courage & Your Career

Journey 2:

Dreams Found Through the Principal of Gratitude

Journey 3:

Dreams Found Through the Blessing of Travel

Journey 4:

Dreams Found Through the Pursuit of a Soul Mate

Journey 5:

Dreams Found Through Powerful Relationships

Journey 6:

Dreams Found Through the Lack of Money

Journey 7:

Dreams Found Through Failure

Journey 8:

Dreams Found Through Death & Illness

Journey 9:
Dreams Found Through Pain, Sorrow & Depression

Journey 10:
Dreams Found Through the Gift of the Holy Spirit

"Many of life's failures are people who do not realize how close they were to success when they gave up."

– Thomas Edison

JOURNEY #1

Dreams Found Through Courage & Your Career

Theme Focus:

Many people have had the dream of running their own successful business. Maybe it's a dream of yours, or a goal you've already accomplished. Perhaps you own a business currently, but feel like it's running your life. Some people stall because of fears that inhibit them from starting their own business and running down their entrepreneurial dreams. Also, I've found that entrepreneurs around the globe do not link courage and the entrepreneurial spirit. I believe that those who harness their entrepreneurial spirit already possess a high level of courage, but don't realize it. Putting their dreams to action despite the risk of failing takes courage. My prayer is that real world stories from successful entrepreneurs and insights that can help run a successful business with more confidence will help make your entrepreneurial dreams a reality.

Chapter I

A Contagious Courage Found in Taking Action

I wanted to start off our journey together by sharing some stories that speak to my humble beginnings. These stories are about the concept of finding the courage to take action, the same courage it took to write this book. I have seen this applied to running down my own dreams in life. The more you have the courage to take action, the easier it becomes to do so in the future. Courage is only one part of the magic we will talk about throughout this book; however, it is certainly a big part of realizing your dreams!

The Kid That Could Sell Ice Cubes to Eskimos

Did you ever think about how you became the person you are today? I think my story has a lot to do with two things: "ice cubes" and "Eskimos." This phrase became one said fondly by my father to me through his brass tacks, tough love parenting style that didn't always mesh well with me as a boy. However, it has since culminated into an epiphany of insight as I look back on my father's charm hidden in his rough ways. My dad always told me things like, "Boy, you could sell ice cubes to Eskimos." I was the kid that was a paper boy at age twelve. I started my own custom magnet factory business at my grandfather's during summer vacations so I could market them in local retail stores. I ran tomato stands at the corner. I moonlighted as a lawn mowing or snow shoveling business owner according to the season. In high school I had three jobs at one time. I suppose I worked a lot because I never had much money growing up, and if I wanted anything like a car, I was only going to get it by working hard to earn it. Sadly, many of our youth today lack that fervor and drive to strive for such endeavors because they have an attitude of entitlement. Often, today's parents give their children anything they want. In doing so they don't realize that most times they handicap their child rather than truly bless them. You can only learn the lessons of youth once. God gives and takes away for a reason, and if we accept that reality, we can instill values of learning in times of little and much.

My father always saw an innate ability in me to sell anything. I never realized it growing up, but I do now. I can sell anything I put my mind to, though to really be successful I've found I need to have my heart fully invested in what I'm selling. That is a key ingredient that cannot be overlooked if you want to find fulfillment in what you do, no matter what the financial reward. An Eskimo does not need to buy an ice cube. He is surrounded by ice and a free, endless supply. The key for me was to realize that if I believed there was a real reason why the Eskimo could benefit from the ice cube presented in a new, more practical, and effective way, it could change the life of the Eskimo. It takes creative vision, an entrepreneurial spirit and the willingness to stand out in confidence by taking a unique stand in a certain marketplace. If you are able to do that you can give life to an idea that could change the world.

Why I've Started Businesses Since I Was Eighteen

The sooner you focus on your gifts, the easier it will be to run down your dreams. I did this. I always went against the grain, and I was always true to myself. I believe these are common threads connecting all top performers, whatever their field. It could be the coach with the unconventional system that leads his team of throwback players to win the championship or the teenager that takes pride in doing the right thing even in the face of massive peer pressure. I believe God has made us all not only in His image, but also to be a unique and special creation. Embrace that truth and remain true to yourself in all areas of your life as you strive to become the man or woman God planned you to be.

As I look back on who I was at eighteen, I can see that I not only believed that anything was possible, I was willing to take the seemingly crazy thoughts that floated in my young mind and put them into action. I remember how I engineered a very small enterprise out of my meager room at my grandparents' house while I attended Millersville University. I had an almost non-existent budget. Staples became my primary supplier, funny enough. I had a strong interest in marketing, advertising, and art, so I channeled those passions into a small business advertising company called The Local Sound. Though I definitely sold my services to local businesses, I never officially formed a real business entity or filed a name with the state. To be honest, I don't even think I realized that was important. I remember designing coupons for Chiropractors and cutting them down at on-campus facilities in their copy shop. It was obviously a very small deal in the grand scheme of things and certainly not a profitable venture in terms of cash flow. However, it taught me something valuable: to get out of my comfort zone. Furthermore, it taught me to step out into the world with my idea so I could boldly face both the potential of success and the high probability of failure. I have since started a variety of other businesses, some successful and others failures, and I've continued to trust God while I walk on with the courage and faith that He has placed into my heart. As someone who has started many businesses, I can say there will be one of two outcomes to a business: success or failure. If you never put your dream into action, then the answer is pretty clear which it will be.

There must be something that is driving you at your core being to motivate you out of the gate. For me, there were a few things. Living in a home where one parent was mentally incapable of working while the other spent a lifetime of working overtime just to make ends meet as a janitor wasn't something I wanted to repeat for my own family. I had a desire to create and wasn't opposed to hard work. I also learned I simply wasn't the sort of person that was cut out to work for someone else long-term. To be honest, if I was working for someone today, I would probably be fired in short order for not being a faithful person to punch in and punch out at the expected times. Perhaps my entrepreneurial gifting qualities make me unemployable! Some people are starters and some people are finishers in life. I know I am a starter. If, like me, you're not necessarily a natural finisher, don't let that dissuade you from doing what you're good at and starting things. I certainly cherish those who are excellent finishers and have surrounded myself with their brilliance.

Everyone's story, gifts, and passions are different. If you are willing to search your heart and determine what drives you most in life emotionally and spiritually speaking, I believe you will find the fire that will drive you to physically and intellectually invest in a dream. Then you will be able to spend and balance the days that God blesses you with by fanning that flame as you live your life. It could grow and change as the seasons of your life change, though the concept will always remain the same. Those that are fortunate enough to realize this truth live life and live it to the fullness that God intended for us all (see John 10:10). I pray you become who you are meant to be and fight the temptation to fit into a practical life that promises security. Just living one day with the mindset of chasing your dreams will help you realize we can't just sit and wait; we have to go for it. So what is stirring in your heart that can become the beginning of your life-long driving force?

It All Begins With Action

So much of realizing your dreams is about having courage to take the first step. The sooner you focus on your personal gifts and talents by seeking to better understand them, the easier it will be to run after your dreams. **If you remain a willing student**, each season of life can teach you to grow in your ability to step forward with greater courage. You never know when your next dream opportunity will appear, ready for you to chase it. As you pursue your dreams with the consistent resolve to take action, you will send shockwaves that will permeate throughout your circle of influence and inspire others to do the same. Never doubt how much this consistent approach to your life could drastically impact the lives of others around you. It all begins with action, no matter your age, race, background, or the adversities before you.

Point of Reflection or Action for Today:

"Ideas are a dime a dozen. People who implement them are priceless."

– Mary Kay Ash

Chapter 2

How Getting Fired From College Helped Me! The College Saga

So when you think of getting fired you rarely find yourself basking in the glory of the concept. My story here might be the oxymoron of that trend. Before I explain to you how I got fired, I suppose I should explain to you what led up to it and more importantly the blessings along the way. First of all, I found myself not happy with learning simply course work as I attended college. Don't get me wrong I am a big supporter of young adults applying themselves in their college educations and making the most of the investment. I just believe I learned that the things you strive for beyond the typical accolades that came with graduating with a high GPA, are many times where the college magic really happens.

What I mean is that you can really learn some street smarts beyond the book smarts and I really encourage you to consider this if you are pursuing higher education now or have family/friends that are doing so. You can learn tons by surrounding yourself with people that know more than you and are willing to invest into your life in a personal way. You could see this in internships, mentorship relationships with professors where you give your time for free in trade for special training, etc. I have also learned that becoming the dumbest person on the team is a sure way for an entrepreneur to soar to peak heights, but I'll tell you more about that later. You could seek out leadership positions within the campus. Also, you could see a need for a new club, organization, or role on campus and you could create a plan of action to become that leader. That is basically what I did and by running after that dream I found that I was setting myself up to be fired.

It all started when I sought out on-campus employment to fund my college expenses. I initially found two jobs working as a computer lab worker and an event setup and tear down assistant. One essential ingredient for my future success (and reaching some of my dreams) was being willing to go above and beyond from an early age. By intentionally doing more than the expected minimum in life, I positioned myself to better reach my future dreams.

I was very lucky to have both jobs and be able to continue to balance my education as well as other activities. However, I chose not to settle there. I saw a giant need for many departments on campus that had websites that were poorly maintained or non-existent. I set up meetings with department chairs to take over improvement of a handful of the departments and even worked for individual teachers. I was paid hourly for the work and was able to do the work while I ran the computer lab because students would only need me from time to time, so I basically was able to bill for two hours at the same time, and my bosses knew this. Like in most jobs, I was allowed fifteen to twenty minute breaks during my shift. Funny enough, my other job as the event setup and tear down assistant typically only took fifteen to twenty minutes though they paid us for three to five hours normally as our pay rate. It never made sense to me, but I didn't argue and the school was fully aware of this. I chose to not take breaks and worked over there on my breaks to be more entrepreneurial.

I also became the leader of the business department computer lab and even helped one of my roommates, Nicholas Bird, become employed in a similar capacity. It was almost like a boss-employee relationship, which foreshadowed Nicholas becoming my very first employee in a future company I created. During that time I further realized an entrepreneurial track by having an internship at Millersville University that counted towards my degree credits where I built my first professional website for a company. I realized I was more than capable of helping people promote their business online.

It didn't stop there, though, as this college saga unfolded. On top of all of this, one of the professors who will go nameless allowed me to teach a business class for him from time to time even though I was an undergraduate. He was comfortable enough to leave the entire class to me so I could teach them how to build country specific websites and in doing so I was paid minimum wage to teach classes I was actually taking myself! I also eventually became a security guard for my apartment complex and was given free rent which would fuel my first home office in trade for working some random evenings or weekends.

I loved the challenge of all of this responsibility; however, the funny thing was I got to the point where I had over 200 billable hours in a pay period though I clearly only worked a fraction of this in real hours. I literally built a first of its kind college earnings potential, by looking for what opportunity existed that others didn't see or were afraid to act on. Each of my managers knew what I was doing and they all approved this so I didn't feel I was doing anything wrong or being immoral because of the fact of full disclosure and being the subordinate as a student worker. However, the director of finance for the university had a different view on the matter. After he realized I was making over $15,000/year as a college worker he met with my roommate, Nick and I, and fired us both. However, much to his surprise, we actually ended up getting a severance package after we stood our ground (by presenting truthful facts) in the conversation.

So then I dusted myself off for the next steps of my entrepreneurial journey during my college years. Before I ever officially launched my first successful business in March of 1999, Sharp Innovations, I went after many other entrepreneurial tracks and didn't allow the on-campus firing to scar me. I was looking through business opportunity ads in the newspapers back when reading the old school treats was still a mainstay. I joined an organization called Usana, became an independent distributor, and started building a down-line through their multi-level marketing system and invested considerable money for a college kid without a paying job. I was courted by door to door vacuum cleaner superstars like Electrolux and went on some wild rides realizing certain roles were simply not for me.

Eventually I sought out on-campus recruitment through our career services department which, ironically, I used personally a year later to hire my own staff to start my business. I was hunted by a power-house financial services firm in Harrisburg, PA. I met their CEO and he said I was a born salesperson and would be a top producer and they paid for me to take a

Life, Accident, and Health Test for the state in which you need to score a seventy. I failed and got a sixty-three but they insisted I try again, and they paid for me. I worked extremely hard though I was never good at test taking and got a sixty-nine. I believe God's hand was clearly all over this. They insisted they would keep paying until I passed and I decided it wasn't for me. Praise God for that decision that was made before I even had a personal relationship with Him because, He nudged me to not go down the wrong path. A passion for entrepreneurialism early on paired with my college employment saga led me to start my first successful firm called Sharp Innovations only a few months later. The last piece to the puzzle was blowing out my knee, but more on that in the next chapter.

Point of Reflection or Action for Today:

"We would literally astound ourselves if we did everything we are capable of."

– Thomas Edison

Chapter 3

Who Thought Blowing Out Your Knee Was Good? The Sharp Innovations Story

Starting your own business and becoming successful is the quintessential American Dream. So many people have this dream, yet never find the courage or support to run after it. With today's technology driven, global economy, it is more feasible than ever for anyone to become an entrepreneur. I was so very fortunate and blessed to have had the courage to pursue this dream and succeed when I was twenty. I would have never guessed, however, that blowing out my knee was the last step to realizing my dream.

I loved playing ice hockey, and was hopeful, despite injuring my knee once before, of continuing  my college sports career. Though after two more knee injuries, I realized my focus needed to change. I found myself putting together a business plan a few months later, I had passion but no real world experience. I launched the business within the same month I had knee surgery and can remember doing my initial work with a knee brace immobilizer. I can say that as I look back over the years since successfully running and growing Sharp Innovations, Inc., that I have encountered many similar stories where business people of varied levels of experience and age found themselves facing major life changes that others saw as periods of temporary insanity when they stepped out in faith to work for themselves.

I started this business with only $5,000 by selling some internet stocks I had invested in and using my college apartment bedroom as my initial office. As I started out, I found major opposition and disbelief from close family and friends that cautioned me to not do this because they believed I was too young and would fail. The timing certainly was ripe for a young entrepreneur to start an internet based business as the turn of the century approached. I am pleased to say that I never allowed that to stop me from running after that dream that was within me.

I can remember so many funny stories as I went through this season of my life, from late night heroics where we pulled off things we never did before for morning deadlines, to driving a truckload of office furniture up a windy hill in an ice storm. It certainly has been a life-changing journey full of adventures that were possible because I allowed myself to step out and believe my dream could become a reality.

I would not be giving credit where it is truly due if I didn't say that the employees on my team over the years have been a driving influence and major reason for our success as a firm. It is clear that many people with special talents and skills were brought into my path. Over time, I realized a gift: the ability to recognize ability in others. God has continued to open up doors and bring new specialists into my path as time has continued showing me that our future could always be brighter than our past. Living life and running a business really is a lot about trial and error and learning lessons as our lives continue.

One of the highlights of my career was when I met Thomas Hopta. We met in our early 20s and had limited real world experience, but were full of potential. Tom began as a sales representative for the firm, which evolved into several other roles, eventually ending up as our Chief Financial Officer, which was his real calling. He has a unique way of making numbers sing a song that radiates strategic insights. Tom taught me the beauty of how different people's unique abilities and gifts can so wonderfully complement others'. Tom is a perfect complement to me. We are able to support each other's weaknesses with our individual strengths.

He has helped me to carry that wisdom forward as I focused on building an increasingly stronger team, as well as helping companies I now coach do that as well. To this day I continue to focus on becoming the dumbest man in the office as I surround myself with increasingly talented people.

Golden Nuggets of Youthful Wisdom

Here are a few golden nuggets of wisdom that came out of my success with Sharp Innovations:

1. Make sure the dream you chase is a deep-seated passion that matches your true gifting in life, not merely the desire to become wealthy.

2. Make sure your business passion is fueled by the desire to make sure your contribution to society is greater than your reward.

3. Make sure you really have a well-prepared business plan in place before you start out so you can have a plan of action to chart and measure against. This is even more so critical if it is your first business.

4. Think through and quantify what you will have to sacrifice in time, life balance, relationships, and economics to succeed in business, so you can discuss them with the closest people in your life.

5. Truly be willing to do whatever it takes to complete the journey, and make sure that your spouse, if you are married, is completely on board with sharing in this sacrifice and believes in your dream. The marriage relationship should be a source of confidence and support, not emotional division.

6. Don't be afraid of surrounding yourself with people that know more than you do.

7. Do your best with the simple things on a consistent basis: say "please" and "thank you;" do what you say you are going to do when you said you would do it, and finish what you start.

8. Focus on making deposits in the emotional bank accounts of your clients and employees that exceed the benefits of your products, services or paycheck. In other words, strive first for deeper relationships rather than more business transactions.

9. Do all you can to reward your staff the absolute best you can, and make that more important than going from rags to riches.

10. Always focus on the cultivation of a future that is bigger than your past. Don't grow complacent in success. Know that failure is possible, but never believe that hope is lost. All things are possible with God.

11. Focus on maintaining a servant's heart as you serve your clients, and those you provide for financially.

12. Nothing is more important than asking God to bless your dream as you step out in faith to pursue it. Ask Him to show you how to run your business in a way that truly aligns with His will for your life.

Ironically enough, I am playing ice hockey today, and have coached youth hockey. That particular dream came full circle, and I thank God for that. It has been a dream that led me towards running down other dreams and a growing passion to help other people do the same. What is your dream? Whatever it is, I dare you to run it down.

Point of Reflection or Action for Today:

"The purpose of our lives is to give birth to the best which is within us."

– Marianne Williamson

Chapter 4

A Road of Convergence: The "9 Local" Story

People often decide to chase a dream when they are at a transitional point in their lives. Regardless of whether their transition involves the death of a loved one, a terminal illness, the loss of a job, unexpected physical disability, an unexpected divorce or broken relationship, some proverbial mid-life crisis or something else, the person is often looking for a new lease on life as they dream. Many dynamics could be surfacing that create a whirlwind of emotions. They can be gripped by personal fears that stall them or showered with new passion that lets them see their life as a blank canvas waiting to be painted. Regardless of how the person gets to these points of transition in their life, they can be an exciting and volatile concoction. (One that affects not only their lives but those closest to them as the drink [that is their life] is shaken and stirred.) I see these transitional places in life as roads of convergence. One of these roads of convergence that affected me personally may help you as you assess the dreams in your heart today.

The Path to a Road of Convergence

I have been blessed with an entrepreneurial fervor and passion that has encompassed many dreams in my life. I walked down the road into the point of convergence with this passion fueling my steps. I was clearly still in my mindset of wanting to successfully launch ten or more companies that would succeed in ten or more industries during my life. My purpose in wanting to accomplish that goal was to make a lasting impact and leave a meaningful legacy behind.

Moreover, I certainly had a passionate focus to find my soul mate throughout my 20s after a broken engagement early that decade. It is pretty natural for a young, single person to have that desire. I am confident that my days in high school working for a chain of card stores, my passion for writing poetry and many other romantic/passionate characteristics that God blessed me with only became blow horns for me as I marched throughout that decade and into the next. I truly understand how God gives and takes away. I experienced a passionate love affair for several years that stopped unexpectedly right before the marriage altar. I took that powerful lesson of love gained and lost, and saw it transformed into passion to help other people find their soul mate in life.

To magnify that internal fire, I was able to harness the passion found in the death of my father after an unexpected one-month battle with cancer. His death strongly spurred me on to realize that you need to go for things in life, because you only live once and tomorrow is never guaranteed. Our dreams desperately desire us to take action so we can see them become realized and birthed in our present lives. I was always very much a go-getter, but I found at that time that honestly there were several passions and dreams that laid in my heart that prior I held out as reservations for some future date that was more appropriate. Sadly, many times like for my father that date never came. That year as well as the next few that followed became launching points into new paths of mystery and passion after I got through the road of convergence that my father's death solidified for me.

The "9 Local" Story

Six partners and I created, launched, and ran a dating service called, "9 Local, Inc.". Though the company was founded on a powerful vision and a

seemingly well-built plan, the business didn't reach notable levels of success in seven months of live operation. Our concept involved capitalizing on massively growing on-line dating revenues and Internet usage stats that existed while growing new dating concepts such as speed dating. We were blending both together, while focusing on a fifty-mile local radius (that was our unique, competitive advantage). We took a gorilla marketing approach and gave away sixty-day memberships to the first 1,000 who signed-up to build our member database. We were able to achieve our goal in about the first one hundred days, and started taking on paying memberships and making revenue. However, we were unable to re-coup costs before a second round of investment would have been required to continue the business. We ultimately failed not because of our idea, but because we gave away too much for free.

The 9 Local experience may have cost me considerable income, since I was the 70 percent primary owner, however the lessons learned were invaluable. No good investment comes without some type of risk. Looking back, I can thankfully say that venture taught me powerful concepts in advertising, marketing, business strategy, business plan development, and creative partnership legality. That knowledge has become invaluable in working with my Internet Marketing clients of Sharp Innovations. It has also helped me better relate to my business/life coaching clientele because of the lessons learned and wisdom gained. I think the entrepreneurial education I received through my 9 Local experience was worth more than I lost in the short-term as I look at how it has and will continue to help direct the remainder of my professional career.

To date, I have started or run seven businesses. I can't say how many more I will get into, but the journey of an entrepreneur is exciting. It is even more exciting if you can truly embrace failures and be motivated to implement change by applying wisdom you gained in both times of failure and success. So it really is about how you see the glass of life. Is it half full or half empty when you look at your past and explore new dreams and entrepreneurial opportunities for your future?

I'll leave you today with a funny memory. I fondly remember a television interview for 9 Local I had on "Behind the Lines" with Diane Dayton in which she asked me about this passion I had for helping other people find their soul mates. She explored her curiosity to see if I would personally utilize my company's services to seek the woman of my own dreams as a single man who could relate to my customers. I assured her I couldn't do that in good conscience because I was one of the guys reviewing and approving profiles of each woman that entered into our database. Could I have squatted the most interesting to me and selfishly contacted them as the owner of the business to see if they were interested in getting to know me first, before approving their profile that just gave them their sixty days of free membership? Yes, but the reality in my heart was that the business was a dream I was running down and God was beginning to show me how my personal passion for finding Mrs. Sharp, needed to shift to a broader landscape about passionately encouraging others to pursue God honoring relationships that would stand the test of time. I'll elaborate on that as the book continues.

I have a final thought as you reflect on the dreams that lie in your heart today. It is a good to think about them, share them with people you trust to gain insight, and to pray about them. However, I feel that dwelling upon them to a point of analysis paralysis (so you never take action of them) is one of the worst things you can ever do. I believe if a dream doesn't seem to stir enough passion in you to run it down, that perhaps it just isn't the right one to pursue. Conversely, if you have a fully acknowledged passion to run down a particular dream, then it is a mission in life that I want to encourage you to go after. Let us not forget that this story would have never happened for me, my partners, and our local community clients without ACTION upon the DREAM at the road of convergence that I faced in life. Dreams require a lot to succeed, however, courage to take action is the first step my friend!

Point of Reflection or Action for Today:

What holds you back the most right now from embarking on your current business or career dream(s)?

Chapter 5

Becoming the Dumbest Person in the Office!

Most people tend to believe that you need to become smarter, more efficient, more wealthy, or perhaps more successful in terms of tangible possessions in order to be in a position to run down their dreams. I would like to challenge that philosophy. Becoming a successful entrepreneur taught me the value of being the dumbest person in the office. Let me explain. I am not telling you that only people with lower intelligence can achieve their dreams. Neither am I saying to be complacent and lazy and operate with low expectations of yourself. Many times those who embrace this concept are quite diligent, hard-working, and humble.

Below are six simple guidelines to becoming the dumbest person in the office and what it means within one's career, so you can more easily run down your dream(s):

1. Become increasingly humble – First and foremost, I believe you need to become increasingly comfortable facing rejection, personal challenge from peers, your team and/or other coaches. You need to always remain open to learning about yourself, how you affect others around you, and how you can improve as a person. If you

take on the role of a humble servant even if you are the CEO of your company, you will be more greatly able to achieve dreams. If you have run your own business already for any period of time, don't be afraid to sweep the floors many years after you launched and grew a business so you can remember your roots, and what it took to even initiate the path of success that you now know. Make sure that no task is ever too small.

2. Surround yourself with people that know more than you in your areas of weakness – It is imperative that you not only know your weaknesses, but that you surround yourself with people that continually can handle those areas more effectively by applying their natural gifts and unique abilities.

3. Build depth into your support team(s) in all areas possible – I have found, when possible, it is prudent to have redundancy at least two people deep in all areas of the company, even if it requires you to use part-time, contracted, or outsourced help. I also like to make sure anyone I hire has more potential than simply an ability to fulfill a role as advertised. This opens up the possibility that they could help you in new ways as the business changes, and gives the team greater confidence to weather any future staffing changes.

4. Always see your future as bigger than your past – No matter how bad the personal loss when a team member leaves, it is critical that you focus on how your business could be better through replacing them (new perspective, new insights, new talents, etc.) or through rebuilding the organization in a unique way, without directly filling the position left by their departure. Continue to hire people that make your support team stronger each time you lose someone or hire someone new. Don't just replace them or hire someone that matches your minimum requirements as to keep up to the level you were at before. Always look to upgrade your team so your future remains brighter than your past through the changes and seasons of life.

5. Become an increasingly stronger delegator – Many leaders and entrepreneurs are poor at delegation. They tend to want to be micro-managers because of what they know and their internal need to feel as if they are in control even if the reality is that they are not. The better you become at more quickly delegating to the

most appropriate person, the more effective you will become in producing consistent results and doing the behaviors you will need to do to achieve the dream(s) that you are striving for.

6. Spend the lion-share of your career time focused on your unique abilities/gifts – Don't waste your time on doing hysterical activity that keeps you busy and simply drains you of your energy/mission. Many times people do tasks that they are only competent at or worse, rather than spending energy on an excellent or truly unique ability which is normally linked to their raw passions. You should focus more intensely on what you do best and try to get to the point where you spend 80 percent+ of your career time there. The clearer you get about yourself by using personal profiling/ inventory tools like Kolbe, DISC or a spiritual gifts inventory, the more likely you can delegate/lead better.

I believe the true beauty in becoming the dumbest person in the office, is that you ensure you are more easily able to run down your dream(s) because you have increased support, clarity, and confidence as you take each step necessary towards your vision!

Point of Reflection or Action for Today:

"If you take a close look at the most successful people in life, you'll find that their strength is not in having the right answers, but in asking the right questions."

  – John Chancellor

Chapter 6

Empowering Entrepreneurs to Become Dream Champions: The Dan Sullivan Story

Dreams Profile with Dan Sullivan

Founder and President of the Strategic Coach®, recognized public speaker, author, and a foremost expert on entrepreneurship in action

So many people possess both courage and the gift of the entrepreneurial spirit. The unfortunate reality is that many of these folks hesitate to fully step out in faith to make their career dreams a reality. The result? They end up not making the contribution to this planet that only they could uniquely make. What a loss for us all!

Dan Sullivan is an entrepreneurial genius. If your burning dream is to start a business, step out today! If you are in the midst of planning a business now or are currently running a business that's running your life, hopefully these insights spur a paradigm shift with your career.

Encouragement from One of the First 13,000 Empowered

I was close to the end of the second year of running my new business venture, Sharp Innovations, when I had an encounter that changed my life forever. I met with Jim, whom I thought might be a business prospect. Though we agreed he did not need my company's services at that time, Jim felt compelled to share with me a recommendation that shifted my life and career in an absolutely profound way.

Jim wanted to encourage me to soar to new heights. Though I only spent a brief couple hours of my life with Jim, I am confident that our conversation was an appointed part of my destiny. He had done the Strategic Coach Program® (created by Dan Sullivan), and thought I would be an ideal candidate as well. I see it as a gift from God, and am thankful for the outward-focused gesture that Jim chose to make that day. If he didn't, who knows where I would be today.

The program has income level minimums because it is focused on empowering successful entrepreneurs who are committed to a lifetime of growth. Though I could hardly even afford the costs of the program—and certainly didn't hit the true income qualifications to join—I somehow still got the opportunity to walk through that door. They have locations around the globe where thousands of entrepreneurs meet on a quarterly basis to work on improving their businesses, growing their quality of life, and striving towards a constantly bigger future. I suppose on some levels people would have said I was successful in business before I interacted with Dan's company, but my affiliation with the program definitely bore fruit. My personal and business income exponentially grew. I went from taking off about five days per year (completely off genuine Free Days®*) to averaging 150-160 days off per year. I started many more businesses and better understood my Unique Ability®* passion and vision for my life. My role as a business/life coach and the realization of this book ever being written has been greatly due to my attendance at the Strategic Coach® meetings. I am so thankful for the remarkable entrepreneurs and coaches around me (including Dan) in my workshops who showed bold courage to do what others only dream of. They have walked alongside of me as I unlocked more of the gift that is the entrepreneurial spirit within me. I thank God for that.

Courage and the Entrepreneurial Spirit

During my research, personal experiences, and interactions with hundreds of entrepreneurs, I noticed something interesting. Entrepreneurs simply do not use the word "courage" to describe themselves or what they do. Dan's personal work with over 6,000 entrepreneurs confirmed this. This is not to say that entrepreneurs don't possess courage, they simply don't describe themselves that way.

Dan says that entrepreneurs have "factory installed," or "batteries included" equipment within that allows them the ability to dream and take action. Entrepreneurs see life as a series of calculated risks and unique opportunities, while the rest of the world simply views it as a risk. Even those closest to an entrepreneur are usual cautiously skeptical.

Two Sides of Freedom

What defines an entrepreneur? Dan describes two key driving life influences: the freedom to and the freedom from. The force of freedom to propels you towards something powerful and positive. The freedom from is an even more powerful concept. People desperately want freedom from limitations, obstacles, and oppression while desiring freedom to be fully themselves in a world that promotes conformity. As I consider how my own career has evolved, I can personally validate both of these freedoms. As a follower of Jesus Christ, I have freedom from sin and self-focus. That's an indescribable gift. As an entrepreneur, the freedom to grow both personally and in a business sense is something I'm grateful to have grasped at such a young age. As I continue to run down my dreams, I am empowered by constantly focusing on the things I do best. Conversely, I work hard to effectively delegate the tasks at which I don't particularly shine. Being unwilling to delegate is a great enemy of freedom. This allows me to focus on ever greater levels of personal growth and evolvement, balancing life, and increasing personal time freedom. For me, freedom to be in business has not been about simply making more money. It's a way of living life that is focused more and more on what matters most each day. It has been a voice of empowerment that allows me to walk more boldly into a life of increasing purpose and deepening meaning.

The Power of Repeating the 10X Model

One of the most remarkable concepts that I have learned from Dan Sullivan through the Strategic Coach® is the concept of the 10x Model™. It forces you to look strategically at what changes need to happen, and determine what new resources and capabilities you would need to reach a goal (such as becoming ten times larger, more financially successful, more profitable, more efficient, less stressed, etc.). It encourages big dreamers to dream bigger! Dan is not merely a creator of tools; he practices what he preaches. Since he began his role as a business coach back in 1974, he has successfully reached "10x" three times, and is working on his fourth "10x" model. In terms of revenue, he went from $20,000 to $200,000, then $200,000 to $2 million, then $2 million to $20 million, and is now focused on the dream of reach his next "10x" goal. He's focused on a lifelong process of dreaming and helping others do the same.

As Dan looks back on how he has reached his dreams during his first three "10x" successes, he recounts several powerful insights. First, the concept of Unique Ability® Teamwork is a key to success and growth for entrepreneurs. This term refers to the great success that stems from getting the right people with the right set of talents and passions in the right roles to propel a business structure forward—and support the entrepreneur's ever-growing vision. In dealing with thousands of entrepreneurs, he has never seen one happy and successful without this principal being true. In practical terms, this has become a constant ingredient to Dan's success. He has seen exponential personal growth in focusing more and more on doing his top two to three Unique Ability® activities really well. He spends his time only doing them and constantly focuses on improving in those areas, while he empowers those around him to do everything else better than he could. This practice gives him the freedom to excel, while he has the freedom from what would slow him down as he runs down his dreams.

If there is anything about courage that truly connects to successful entrepreneurs, it's their need to constantly grow in their ability to delegate and promote authority to others within their teams. They trust that other people will do a great job and can cooperate in achieving success. Dan realizes it is extremely important to surround yourself with people with varied capabilities. Furthermore, to keep great people on the team, they need to be properly rewarded. They need greater authority, responsibility, and a sense of achieving a greater purpose in the world. Entrepreneurs should encourage people to grow and learn from experience and circumstances as they pursue new goals and dreams.

Batteries Included! Entrepreneurship in Action

You can't talk someone into becoming an entrepreneur. They come with batteries included while disregarding fears and obstacles in pursuit of dreams. Entrepreneurs are lifelong dreamers. But the question they are inevitably forced to answer as they consider the future is "how big do you really want your dreams to be?" Dan encourages only working with motivated people that help you to flourish and grow as you walk towards your dreams in life.

Many of the world's top-performing business owners regard Dan Sullivan as the person to teach you how to be a better entrepreneur. Being so results-oriented, entrepreneurs are a demanding audience. Dan enjoys rising to the challenge. "Always test your ideas out on check writers (people who can pay you for your idea)" is one of his mottos. For over thirty-five years, he's been refining his methods and learning from his own experience as an entrepreneur, as well as from his clients' experience—engaging in over 50,000 hours of conversation with more than 6,000 of these successful business leaders. Dan sees his central purpose as a coach as helping people become "unmanipulated"—liberated from external forces like industry constraints, economics, and politics, as well as internal forces, like their thinking, their habits, their past-based assumptions, and the messes in their lives. When they gain this freedom, they begin to see and capture all the opportunities in their situation. His marketplace predictions consistently come to pass—and this has earned him a deserved reputation as a thought-leader in business. But his passion always comes down to helping entrepreneurs.

Dan pointed out to me a key distinction between successful entrepreneurs and non-successful entrepreneurs: successful entrepreneurs make a decision that there is simply no alternative to the pursuit of their dream. They are passionate, relentless, and unwavering. They acquire whatever skills, capabilities, resources, knowledge, or changes are needed to see their dream(s) come to pass.

Pioneering a New Kind of Experience-Based Education

Dan is spurring people on to learn not just through books, but also through practical life experience. In other words, don't exclusively base your understanding and limitations on a theoretical model—be courageous and test the balance and boundaries on your own. His passion for education is based upon life experience and valuable lessons learned only through trial and error, rather than solely the book learning. He's committed decades of his career to cultivating and spreading this message to entrepreneurs who will become the next Industry Transformers™. He is watching exciting progress of entrepreneurs from his client base take this model globally into what he believes will become thousands of industries one day. He shared an example of a client working in Rwanda who is helping people pursue entrepreneurial dreams in their country through this educational model. Dan's firm is happily encouraging this effort through a charitable support role.

Dan has a lifetime passion for building creative thinking exercises that are focused on people's life experiences and helping them think about their life and dreams in a whole new, fresh way. This educational approach strongly advocates searching out the pertinent success of others to help steer your life path. Dan is in the game for good. He is a lifer that believes he is going to die on stage educating, empowering, and impacting people about the entrepreneurial lifestyle and success in the pursuit of dreams.

I would highly encourage anyone to review the Strategic Coach® website as they pursue their entrepreneurial dreams. Even if you, like me, do not qualify for their programs initially, you can still benefit from the abundance of excellent online resources. Let me encourage you also to consider seeking out successful mentors and coaches that can help you find your courage and bring clarity to your dreams so you can take action. Who do you know who can be your next dream mentor?

Feel free to visit my life/business coaching website at: www. livewithpurposecoaching.com for a growing archive of videos, articles, and tools that will help you achieve your dreams.

* Additional information on Dan's firm that empowers entrepreneurial dreams is available online at www.strategiccoach.com. Unique Ability®, Industry Transformer™, and Free Days® are registered trademarks and copyrights created and owned by The Strategic Coach, Inc. All rights reserved. Used with written permission.

Point of Reflection or Action for Today:

"Always make your future bigger than your past. Every entrepreneur's number-one responsibility is to protect their personal confidence. Treat mistakes as learning, not failure."

– Dan Sullivan

Top Insights Summary from

JOURNEY #1 Dreams Found Through
Courage & Your Career

1. **A Contagious Courage Found in Taking Action**
   - The sooner you focus on your inner gifts by seeking to better understand them, the easier it will be to run after your dreams.
   - Each season of your life can teach you to grow in your ability to step forward with greater courage.
   - Be ready to take action, because you never know when your opportunity will appear.

2. **How Getting Fired From College Could Help You!**
   - Be willing to go above and beyond. By intentionally doing more than the expected minimum in life, you position yourself better to reach your dreams.
   - Failure many times is needed so you can be directed towards the path that you are truly meant to go.

3. **Who Thought Blowing Out Your Knee Was Good? The Sharp Innovations Story**
   - Many times when one of your dreams dies, it gives birth to a bigger one.
   - Being too young (or even too old, for that matter) should never be used as an excuse to stop the pursuit of your dreams.

4. **A Road of Convergence: The 9 Local Story**
   - Fear and analysis paralysis will stop your dreams dead in their tracks, so dare to step out courageously to take action on your dreams.
   - Many times the greatest lessons in life are realized (and leveraged for the future) in the midst of a courageous beginning, even if it leads to failure.

5. **Becoming the Dumbest Person in the Office!**

   - There is wisdom in learning that there is power in surrounding yourself with increasingly greater capabilities forever.

   - Being smarter, more efficient, more wealthy, or perhaps more successful in terms of tangible possessions, isn't always the best to focus on when it comes to pursuing dreams.

6. **Empowering Entrepreneurs to Become Dream Champions: The Dan Sullivan Story**

   - Surrounding yourself with inspiring, motivated dreamers who have shown courage to take action, can many times be exactly what you need so you can embark on your dreams.

   - Embracing the school of life experience can many times teach you more as you run after your dreams than just traditional educational institutions.

JOURNEY #1

Dreams Found Through
Courage & Your Career

Running Down Your Dreams—Taking Action!

For current business owners/entrepreneurs:

What new entrepreneurial dream is being held back today because of fear, complacency, or your anxiety that it is too big? Write about it in the space below, assign a go-date for you to take action, and journal about what your next action should be to make progress towards the dream.

For aspiring business owners/entrepreneurs:

What new career dream, entrepreneurial dream, or business do you desire to start? What is holding you back? Write about it in the space below, assign a goal date to start your business (if that is your dream), and journal about what your next action should be to make progress towards the career dream.

Dreams Journal

My Dream's Name: _____

My Go Date: _____

For more free resources to help encourage you in your pursuit of dreams found through courage and your career, please visit: www.livewithpurposecoaching.com.

"As we express our gratitude, we must never forget that the highest appreciation is not to utter words, but to live by them."

– John F. Kennedy

JOURNEY #2

Dreams Found Through the Principal of Gratitude

Ch. 7 - A Passion for the Gratitude Focus

Ch. 8 - Inspiration to Give Beyond the 80-10-10 Model

Ch. 9 - Becoming a Creator of a Brighter Future for Others

Theme Focus:

Too many people in the world are focused on themselves. A self-serving appetite slows people down from living a life full of true peace, deep purpose, and meaning. Fortunately, this weakness has an antidote: the Principal of Gratitude. If you focus passion and energy on the world around you in an intentional manner, it reflects a heart full of thankfulness. You will see the world through an outward, not inward, focused lens. May you be motivated by the stories shared here and propelled towards new and better dreams!

Chapter 7

A Passion for the Gratitude Focus

By focusing on the concept of gratitude God has taught me the importance of proactively seeking to do the unexpected. Many times I've found myself asking God to remove my own selfish visions and life ambitions and replacing them with His more beautiful vision for me. The Holy Spirit has placed a call in my heart to spend the rest of my life becoming increasingly focused on blessing others while inspiring them to become increasingly grateful in a perpetual and proactive way.

Let's face it, we all currently have or have previously dealt with close relationships in our professional or personal lives that have been chronically negative and pessimistic. Many times, we allow these relationships to penetrate our hearts and not just get us down, but hold us down. We become less effective within our career and life in general. Many business owners and leaders are good at planning a brighter future for themselves, but many forget that you should also focus on creating a brighter future for your team and clients. Indeed, that should become the ongoing fuel that drives your business and strategic outlook.

I challenge you to work, lead, and live differently. I challenge you to grow a heart of gratitude. In doing so, you can develop a life-long attitude of appreciation. It's one thing to simply be thankful as positive things happen to us, it is another thing altogether to cultivate a proactive gratitude focus in your daily living. Ideas like a daily gratitude journal as a part of your behavioral plan, offering intangible perks to co-workers/employees, or reaching out to your team or clients through unexpected means of communication can start to reinforce this concept.

If you start doing proactive gratitude behaviors, you'll find new ways to appreciate what is beautiful in the world, despite your circumstances. If you become keenly aware of your daily attitude and how it affects your behavior, then you can truly see great change. In doing so, you begin seeing value and appreciate aspects of your career and life that you couldn't see before. It validates that your future can always be brighter than your past.

Incorporating Proactive Gratitude Habits into Your Life

Though there are endless possibilities in how you can see gratitude transform your life and career, the following are a few ideas to encourage you in taking the first steps:

- The Daily Gratitude Focus Journal – Spend time each day doing or saying something that reflects a heart of gratitude and encourages someone else, then write down what you did. It can be as simple as praying for someone or contacting them unexpectedly. By practice, it begins to change you from the inside out.

- Weekly Gratitude Focus – For those who feel like the daily gratitude focus journal concept is too much, make it weekly.

- The Fifteen Minutes Per Day Factor – People often give the excuse that they don't have enough time to do things they should. I believe a great approach to building a heart of gratitude is to start out by spending fifteen minutes per day thinking through all of the blessings that are in your life. Write them in a journal. Pray about them. Meditate on them. Share them with your family at a meal and encourage meaningful dialogue. Make your fifteen minutes of gratitude a priority.

- <u>Be Grateful for the Small Things</u> – People often obsess over their goals: landing a dream job, building a nice home, finding a soul mate. In so doing, we miss out on life's small blessings. Focus each day on finding at least one small thing that you are grateful for, like seeing a child smile.

- <u>The 21-Day Gratitude Focus™ and The Gratitude Principle™</u> – These are concepts from the Strategic Coach®, Inc. The 21-Day Gratitude Focus is a great tool for allowing you to take a twenty-one-day journey to build a heart of gratitude that can reshape your outlook on your life despite your circumstances. It is a simple resource that can be purchased on-line. I like to give this to my coaching clients to use personally.

Reflecting Gratitude Through a Heart of Appreciation For Others

Many successful leaders I have met lack an ability to give credit to those around them for their success. Here are a few ideas to counter that trend:

- If you show ongoing appreciation for the unique value and abilities in others around you, you will see significant growth in your own leadership and find a deeper sense of peace over time.

- Appreciate the opportunities you have now and take advantage of them, despite your circumstances. You can respond by looking for ways to bless people. It's a choice.

- You can show gratitude toward your greatest teachers and continue to learn from them. People should always remain teachable, no matter their role or circumstances. On many occasions, I was able to have a deep, heart-to-heart conversation with one of my dear teachers, Ed Staub, from Staub & Associates. His shared love for others while serving God and paying meaningful deposits into the lives of other leaders like me is inspiring.

- Going the extra mile to really connect with your clients, co-workers, family, and circle of influence is key. It could be through meaningful cards, articles, gifts, or contacts that would connect with each person in a meaningful way.

Becoming a Plank on the Bridge to God's Heart

So how can you still do the unexpected small things for God's glory, while making your life a solid plank on the bridge that spurs people on in unexpected ways to search for God's heart? Here are some ideas for you:

- Pay for someone's coffee in a Starbucks or Dunkin' Donuts drive thru and give the teller a note that says: "I know you don't know me, but I wanted you to have a great day full of blessing. I pray that God blesses you."

- Give a good parking spot you get to someone that comes in right behind you.

- If you get caught in a storm, share your umbrella with someone who doesn't have one.

- Go to a hospital and donate a pint of blood.

- Help an elderly person with their packages or groceries to get them into their car.

- Baby-sit someone's children so they can enjoy some quality time as a couple.

- Read articles at a center for the visually impaired.

- Serve lunch at a soup kitchen.

- Write a note of encouragement to someone in your life that wouldn't expect it.

- Take your neighbor's children to school to help them when they need it.

- Take in a foreign exchange student.

- Help box or donate items to the Salvation Army/Good Will.

- Jump-start a car for someone that needs help.

- Stop in and offer to walk some dogs from a local animal shelter if they could use the help.

- Cook a meal for an elderly couple or widow you know or offer to pick up their groceries one week.

- Help at a work day at Habitat for Humanity or with a local church.

- Help someone move and give up your day. Everyone knows time is precious.

Keys in giving to remember:

1. Seek no recognition and try and go unnoticed as best as possible, unless those you bless ask why you do it then it creates a natural response from your heart. Don't tell your friends or co-workers about all the great things you did.

2. It is important when you give something to someone that it be given with the right spirit, not through a sense of obligation.

3. I was reminded of how a small gift when it is given can be a magnificent gift as it is received in the eyes of whom you gave it to.

I want to encourage you to reflect on who you are today, and who you want to become. You can find yourself full of gratitude for those dreams and visions. I know I am extremely thankful that God has placed them within my heart and allowed me to not only access them, but see them for the gift from His hands that they truly are. As I write this at Christmas time, I want to remind you again of the true meaning of Christmas (that we celebrate annually). I want to remind you how God did the unthinkable, becoming a child that would one day show us His desires for us all, while creating a door into a life of abundance with Him that goes well beyond this life. I personally believe no other act will ever allow the world to develop hearts that can be filled with gratitude more deeply. His undying love remains open to us all, and as we celebrate the birth of Jesus Christ each year.

In closing, I pray He would touch your heart today and give you an amazing outlook on your life as you prepare to continue your journey with proactive gratitude. I hope you embrace the opportunities of each new day He blesses you with. If you do that, I believe you can not only run down your dreams, but you can also inspire others to do that very same thing as you live a life full of deep purpose and meaning.

Point of Reflection or Action for Today:

"Develop an attitude of gratitude, and give thanks for everything that happens to you, knowing that every step forward is a step toward achieving something bigger and better than your current situation."

– Brian Tracy

Chapter 8

Inspiration to Give Beyond the 80-10-10 Model

Money, religion, and politics are typically taboo or private topics. Adults grow up with these mental tapes playing in their subconscious as they walk through their daily lives, and many times don't even realize how much powerful influence these mental tapes have over the life they live and the decisions they make. Though this concept could be true of all three topics stated above, I would like to focus on money as we look at the dreams that lay on your heart today, and you prepare yourself to perhaps realize new dreams in your life upon reflection.

I do recognize that those reading this will be coming from an extremely diverse financial background. Regardless of where your financial status currently lies be it amongst the poor, the middle class, or the upper class, I can assure you that these concepts are universal for all human beings in God's eyes. If you really want to get to know someone, you can look at how they spend their most precious resources like their time and money. That isn't to say that wealthy people who have nice things, travel, enjoy luxuries and the like should be labeled as pretentious, self-focused individuals. It is more important for you to look at how they use their influence and to what proportion it impacts their life overall. It might be true of many wealthy people, however, you can find people who invest their time, money, and mental energy in the pursuit of increased wealth in negative, self-consuming ways at all economic status levels.

You can be a prisoner to wealth and the pursuit of it very easily. For many, to counter this tendency you need to re-evaluate what is important to you, and what is truly driving you in life. You need to establish out-ward focused boundaries with your finances. You need to ensure that you are more concerned with pro-actively striving to make an increasingly larger contribution to the planet, than you are about pursuing a comfortable life rooted in financial security. I don't mean to imply that there is any lack of wisdom in the development of financial intelligence, success, growth, or security my friend. I simply desire you to look at how you approach the all mighty dollar in your life as it relates to the pursuit of your dreams. If you do that, I am confident that greater clarity of current dreams and realization of new, powerful dreams can be born in your world.

What is Tithing, Really?

I acknowledge that it is very possible that you might believe that the Bible is not the inerrant word of God, and because of that you might not want to invest your time in reading it and applying it to your life. We are not under the law to give 10% per say. Rather than being tied to a specific amount, tithing is giving freely out of thanks. I surely don't desire to deliver some sort of canned church sermon to you here in hopes of seeing you give 10 percent of your money to a local church. I do pray that you would see the wisdom in a solid foundation of stewardship.

Well built financial plans are no different than well built homes. I believe Tithing is that firm foundation, financially speaking. Tithing refers to the practice of giving one tenth of one's income for the work of God (the words "tithing" and "tenth" have the same roots). It could be to your local church and the ministries they support, or to other organizations that serve the needs of this planet that God cares about as you read through the Bible. If you haven't read the Bible for yourself, then you starting with the support of a local church is a great recommendation my friend because these people serve in spiritual ministry roles to serve people for God, and only can operate from the contributions of the community.

The Bible records many accounts of people giving thanks to God through tithing of their possessions. This offering was understood by the Israelites to be a response of gratitude and an expectation. Jesus and the apostles assumed that the tithe was a healthy guide to one's financial stewardship; and Paul follows the same logic in emphasizing that believers should give proportionately, as God has blessed those who believe in him (see 1 Cor. 16:2 and 2 Cor. 9:6-12). Nowhere in the New Testament of the Bible is tithing repudiated.

Tithing isn't simply for the church-goers or for Christians my friend. This very day, some Christians do not tithe because they have been taught that they are not under the law of the Old Testament, but under the grace of God today. While this is a true statement, God did not institute the tithe to bring us under the law, but to get blessings to His children. We're under grace that we might establish the law; not turn from it. Jesus said that He didn't come to do away with the law, but to fulfill it (Matt. 5:17-19). Because He fulfilled it, we are to establish it and one of the ways to do that is through the tithe.

Many Christians understand tithing to be a loving, freely chosen response to God's gracious provisions for our life—God's grace! Tithing is understood by many Christians to be a very helpful discipline of one's spiritual life. I believe it goes much deeper than that. It affects how you spend your money, which changes how you make decisions of all sizes in your life and through that you are forced to become more disciplined and more outward focused (two things I think nobody would find fault in). That being said, let us continue on the journey of discussing some financial stewardship boundaries as you get clearer about your dreams and how you could pursue them in a passionate, new way.

The 80-10-10 Model

Let's take the Tithing concept a bit further and put it into a workable and realistic framework for financial stewardship and personal financial management. If you have a sound game-plan on how you will operate your financial life from a core set of principles, then you have the advantage of pursuing all dreams in life with a basis of wisdom. Too many people want what their heart wants, and will do anything they need to get it. They want the quick buck. They want possessions they can't really afford. They drown in bad debt, and almost try and kid themselves it exists so they can incur more without feeling guilty. It is vicious, never-ending cycle in people's lives which can destroy families, businesses, and lives. A different approach (The 80-10-10 Model), can bring forth limitless peace and power for those that apply it to their lives for the first time.

A balanced approach to financial stewardship is described by many as the **80-10-10** model or rule—giving 10 percent, saving 10 percent, and spending wisely 80 percent of their income. Some find that they can even live on less, and thus increase their percentages of savings and giving. The brilliance of this format is that if you learn to live within less than your earnings (80 percent) you can better adjust to unexpected financial difficulties, and you never push the envelope by living beyond your means which normally brings a barrage of stress and anxiety with it. Life is hard enough without that burden. So the first thing you should do is look at your existing personal financial budget if you don't operate on 80 percent or less of your earnings, and you assess what changes would need to happen to get to that point. Focus on accomplishing that, no matter the sacrifice. You simply need to learn the lesson of spending wisely, regardless of how much you make. No matter where your finances are today, they are probably affecting how you pursue your dreams. Remember change is possible. There are no unrealistic goals, only unrealistic timelines. That's 90 percent of the equation. Let's talk about the remaining 10 percent.

The idea of paying yourself first can simply be explained as setting a guideline where 10 percent of the income you have goes straight into investments. It doesn't matter if it is a money market account or other financial instruments (stocks, mutual funds and the like). It does, however, need to be a separate account though so it is not co-mingled with other accounts and is trackable. This becomes the foundation for your "Dreams Fund." As you keep on living, plan on tackling the dreams in your heart that require investment. Continue to build financial flexibility into your life so you have a structure to capitalize on new dreams that present themselves. Part of the brilliance of the model is that it keeps you out of bad debt patterns and gives you better leverage to work with lenders for loans.

This model works, but you need to commit to it. You don't need to make six or seven figures per year to be ready. Actually, many times there are increased difficulties with increased levels of assets and wealth. It is actually easier to simplify your life if your family has lower earnings since there are less things to cut out that may have a great influence on your lifestyle. The wisdom that people of lower economic classes can impart to their children and those around them that watch them live under this model can be so impactful, that it could cause others to become inspired to do the same thing and approach their dreams in life differently. What a blessing that is to see!

Reverse Tithing

Rick Warren is one of my favorite authors. His best-selling book that sparked a spiritual revolution is The Purpose Driven Life. Though this book touched my life in a personal, life-changing way, today I want to focus on how it changed the author. Rick and his wife Kay, were married over thirty years ago and they began with the traditional 10 percent tithe, and focused on increasing their giving by 1 percent every year. This is a wise and doable approach that I have personally seen become successful and meaningful in my own life. Rick now operates financially under a reverse tithe by giving 90 percent of his earnings.

The power behind his story isn't in the fact that he gives that amount, as Rick himself comments on how easy it is for him to give the 90 percent back to God now since his Purpose Driven Movement has existed. He remembers four key components to how he handled this financial life change. First, in spite of all the money coming in for Rick's ministry, he would not change their lifestyle one bit. He made no major, personal purchases. Second, shortly after, he stopped taking a salary from the church. Third, he set up foundations to fund an initiative they call "The Peace Plan." It is one to plant churches, equip leaders, assist the poor, care for the sick, and educate the next generation. Fourth, he added up all that the church had paid him in the first twenty-four years since he started the church, and he gave it all back. It was liberating to him to be able to serve God for free.

The true power is in how a person of power, influence, and faith could trust God by caring for those less fortunate. He does so by intentionally giving 90 percent of any earnings, so he can ensure that strong boundaries are in place in his life, so the wealth does not go to his head, and negatively impact his influence that he has in the world. If we could see our other celebrities and sports stars implement this concept, just think of how much change could happen on this planet to help the less fortunate. So for those of you that are blessed to have growing wealth, I pray that you would challenge yourself to dream about how you could use this to leave behind a legacy in life that will outlive your last breathe. For the rest of us that might not be able to choose this very day to reverse tithe because of realistic financial limitations, it is my prayer that we would ask God to grow a desire within us that would want to see this dream become realized in our lives so we can see what God would do with it to impact those less fortunate in the world (widows, orphans, and the truly needy).

Ways to Increase Your Giving

Your dreams can be shaped and re-shaped by increasing your giving. You can do this in a practical way by doing it gradually (Growth Giving). Growth Giving is done by increasing your giving by 1 percent of your income every year as you prayerfully consider the pledge for the coming year. Another method would be to increase your giving by one dollar each week. For instance, if your current giving level is $20, give $21 next week, $22 the week following, and so forth. Eventually you will reach a tithe or whatever goal you feel that God is calling you to give. You can start anywhere and passionately walk out a mission to increase your giving as a foundational part of your life.

How will you use your influence now and in the future as you pursue your life dreams? Money is undoubtedly one of the most influential forces on this planet. It has the power to change people in a multitude of ways as you look at any individual and see how they focus on utilizing their influence. Cheerfully giving is living to leave behind something that will outlive you. Knowing that truth, it is clear that considering how you utilize the influence of any earnings you have can alter the path of your life and dreams. Freedom in how you spend your time and money and living a well-balanced life holds much deeper meaning than maximizing your earnings, because I can ensure you that you will not take any of it with you when you breathe your last breath. My ultimate prayer for you today is that you would never stop striving to give more and that you would ask God to change your life forever by teaching you how to embrace one of his greatest gifts—the gift of giving!

Point of Reflection or Action for Today:

Malachi 3:10 (New International Version)

[10] Bring the whole tithe into the storehouse, that there may be food in my house. Test me in this," says the LORD Almighty, "and see if I will not throw open the floodgates of heaven and pour out so much blessing that there will not be room enough to store it.

* God has blessed those who believe in him (see 1 Cor. 16:2 and 2 Cor. 9:6-12). Nowhere in the New Testament of the Bible is tithing repudiated.

Chapter 9

Creating a Brighter Future for Others

Many business owners, entrepreneurs, or dreamers launch their ventures focused on reaching their dreams before they ever stop to ensure that they are setting out to do so in a way that is focused on creating a brighter future for others first. I am honest enough to admit that I have done this several times. My prayer is that through these stories you will learn from the mistakes I made as well as countless others before me. I am hopeful that these stories will inspire you to pursue any career or business dreams that you have by approaching them in a brilliant, diametrically opposed way as compared to the vast majority of your peers. I am hopeful that it won't take you long, like it did for me through several business ventures, to realize this as you continue running down your dreams.

My entrepreneurial career started out by my ambitious pursuit of what I called my 10x. The goal was simple in definition yet bold in ambition; to start ten or more successful businesses in ten or more industries. I even went further to desire to employee 1,000 or more people and help them to become matched with their unique abilities. I actually had an employee named Melissa visually chart this out as career motivation. There is nothing wrong with charts (it still exists today as a memento); however, what was behind my drive needed some drastic altering. Typically, it is in an entrepreneur's blood to create and be a part of many business ventures in life, even if the world around them cannot understand their insatiable passion and drive that collides with change and risk. My life to date validates this.

People who listened to a wet behind the ears twenty-something dreamer didn't necessarily find fault with my intentions or approach. The problem was that most people simply offered validation to pursue anything that was bold and ambitious, even if a self-centered drive was at the center. I did not realize it then, but the years after proved that my 10x dream was corrosive and full of unrealized, self-centered motivation. The problem was that what was driving my dream was my pursuit of success which would be deemed by chasing a better life full of creature comforts first. It focused on doing that before focusing on new ways I could become a more significant blessing to my team and clientele first with each major career destination I set sail for upon the entrepreneurial winds of change.

The Destiny River Properties Story

I was fortunate enough to collide with my first personal venture that was engineered from day one in a way that was focused on a bigger future for others. I created a real-estate investment entity called Destiny River Properties. Like most ventures I engage in, I looked outside of myself to see who knew more than me. I believe the quicker you recognize your weaknesses, and find specialists that are further down the path you are traveling on, the better chance you have of reaching your dream or surpassing them on your journey. I assembled a team of real estate, legal, and financial professionals to help me with the numerous areas of the real estate industry that would simply go beyond my own personal gifting, and could easily contribute to my failure. I even hired a real estate coach because of my belief in tapping into the resources of others that counter my weaknesses.

destiny|river
properties

I launched forward and purchased a series of real estate investments after analyzing many properties of various types. I focused on implementing what seemed like a solid tenant screening process to aid in the property management strategy we developed. However, this story is not one merely about real-estate investment and dreams about becoming financially free through such investments. It is actually more about seeking to re-define money's purpose in my life. My goal for creating a bigger future for others upfront was focused mostly on two aspects.

First, I wanted to begin an income shifting model in which I would begin to pay myself less through my main business, as my passive income (something that grows in the background without you doing anything like a money market account with interest that grows your money regardless of you doing anything)from Destiny River Properties began to grow. I wanted to do so as a means of offering back a stream of my income to benefit the team members that worked so hard over the years helping me to see Sharp Innovations become the stable, successful business that it is. It was important for me to do this because I wanted my team to know as I spread my time between both ventures, that I was not doing this through selfish motivations.

Secondly, the concept beyond the name was that I wanted to work forward from a typical tithe (10 percent giving of your earnings) towards a reserve tithe (90 percent of your earnings) over my lifetime. I wanted to take the passive income that was built to go beyond supporting my future family's financial stability and dreams. I wanted to ensure that the massive goals I set for myself in lifetime giving amounts would become a central focus to this venture and any future success. It was what I call a triple win of sorts that focused on a bigger future for my team, my future family, and the needy in the world as a primary focus. I passionately desired to reach my life destiny as I journeyed further down the river of life seeking the source in which I was given life, hence the name Destiny River Properties.

I realized as I continued to journey down this river towards my dreams, that it was a valuable life lesson, and a strategy that was to be placed on hold for some time so I could follow the path that I felt God wanted me to walk forward into the new roles I serve today including writing this book. Today some real estate is still passively managed by others on my team, and I can't say that this dream is a completely dead one. If I feel led to engage in new real estate ventures over time I will gladly embrace them, as long as the triple win approach can remain a founding principal. Currently, I am happy to continue to split the proceeds with a dear team member that supports the venture, so even in smaller means it still continues to this very day to produce a brighter future for him and his family. It is my prayer that if you have engaged in this field in any way or if you ever do that perhaps some of my story can inspire you to modify your plan so you can become a greater blessing to others and their future my friend!

The Burning Bush Creative Story

One year after starting Destiny River, I was fortunate to be a part of another story that was focused on creating a brighter future for others. My management and creative teams worked together to build a business plan and corporate identity for an entity called Burning Bush Creative. It was the anti-advertising agency that was going to be born right before the economy shifted and we faced a global recession. It was to become a sister company of our internet marketing firm, Sharp Innovations, Inc. We were diversifying to bring traditional marketing specialties to our clients as we focused on truly becoming a one-stop shop for them. Our strategy was clearly set on bringing business ethics to the foreground in an industry that was notoriously unscrupulous, by basing our entire operation upon biblical wisdom. We were determined to deliver quality products and results for clients, while ensuring that the way we did business was what mattered most.

This story is one about a business planning venture that has yet to be born in regards to an actual business. While that might  be a true statement, who knows what God has in store for our futures. The business plan sits ready to execute like a champion horse that is revving to leave the starting gates at the Kentucky Derby. I felt sharing it was a great idea to show you that your dreams could receive answers to prayer from God in the form of: yes, no, or not now. The third answer we tend to struggle with most as humans, even more so in a culture today that tends to want everything immediately. Furthermore, the concept of creating a brighter future for others is one that I pray you see as a fundamental life choice throughout your entire career. It doesn't require a live business to implement. It begins with the creation of the business plan and clarifying the passion behind what is driving it. Many times the things we start off well in life have a much better chance of coming to fruition.

I believe we were obedient to God by waiting, and through it He opened up a massively larger vision that has become very successful. Now, I realize that all of our dreams should be put through a filter of sorts by seeking God first to make sure the venture you are pursuing is focused on God's will for your life above all things. You do this despite any opposition from a world or industry that wouldn't embrace your doing so. In this case, the Advertising industry would many times rather you fit in, care about your image, the financial bottom-line, and keep up with the Joneses than do the right thing in the name of integrity.

Looking back, I believe I had a heart focused on creating an opportunity not only for financial growth, but character development and creative expansion for the creative team around me. My heart was in creating something that would further support them (and their dreams) and allow the depths of their passions to be unleashed to benefit the world in an even bolder way. It is still the passion of this business plan that waits for assurance that the timing aligns with God's purposes.

Reinventing Yourself by Planning a Bigger Future for Others First

You might not like Starbucks, but there was one day where three of us really needed to have a drink at one. I needed to share what was on my heart, and ensure I found out what was on theirs before any actions happened. My key managers, Tom and Paul, have been a blessing to me for many years in business. I am fortunate to know them and be able to work alongside of them. Realizing that during our heart-felt conversation, I explained to them my fears, dreams, and my visions for the three of us. I recognized that we were only going to walk forward into a brighter future together, if I built a plan upfront that focused on creating a bigger future for them.

It is well researched in books like Good to Great that one of the greatest shortcomings of any successful entrepreneur is that they do not create a company culture that not only embraces ownership succession, but truly has a plan in place. I might still be fairly young when compared to many other successful entrepreneurs, and I might not have any plans of leaving any of my companies at this time; however, I am glad I realized the value in building for the future well in advance. To do that, it many times requires some creative planning. My vision for the bigger future for Paul and Tom would become a hybrid strategy.

Paul would continue to grow and eventually became the new president of Sharp Innovations, with full decision making authority that only I had previously as CEO. Tom would now have performance based incentives to show gratitude for his unique ability to excel in support of multiple businesses for me. They both would be offered partnership in Sharp Innovations that they invested many years of their life building and running with me. All of these changes and plans needed to be something we all felt good about before any new strategic direction would be initiated. Showing your key people you truly care about them, and want to know what is on their heart proves that you truly want what is best for everyone involved. It also ensures you don't have mutual mystification that you find out about after it is too late. You don't want to find out later that they didn't support the great new directions or ideas you had envisioned upfront, and because of that it never becomes a rewarding or sustainable future company model. Many times you lose your key people because of such ill-advised decisions and with it the passion of the entrepreneur can even become something that dies. I should also add that though I focused first by ensuring a brighter future for my managers, we all then reaffirmed a commitment to maintaining and growing a company culture that embraced a bigger future for the entire team of the future company, no matter what adversity we would face over time.

As you run down your dreams, always see your future and the future of those around you, as bigger than your past my friend! This should remain true no matter how bad your personal losses are when you go through financial struggles, recessions, or key staffing transitions. It is critical that you focus on how your business could be better through replacing them (new perspective, new insights, new talents, etc.) while planning a brighter future for everyone, not just yourself. The beauty found in adversities is seen through our response to them. Perhaps it will be through rebuilding the organization without filling the position left by someone's departure, or re-engineering the strategic focus of the organization that was maintained through complacency fostered during seasons of success that lacked of perpetual focus towards a brighter future for others.

Only God knows what truly lies in my management team's futures together or separate from a career perspective. However, the same principal I applied to how I have handled our relationships then, will always apply.

I pray I learn to grow to deploy this concept in increased measure all the days of my life. Moreover, I pray that you can do the same for your employees, partners, co-workers, family, or others who are deeply engaged in working alongside of you as you run down your career dreams my friend. By focusing on ensuring a brighter future for those you care about most, as you walk out your passions in life, you have a unique advantage as you continue your walk based upon a firm foundation, not the sinking sands of human selfishness.

Point of Reflection or Action for Today:

"Each of us will one day be judged by our standard of life, not by our standard of living; by our measure of giving, not by our measure of wealth; by our simple goodness, not by our seeming greatness."

– William A. Ward

7. **A Passion for the Gratitude Focus**

    - The pursuit of your dreams can become so much richer when you inspire others to do the same through a life that reflects a grateful heart.

    - Implementing intentional, consistent, pro-active focus on showing gratitude will change your life.

8. **Inspiration to Give Beyond the 80-10-10 Model**

    - A person with a heart that passionately desires to give beyond what is asked or expected, will live a life of deeper purpose.

    - Embracing the gift of giving can lead you to an amazing life driving purpose and legacy.

9. **Creating a Brighter Future for Others**

    - Always make sure your contribution to the world is greater than your reward as you pursue your dreams.

    - Always seeing your future as bigger than your past becomes the life fuel for running down dreams.

    - You will live a life of greater purpose and meaning when you focus first on how your dream can create a bigger future for others before you pursue it.

Running Down Your Dreams—Taking Action!

Who is in your life that you could intentionally show gratitude, love, and thankfulness to for what they have meant to you in your life? Perhaps it is someone that has been on your heart for quite some time. If it is not an individual person then perhaps it is a cause or organization? One that you feel led to get involved (or further involved) with? What could you commit to doing for them now (or perhaps an on-going basis) to invest into their lives (or cause) while living out the principal of the gratitude focus?

Write about it in the space below; assign a goal date for this existing or new dream and journal about what your next action should be to make progress towards living a life full of genuine gratitude!

My Dream's Name: _____

My Go Date: _____

For more free resources to help encourage you in your pursuit of dreams found through the principal of gratitude, please visit: www.livewithpurposecoaching.com.

"The World is a book, and those who do not travel read only a page."
     – Saint Augustine

JOURNEY #3

Dreams Found Through the Blessing of Travel

Theme Focus:

Most people have had a dream of traveling somewhere they have never been. It seems the more people travel and experience new lands and cultures, the more they become enamored with doing so throughout life. There is so much to learn from people as you see life through their eyes. There is such vast beauty as you travel throughout the landscape of the picture of God's creation. It testifies to the very fingerprints of God. I believe too many people limit themselves by not traveling. Regardless of your passion for travel or the lack thereof, we can all learn something. My prayer is that through some amazing, real world stories shared within this theme of the book that you will be inspired in a fresh new way to pursue your dreams in life.

Chapter 10

Take a Year Off to Live Your Dreams: The Hemphill Family Story

Dreams Profile with Jim Hemphill

CFP®, Managing Director & Chief Investment Strategist of TGS Financial Advisors

Do you have a dream so exciting it scares you? My friend, Jim Hemphill, certainly had one like that. I met Jim through The Strategic Coach®. We have been attending quarterly workshops together for many years. Several years ago, Jim and his wife resolved to make one of their dreams a reality. His dream was one that many people have, but rarely take action on: to take one year off from work and travel around the world with his family on an epic journey of growth, education, and enrichment.

I remember hearing of his goal, and then, a little over a year later, hearing the story of the completed trip. The story was a blessing and encouragement to those who were already very empowered individuals.

Hearing about the Hemphill family's adventure challenged each of us to dream bigger. My prayer is that the insights and lessons learned through Jim's story will encourage you to stretch your mind to dream big.

A Unique Challenge Faced By Leaders

Someone who does not own a business, reading this story, might think, "Well, if I was in business for myself (like Jim) it would be easy to take off a year and travel around the world. I would have more resources and greater control." In some regards that might be true. With ownership comes responsibility. A business owner can build in more flexibility, but that flexibility does not come cheap. You can't simply quit your job or pick up and leave, even if you have a phenomenal management team.

As Chief Investment Strategist at TGS Financial Advisors, Jim specializes in money management for high net worth individuals, with special expertise in the areas of retirement transition and retirement cash flow planning. He is responsible for coordinating the firm's investment research initiatives and for recommending changes to the firm's investment committee. He also works with over one hundred client families, some of whom he has known since the 1970s.

As he approached his dream of traveling one year around the world with his family, Jim quickly realized he was confronted with some major obstacles due simply to his responsibilities within the firm. He couldn't leave a client base who was counting on him, and he couldn't easily leave employees—with families—as he pursued this dream. It clearly requires a lot of coordination, resources, and planning to uproot your life and the lives of your family.

Jim dedicated decades of his life to building his business and certainly did not want to see them destroyed by embarking upon such a dream. Following this type of dream, means dealing with unique challenges. It also requires a willingness to sacrifice. In Jim's case, he gave up more than one-third of his income.

Learning to Confront and Embrace Big Dreams

Jim's family has a tragic family history of colon cancer. Three of his close relatives died of the disease by their early 40s, including his mother. Jim didn't want to delay his dreams into a future that, in the case of many in his family line, did not materialize. Through that impetus, he was aware of his mortality earlier than many people. It was a strong motivation to do something remarkable with his life. Jim and his wife, Amy went to a couples' Strategic Coach® conference. During the conference, they worked on developing a vacation plan that led to Jim's world traveling dreams.

At first Amy thought he was insane, and said so. She did not think this idea could be practical for their family. But three days later she called him at work and said that after further thought, reflection and prayer, "We have to do that." She realized that if they didn't make the commitment then, they probably never would have. Making that initial commitment was only a beginning. A decision is not an event; it is the beginning of a process. They had to overcome massive barriers to make the trip happen. As they began to plan, they also began to realize the size of the risk they were taking on. Doubts crept in. At one point, Amy suggested that they move the trip back by another year. As they discussed this option, it triggered an emotional storm. Finally Jim delivered an ultimatum—we go on schedule, or we don't go at all.

The stress actually diminished. They learned that, once committed, you need to run after a big dream in an uncompromising, even inflexible, way. Only in that way can you muster the energy to overcome what otherwise seemed impossible obstacles. Jim and Amy learned through experience that you have to proceed without certainty, trusting in God that everything will work out according to His plan.

Simple Beauty:
Daring to Take Action When Others Would Not

If the financial markets had collapsed in the summer they began their trip instead of the following summer, they would have had to abandon the trip. They would have lost many of the funds they had already paid. Events beyond their control could have ended the dream at any time. The success of their trip was really a gift. It was a demonstration of the amazing beauty of God's timing in our lives.

Risk is part of life. You can't wait for a time without risk to pursue your dreams. God doesn't place limitations on the size of our dreams either. Many times He speaks to us through our dreaming. From the beginning, God has spoken to us through our dreams. If we listen, our lives can change in ways we could not imagine. There simply are no accidents in life. "You don't reason your way into dreams," Jim says. Sometimes those dreams God delivers as words of knowledge* simply seem ludicrous to us at first. It doesn't mean they are not possible, or that we should refrain from taking action.

A Rich Bonding Experience That Will Live Forever

When we talked, Jim spoke of the trip as a rich bonding experience that will live forever in his family's memories. They all developed a deep sense of gratitude as they experienced God's creation and the blessings of travel. Many times, travel helps you to appreciate your home life even more upon your return. Moreover, he realized through his worldwide travels how similar humans are despite their unique historical or cultural distinctions. He was reminded how almost everyone wants similar things out of life (a better life for kids/family, to make progress in life, to have purpose and meaning in life, etc.).

Though there were many highlights, here are a few of the most meaningful to Jim. Their first Christmas after the trip, his ten-year-old daughter sent a letter to Santa. She asked for no gifts. Instead, she asked for those less fortunate to be blessed, for their needs to be met. It was a touching experience to see what God did in the heart of his child. It went well beyond the amazing physical beauty she saw in the year of travel. It created a life-altering passion within her.

They had so many special places they fondly remember: the museums of Paris and London, a villa in Italy, the waves of the Indian Ocean at a beach in South Africa, the red glow of sunset on Uluru (Ayers Rock) in the middle of Australia, the gentle people of Bali. In Bali, twice a week Jim and his son Jack would wake up at 5 a.m. and walk through the Sacred Monkey Forest before dawn, walking for forty minutes to the only place with a reliable internet connection, so Jack could keep up with his online school classes. Jim learned that there is something special in today's modern world about having extended quality time with your family, without the distractions of technology and day-to-day activities. He and Amy believe they are more profoundly connected to their children than most modern parents. What one word best describes their feelings about their trip? Gratitude, overwhelming gratitude to God that they could experience this adventure, that they all came back safely, that they got along so well and learned so much. At the end of their days, each of them will be able to look back and bask in the beauty and realization of this dream.

You Don't Reason Your Way Into Dreams!

Just because his family accomplished their "one-year dream," it is actually one of many related, grand dreams that Jim had in regards to travel. Another lifelong dream was to go to the World Cup tournament. Jim and his son accomplished that goal during their visit to South Africa. Other related dreams he has now are riding coast to coast on his bicycle, hiking the Appalachian Trail, bicycling through Europe, and completing a special trip with each one of his kids separately like he did at the World Cup with his son. He also wants to finish his book that goes into greater detail about his year-long journey, an expansion of the blog they kept during their travels.

Each travel dream can be different in location, length of time, cost, etc. However, with travel or any category of dreams, one concept remains true: you don't reason your way into your dreams! You pursue them with the belief and understanding that all things truly are possible, and worth pursuing as you live a life of purpose and passion. "Always have a dream that scares you in life," Jim says. Then, take your first step toward it by believing it is possible. There are so many undiscovered dreams and so much beauty in the world around you that eagerly awaits you. You definitely do not need to be an entrepreneur to embark on dreams that scare you either. Jim's dreams might not be your dream or even remotely inspiring to you; however, I pray that Jim's story will spur you on to run after your dreams with a new fervor and belief in what seems impossible.

* A Word of Knowledge is a supernatural revelation of information that is given by the Holy Spirit. It is not something that the person who gets the word knows by their own senses, rather, it is supernaturally revealed by the Holy Spirit. It has to be something that you are totally unaware of prior in order to be a word of knowledge. See 1 Corinthians 7:10 for more context.

*Additional information on Jim's firm is available online at www.tgsfinancial.com. You can read his family's blog at www.travelpod.com/members/oneyearaway.

Point of Reflection or Action for Today:

"It is for us to pray not for tasks equal to our powers, but for powers equal to our tasks, to go forward with a great desire forever beating at the door of our hearts as we travel toward our distant goal."

– Helen Keller

Chapter 11

The Speed of Love

It's amazing how quickly God can work through us to love another person we don't even know. With that in mind, travel isn't just a means of personal discovery, it can also be a way of intentionally serving and loving. I'm not saying you have to be a missionary to see this, but I am saying that it can be a great way to get some perspective on how good we have it in America. Maybe your mission's field is the needy in your local community. Or maybe, if you're blessed enough to travel, you'll discover it by trading one destination in for another, like down the street in a spot you usually avoid.

I know that for me personally, mission work has given me incredible insight. In Ecuador, Rita taught me greater depths of love than I'd ever known. I used my strengths to help her with her business and encourage her, but the help I was able to give seemed dwarfed by what she and the Ecuadorian people taught me. I was floored by the humility that was evident in their lives every single day.

Just Show Up —
The Aftermath of the Earthquakes in Haiti

As a Christian, I need to take God's plans into consideration when I travel or go on a mission trip. My plans were to help a cleanup team after Hurricane Katrina. God's plan? Just show up. And not in Louisiana. In Haiti. I could not fully explain why, I just knew I needed to change my schedule and be ready and willing to serve Haiti. Fear, uncertainty, anxiety, doubt, and feelings of inadequacy as well as many other emotions ran through my veins.

My first experience in Haiti was searching for my bag in a disorganized pile sitting just off the runway. After (luckily) locating it, I met Marcio. He was my team's driver. Marcio would be the one to transport us to the tent communities we would be ministering to. He told me about how the devastating earthquakes happened one after another. He told me it was like something out of the movie Transformers. I was convicted as those in Haiti thought the world might be ending, while people like me were surrounded by comforts. Marcio kept telling me what that day was like. The ground ruptured like an oceanic tidal wave, cars flew through the air into buildings like a ping pong ball bouncing across a table. Buildings folded like blades of grass under a lawn mower. He could not fully explain to me how difficult it was to hold the hand of a dying girl as her body grew cold. He couldn't get her out of the rubble or speak her language, so he simply held her hand until she stopped breathing. The rubble included mass graves of burned bodies in the streets. During my visit, there were still dead Haitians in the rubble that weren't found until months later.

Marcio's tears spoke louder than any of his words could. He exemplified the speed of love, and how quickly God can move through willing hearts and hands. He not only loved the people of Haiti like they were his blood relatives (though he was an American), he showed me how a man could be open, vulnerable, and full of love with another man even if we were complete strangers. God made man in His own image (Gen. 1:27), and since God is love He proved to me how loving we could be to one another as I interacted with Marcio. For that I'll be forever changed and thankful.

There were so many moments during that week where I learned about the speed of love as I reflected on my dreams in life, the true purpose and focus on my life and the dreams I wanted to continue to pursue when I returned state side. In reflection, I learned that you can learn to love people of another race, language, and country more deeply than so many people you interact with locally on a weekly basis. My team was stretched to step out of our comfort zones and to learn to love people we have never met more deeply than ever. It was initially even more awkward because we had to communicate through translators, though we quickly learned to love the people and the translators deeply for helping us in our time of dependency and need.

It was a blessing to work alongside of the Haitians digging ditches for foundations, playing with their children, bringing food and supplies to their community, working with the local church, as well as teaching them how to put up tarps over their makeshift tents (sticks and torn bed sheets they saw as a home). These beds in which they were sleeping on were rocks in the mud. I remember one child that was so proud of the tent he and his mother lived in that he wanted to strike a pose and wanted me to take pictures of him in it. Most children in America would not have made it one night there without massive complaining. However, this boy was humble, peaceful, proud, and content with little. There were many other amazing stories like translators using their heads to literally break sticks for people that we were helping to tarp. Several children including one named Babosh, became self-appointed workers within our team. They became our brothers and sisters so quickly. They knew we loved them and they made it easy to do so by being so open to showing us love while freely receiving ours. We were blessed by a Haitian church that was so passionate that any atheist would shudder at the reverence, awe, and power of God that was seen through the faith of a people in such dire need. We did not need to understand their Creole words spoken during worship, though we could feel the speed of their love sweep through that tent service we witnessed in a mighty way.

I cannot do justice through mere words to explain to you how thankful I am that I was obedient to God and simply showed up in Haiti as I was prompted to do in my spirit. Haiti is a spiritually re-born nation ready to rebuild physically like never before, as it teaches the world how to love more purely. They are actually sending missionaries to the United States and other countries to teach them about God and the speed of love! I love the spirit of the Haitian people, and I pray you get an opportunity to experience such love first hand through travel. It will change your life if you open your heart.

A Day My Family Grew and I Learned About Love:
A Journey to Belo Horizonte, Brazil

I have been sponsoring two children (Ingrid and Cleiton) from Brazil through an organization called Child Fund International (formerly Christian Children's Fund) for several years. It was my first experience in sponsoring children in need, and it has it taught me so much about the speed and depths of love! For several years we wrote to each other and sent each other pictures through the translation service of the organization. They drew me pictures and shared from their little hearts as they reached out to me in love. They were truly like the little brother/sister or children that I never had to date in my life. I always desired and they dreamed that one day we would be able to actually meet each other. Fortunately, that day happened as I journeyed through the east coast of Brazil one summer.

I could not tell them initially because of the wishes of the organization, but only weeks after our last letter, I was set to come to meet them with many other sponsors as a surprise on a study tour of the nation of Brazil. There were so many highlights that I experienced in that country, and so much I learned about God and love through the hearts of the Brazilians. However, nothing was more special than the one day I spent with my sponsored children. I was blind folded early that morning and led down through the scenic landscape of the resort that we brought the children to. They had never seen a swimming pool until that day, and they were exposed to a five-star experience with ponies to ride and countless other first-time opportunities for the children to enjoy. I met their mothers and other family members and teachers. We shared gifts, tears, and hugs. We played like I have not played in decades with such a youthful vigor and passion. We did so many goofy and fun things. We danced the night away and though our last embrace was sad, we left each other with memories that will never fade away. Through the imprint of the hands of God, he taught us about the speed of love that day. We still write to one another to this very day and it is wonderful to watch them grow up and remain a meaningful part of their lives.

There are many great organizations if you ever want to look into the benefits and opportunities found within sponsoring a child personally or as a family. What a great opportunity to teach your children about the speed of love by allowing them to lead a new relationship with a new sponsored sister or brother that you adopt into your family unofficially speaking. World Vision (www.worldvision.org) and Compassion (www.

compassion.com) are two other great organizations for you to look into if you have not already. I believe you can learn about the dreams of others, help encourage others to reach their dreams and find new dreams become born in your life through such experiences.

Going Where Your Gifts Are Needed:
Ecuador Instead of Peru

Many of us spend so much energy planning out what we want to do in our lives. Many times we forget that God always has a plan for our lives (which includes each day). One spring I was set to go to Peru and serve the people of that nation who were in need. I was willing to do anything they needed. I picked Peru because for some unexplainable reason it was always a nation on my bucket list of places I would want to go one day. So when I had the opportunity to serve as a short-term missionary, it was a no brainer for me to select that country over countless others. Literally weeks before I was going to leave for the trip, God showed me yet again that He has plans that are far greater than our own. My trip to Peru and several other opportunities to go there during different weeks were all cancelled for various reasons. It was frustrating and I was honestly angry because I desperately wanted to go and serve.

I prayed to God and asked for direction and in his consistently, faithful love he delivered to me through a phone call from LifeTree Adventures (the organization I was scheduled with to go to Peru). They called me and told me of a need they had for my true passion and gifting in the country of Ecuador. They had people in the community they were serving who had dreams to expand their small business as well as people that had dreams of starting a business. They asked me to come in to do business coaching through a translator. I even wound up teaching a business ethics and encouragement class at the local church in addition to other missionary aid efforts I was fortunate to provide while working with the families of the community, the neediest children, and the pastor of their church. I bonded with one woman's dream in particular during my journey. Her name is Rita. Through this lady, I felt God allowed me insight into the concept of the speed of love. Below is a poem that was written for my life/business coaching website (www.livewithpurposecoaching.com). I think it explains our story very well so I'd like to encourage you to read it today.

A Poetic Offering: The Speed of Love

I have been blessed to travel around the world early in life,

Today's technology driven world makes it much easier to travel across continents in a blazing pace,

Though as I have traveled I found it hasn't been the places that were most impressive,

Nor was it merely the amazing people I have met that have become appointments from God,

There has been something much more special that was reinforced to me recently as the golden nugget of truth,

Simply put it was a concept I'd like to call the speed of love,

Sadly I find in the United States more than other countries we live in a self-centered, blind sort of way many times,

We make sure that our children are reinforced that talking to strangers is a bad thing,

I am not naïve enough to believe that lesson is permeated with illogical basis for our youngsters,

Though it is robbing them of an internal gift of wisdom, love, and blessing,

It shows up in the way I have seen people of other lands open their hearts from the first moment,

Like a child who gasps his/her first breathe exiting the mother's protective womb,

Recently in Ecuador I was overwhelmed by signs of immense affection from children and adults,

They sought nothing in return and merely desired to make sure they conveyed how much my visit meant to them,

What do you do when people from other lands cross your path in life and back at home?

I pray we could say the same for us about how we show others love,

The Lord has made it clear to the most giving person that without love we have nothing,

I firmly believe our lives are full of appointments from God, in which certain people were meant to cross our path,

Sometimes your heart can be touched in a deep, meaningful, and unexpected way,

The key is for us to open ourselves up to the unknown and potential goodness found in each new person,

While seeking God asking him what He desires for us to do to be a blessing to that person,

Rather than placing inappropriate judgment or focusing on what we could get from a relationship with them,

One great example of this for me was a woman named Rita from Quito,

Though we spoke through translators to communicate with one another,

Though we came from economic classes and lifestyles that were as different as night and day,

No barrier existed when it came to expressing and showing each other heartfelt love,

It didn't stop her tears from penetrating the depths of my soul as they streamed down her face,

It didn't stop the back of my hand from gently wiping them away and reciprocating love to her,

Nor did it stop her being filled with hope and me with encouragement to inspire her to run down her dreams,

The amount of time we spent together was limited but clearly irrelevant,

God proved to me that nothing limits His work including time,

Tomorrow is truly never guaranteed to any of us,

Today is full of opportunities to extend love that you will never give unless you truly open your heart and eyes,

So I pray you live today in a way that shows how you value the beautiful speed of love...

Taking Action On/Creating Your New Bucket List

Since I wrote the poem about Rita, I am thankful to say that I was able to help her church with funding that was needed to accomplish the growth phases she desired for her business and I have received pictures of her progress. I truly pray that she continues to dream and believe in God's ability to inspire and fulfill her dreams. I am sure the story of Rita and me is something that happens all of the time throughout our world and many times it happens in a wonderfully covert sort of way through humble hearts of the givers. The only reason I shared how I helped her financially was to state my final point for you today as you reflect on your dreams. It all begins with taking action. If I did not take action then the speed of love that was evident would have died as something I experienced yet denied a loving response to. For me, a new dream was born out of these lessons surrounding the speed of love. The new dream is to be a short-term missionary to serve those in need around the globe as I continue to strive to live a life of deep purpose and meaning that honors God.

Do you have a bucket list (a list of dreams, life goals or destinations to travel to)? If not, I encourage you to grab a notepad today and do so. That could be the very next action that could inspire new dreams in your life, or give you clarity on running down the dreams that might have been floating around in the background of your mental conscience. I encourage you to dream big. Stretch yourself and write down things that seem unreachable, and then ask God to confirm what is best for you to pursue. Asking God questions through the power of prayer is all it takes if you desire Him to give you ears to listen and a heart to receive clarity about dreams and inspiration for new ones. What place is calling out to you today my friend? I pray you would open your heart to ask that question to God and be ready to be inspired by new dreams surrounding the blessings of travel.

Point of Reflection or Action for Today:

James 2:5 (NIV)

[5] "Listen, my dear brothers: Has not God chosen those who are poor in the eyes of the world to be rich in faith and to inherit the kingdom he promised those who love him?"

Chapter 12

The Real Gifts Found in Traveling!

I have been fortunate enough to have ability to travel extensively. I realized that after taking a few trips out of my local region, that there was a whole big world out there that was ready to be explored. I have been fortunate to have met so many amazing people as I have traveled around the world. I have also seen my life completely re-shaped and be used to touch other people, while being touched by others in unique and unexpected ways. I now have a true life passion for missionary work which was something that never was on my radar screen for nearly the first thirty years of my life. Below are some of the real gifts that I have found in my travels. I pray they inspire you today as you run down your dreams!

A Life with a New Landscape

Too many people in our world see the horizon each day and leave it at that. The horizon is simply seen as a vantage point from where you are standing at that moment. The world offers a landscape so much broader than most of us ever even venture out to explore. I know there are many people that see themselves as home bodies and find traveling to be something they dread vs. something they have passion for. Though I can't relate personally to that mentality, I know it is real and have seen it in the lives of many who are close to me. Other people have dreams of traveling places, yet never step out in faith to make it a time, financial, or life priority. They wait for the years in the future when they will do that. The sad part for many people is that time never comes before they take their last breath on Earth.

Parents have a direct influence on our lives during what my pastor, Steve Cornell, calls the Eighteen-Year Factor. It is the first eighteen years of your life and how it has profoundly shaped you in a unique way. If you are a parent as described above that dreads travel or never made it a priority in life, then you have profoundly affected another generation and more likely several to come not only in how you have hidden these gifts from others, yet you might have conversely lit a fire in them to explore the landscape of the world that has been withheld. I do truly understand that for many families that they were not able to afford to do extensive travel because of their financial constraints. This is true in even the richest nations like the United States. I grew up in a home where we were on food stamps, and didn't have much money. We didn't travel really at all besides annual day trips or weekends both because of economic reasons and parental eighteen-year-factor influence. So, I truly feel like I can relate to many people because of living a life that has walked both sides of this coin of traveling or not.

It has been amazing to see how much I can see my perspective in life become re-shaped through the blessings of travel. Though I might not have been able to experience this as a child, my travels later in life definitely altered my entire life path. I would like to encourage all parents reading this to do whatever you can to make traveling a priority for your family. Frequency isn't the main concern. It is found more in the simple fact of the doing: taking action to travel, opening your family's mind and exploring the future together through new lenses. If not for your benefit, then I pray you see traveling as a blessing of education and life perspective formation of that of your children. They will become deposits that will last a lifetime. My understanding of the world is an active and growing platform of education. Traveling has been a teacher like no other. I have developed amazing lifelong friendships, found faith in God, seen my direction in life completely shifted, and further understood what true love is (as well as the depths of love that the human heart is capable of). I can say that these blessings were all largely found through traveling. Just imagine how beautiful the unknown landscape could be if you spread your wings to soar through it?

An Artist Like No Other

Most of the world would agree that Picasso was one of the greatest artists to ever live. I believe the blessings of travel have taught me that we need to look beyond the human Picasso to see the true Creator and Artist behind him. As I have traveled, I have seen so much evidence of God's handiwork, including the Great Barrier Reef in Australia and the vastness of the Grand Canyon. You can almost find yourself lost in the sheer size and majesty of places like those. It definitely puts in perspective how small we are in the grand scheme of life and how amazing the world truly is. If you ever venture to places of convergence like Alaska you will see how the vastness of the sea, wilderness, and mountain ranges create a place of artistic brilliance and mystique. I don't understand how anyone could deny a creator and author of life in places like those. They are simply unexplainable and incredibly beautiful fixtures of art on display for all of creation to enjoy each day. The destinations I mention are surely not a comprehensive picture of the amazing diversity found in creation and culture throughout our globe. You will see God's handiwork show up no matter where you go including your home town. You will find it each day within the smallest of creatures on this planet, to every plant that has given way to life, to the amazing wonder found in the changing weather of each day. For those that take action to travel they are able to experience the artistic beauty found in different cuisines, cultures, and societies that they become exposed to. They are true gifts that can speak to our hearts.

New Dreams and New Life Fuel

So my travels began with a selfish hunger to experience life. Instead of viewing travel as a gift, I viewed it as a right. After growing up in a home where traveling wasn't a priority or really even a possibility, I had earned the right to travel. I fondly placed pins on two maps of the city and country as I noted each and every place that I was able to venture to. Enjoying the fruits of your labor and seeing the world is something I do embrace, so I am not trying to discourage anyone there. I even continue to this day with the concept of charting my path of travel blessings on those maps. I am simply trying to state that my early travels were very self-focused and all about my entertainment value. As time continued on, I found myself being truly touched by the amazing love seen in those that faced poverty well beyond anything I ever experienced (even in my days on food stamps as a child). I have met people that have nothing by the measures of the world, yet they tip the scales with their abundance of genuine love for life and others. They demonstrate this each day as they live their lives in places that we see as remote from the creature comforts of more modern economic and social climates that you commonly find in the first world nations.

Fortunately, my dreams to explore life and conquer the world shifted to a platform of new-found, outward-focused passions that fuel my travels now with fresh perspective. The concept of doing short or long-term missionary work was the most foreign concept to me earlier in life. Now it is my true hunger that dwells within my spirit. I thank God for taking me through a path that stirred this passion within me. As mentioned, I was fortunate enough to meet two of my sponsored children from Brazil: Ingrid and Cleiton after years of letter writing. We spent a magical day where the children were able to experience things they never dreamed of as we shared in a depth of love that transformed our letter writing to this very day with exponentially deeper meaning. We all learned that love knows no age, distance, or language boundary. During travels to Ecuador, I was able to learn about the speed of love and the depths of love found in the human heart. Though I went to serve the people of Ecuador, I can say they blessed me more by simply showing me how they humbly live their lives day to day. Other travels like helping to lead a Bible camp for youth in the Australian wilderness called Impact and taking a journey to the Holy Lands in Israel where the bulk of Jesus Christ's ministry took place has also certainly become a fuel injecting catalyst for my growing Christian faith. They have all given my dreams a new life fuel.

One Check You Can Take to Any Bank

You only live once in life, so why not live a life of passion and purpose? Why not explore the landscape of the world by walking out past that horizon you see? I can promise you that you can't take anything with you to the grave even if you try and bury your wealth with you. That is one check you can definitely take to the bank.

I encourage you all to see life as doors of opportunity to walk through and experience while balancing that with fiscal responsibility. I understand that we need to be good stewards of the resources we are given in life. I do believe, however, living like you are dying each day and pouring out your heart to the world through passionate forms of true love as you travel, is an amazing way to live life. It is my prayer for you that you would experience that approach to life for all it truly is. There are no unrealistic goals in life no matter where you want to go or what your financial picture looks like. There are only unrealistic timelines. Dreams can become truth through not only thought and planning, but action. Action requires faith and belief that God could help you accomplish the travel dreams within your heart. Traveling experiences can open you to new seasons within your life and alter your life path forever like they did mine. They can also allow the person God made you to be uniquely come alive to better the world on a broader landscape if you open your heart to the unknown of each day. Traveling can teach you how you can bless the world while you grow and learn. Now that is a true triple win! God will open doors for you if you set your desires before Him and they align with His purposes for your life. I truly believe that, my friend...

Point of Reflection or Action for Today:

"Do not go where the path may lead, go instead where there is no path and leave a trail."

- Ralph Waldo Emerson

Chapter 13

Re-engineering Global Economies to Fuel Dreams: The HOPE International Story

Dreams Profile with Jeff Rutt

Founder/Chairman of HOPE International, (a Christian Micro-Enterprise Development Organization) and CEO of Keystone Custom Homes

Jeff and I first met when my firm, Sharp Innovations, Inc., did technical support work for his firm, Keystone Custom Homes. He was a client for some time, though at our initial meeting HOPE International, the dream of this book, or my role as a life coach, author, and speaker for God's glory wasn't even on the radar screen. I was not a Christian at that time, and I certainly didn't ever consider being a missionary as I reflected upon my dreams and what I wanted most out of my life. To be honest, I simply considered my interaction with Jeff to be a mere transactional business relationship with no real deep connection. That was before I could see what God was doing in our lives and how our paths would cross again multiple times in completely new ways.

The story of HOPE International was born through a beautiful coalescing of courage, the depths of true love for the less fortunate in our world, obedience to God, and the blessings of travel. My prayer is that their story would touch and inspire you today in a unique way as you further reflect on your own dreams and purpose in life!

A Foreshadowing to a Shared Life Call & Passion

Before I officially launched into a new role as a business/life coach, Jeff was one of the first people with whom I met to test pilot what I believed was a unique gift that God gave to me. Though we have not continued into a long-term coaching relationship, our interactions have allowed me to better understand his passion and purpose within the new part of his career through HOPE International. HOPE became one of my first points of reference as I continued to explore my new-found zeal and calling to the global mission field as a short-term missionary. Jeff and I both share a passion to help empower the less fortunate in this world to pursue and reach their dreams, while sharing the truth of God's love for all people. Years later, as I write this chapter, Jeff's story and the launch of HOPE has been a key motivator in my own passion for short-term missions and personal travel that is designed to promote God's glory and blessing for others.

HOPE International was born out of true courage. Many times people feel as if they have a dream for their life that they will pursue one day in their future. For "one day" when the timing will be better, and perhaps "one day" when more people support them in walking their dream out in faith. Jeff's dream that became HOPE International is proof that there may be no better time than today for the realization of personal dreams.

Jeff saw a huge need for global help for the impoverished people of this planet who hold tight to dreams that might never have a chance to be born. Even though Jeff was in the midst of a successful real estate career, and growing his construction company (Keystone Custom Homes), he felt as if God was calling him to have courage to do more. He remembers meetings he had with trusted counsel. One gentleman in this group, Jeff's attorney, strongly urged him to forget about this dream, out of genuine care and love for Jeff. He thought that perhaps Jeff was in some sort of mid-life crisis. I am proud to say today that we can all express sheer thankfulness that Jeff never wavered in pursuing the call that God put on his heart that became the birth of HOPE International.

Dreams Come in Pieces

In reflecting on how HOPE came to be, Jeff made a profound comment: "The thing about dreams is they come in pieces." Jeff Rutt didn't set out to found a leading Christ-centered microfinance organization, but by the time God brought all the pieces of his dream together, he had.

What began as an unsettled feeling after returning from a short-term mission trip quickly blossomed into a deep desire to make a difference beyond his two-week commitment. Jeff joined his church in sending shipments of aid to the city of Zaporozhye, Ukraine. Following the collapse of the Soviet Union, the families residing there were struggling to make it through another bitterly cold winter.

When Jeff later traveled to Ukraine, a pastor asked him to "help in a way that wouldn't hurt." The aid shipments, the pastor explained, were depressing local industry and initiative, creating a dependence on American charity, and stripping the Ukrainians of their dignity. A vision began to form in Jeff's mind of providing the people of Zaporozhye with a viable solution for their desperate poverty. In his vision, he helped a handful of people—not even the entire city.

Research led Jeff to the concept of microfinance. "I felt God leading me in that direction," he explained. "I could see these industrious people who wanted to make a better life for themselves and their families. We had this tool to help them turn hard work into provision and I could visualize how it would work." Even so, Jeff's dream was to help a handful of people. He couldn't imagine reaching the entire city of Zaporozhye when he issued the first twelve loans.

After the loans in Zaporozhye proved successful, Jeff decided to expand HOPE's ministry to the rest of Ukraine. Only years later did Jeff realize that what began in a small Ukrainian city could become a global initiative focused on bringing solutions to both physical and spiritual poverty to countless suffering families. Jeff has learned not to put limits on his dreams. "It's hard to define my dream for HOPE except to say that we're going to continue to trust God to send us in the right direction. There's amazing potential," he says.

HOPE's Focus on Micro-Financing Sustainability

HOPE's purpose became one of providing solutions for sustainability through micro-financing. They stand for the direct opposite of the typical model of short-term relief efforts that many times only become a band-aid for third world nations—even when the aid is seen as pure heroism from the vantage point of most giving communities. Following the fall of the Soviet Union, Jeff traveled to Ukraine numerous times as a member of a church delegation, transporting containers of food, clothing, and medical supplies to the city of Zaporozhye. After several of these visits, it was then that the local pastor made his profound comment to Jeff and told him honestly that the shipments were not helping. Instead of handouts, the pastor felt that his community needed a hand up.

Though people were accessing needed supplies, they had become dependent on American charity. In addition, local businesses could not compete with the free handouts. The well-intentioned aid shipments were actually doing more harm than good by depressing local industry and initiative. Jeff returned from the trip with a strong drive to find a solution. He focused on better understanding and refining the concept of microfinance (providing small loans and savings services to entrepreneurs in developing countries), which then was a little-known poverty alleviation strategy. He applied this tool with great success in Ukraine. HOPE International was borne of this effort. As Jeff and HOPE's staff and board realized the enormous impact they could have on the poor through microfinance, they expanded their effort to other countries. In 2004, Peter Greer joined HOPE as president, taking on the day-to-day leadership and releasing Jeff to serve in a visionary capacity for the organization. This move ushered in a period of strategic growth and increased public awareness. Under Peter's leadership, HOPE articulated its four distinctive features: focus on microfinance, intentional witness for Christ, commitment to financial stewardship, and dedication to the hard places around the world.

Today, HOPE continues its focus on providing hope and dignity in the lives of families in the hard places of the world. They have a passion for sharing the gospel of God's love to the broken and less fortunate while ministering to the families they are supporting. They go far beyond the simple financial aspect of the ministry. Their work looks different in different places. Their mission is to invest in the dreams of the poor in the world's underserved communities so that they might be released from physical and spiritual poverty. Their method is to offer small business loans, savings services, biblically-based business training, and mentoring and coaching from a Christ-centered perspective. Their motivation is to share the love of Jesus Christ as they strive to identify with the poor and care for their physical and spiritual condition.

Their loan officers manage from a three-fold vantage point: the head of a banker, a heart of pastor, and the soul of a missionary. As they pursue excellence in micro-financing with an intentional witness towards spiritual poverty, they conduct biweekly loan officer meetings and prayer meetings. (The community is invited to the prayer meetings, but those receiving the loans from HOPE aren't bound to participate in them.)

They have been greatly encouraged to see a broad spectrum of people of faith, including Muslims, see the true heart of HOPE, and through that see their life dynamically changed by God. The stories are too numerous to recount with full justice in this chapter, but let me offer just one inspiring example: the story of Kande from Congo. HOPE helped him to transform his family from a lifestyle that had their children sleep on their stomachs to suppress their severe hunger pains, to one more fortunate through a successful small business that provides copy services to the local community. It was such a sweet follow-up for Jeff to have with Kande several years later as they could both express the joy of what had happened through the dream that fueled what is HOPE International.

The Heart of a Founder of HOPE

Jeff encourages people that when a need is there, dealing appropriately with that need should determine our actions in life. He feels people should use their God-given talents to meet the needs of the world around them. You can use your God-given passions and talents to meet the needs that exist right in front of you. Be encouraged that dreams are often times found through the blessings of travel and stepping outside your daily routine. You are then able to see new dreams borne in the same way that the HOPE dream was birthed. God has taught Jeff much through experiences in serving others. However, you certainly do not need to leave home either to experience and share in the passions found through the mission, purpose, and motivation of HOPE International. People in your own hometown this very day are in desperate need of love, support and compassion, and could easily become a grafted part of the next season that further defines your purpose in life.

HOPE is focused on growing their organization by doubling their global, micro-financing loan portfolio in the next three years from $25 million to $50 million. Just imagine how many dreams can continue to be shaped, born, inspired, and fueled by the dream that sparked with Jeff's courage! The time to move forward could be right now for you, my friend! If God is leading you, then the need to follow is when He is leading—not when you are ready. You can wait for a better time to come in life to take action on your dreams, but that time might never come. Do you feel God nudging you towards a new dream or direction in life today?

*For more information on HOPE International, visit www.hopeinternational.org.

Point of Reflection or Action for Today:

Jeremiah 29:11 (NIV)

[11] I know the plans I have for you, declares the Lord, plans to prosper you and not to harm you, plans to give you a hope and a future.

Top Insights Summary from

10. Take a Year off to Live Your Dreams! The Hemphill Family Story
- Always have a dream that scares you in life, and then take your first step towards it by believing it is possible.
- There are so many undiscovered dreams and so much beauty in the world around you that eagerly await for you to discover them.

11. The Speed of Love
- The speed of love can break down any barrier that dares to stand in the way of a dream.
- Love has the ability to give birth to new, life-long passions and dreams.
- You can learn much about what matters most, and how to love more deeply through your interactions with those less fortunate.

12. The Real Gifts Found in Traveling
- Traveling can help you broaden your perspective in life, as well as gain clarity about your purpose and direction.
- Any travel dream is more achievable when you view travel as a gift.

13. Re-Engineering Global Economies to Fuel Dreams: The Hope International Story
- Micro-financing is an incubator for so many beautiful dreams around the globe.
- You should focus on using your God-given passions and talents for the betterment of the world around you.

Running Down Your Dreams—Taking Action!

For those who are passionate about travel:

Where have you always dreamed of going most but have never made it to yet? Think about the reasons behind why you want to make it to that destination. Perhaps it was a dream fueled by someone dear to you. Perhaps it was a place they always wanted to go, but never made it to before they passed away. Perhaps you have no real reason, but have always dreamed of going there. Write about your dream in the space below; assign a go-date for you to take action, and journal about what your next action should be to make progress towards the dream.

For non-travelers:

Who do you know with a travel dream that you could contribute to today to inspire them to take action on it? If you had no constraints in life, and had a magic wand that could take you to one destination for free, where would it be? Write about your dream in the space below; assign a go-date for you to take action, and journal about what your next action should be to make progress towards your dream or the dream of someone you care about.

My Dream's Name: _____

My Go Date: _____

For more free resources to help encourage you in your pursuit of dreams found through the blessings of travel, please visit: www.livewithpurposecoaching.com.

1 Corinthians 13:3-5 (NIV)

[3] If I give all I possess to the poor and give over my body to hardship that I may boast, [a] but do not have love, I gain nothing. [4] Love is patient, love is kind. It does not envy, it does not boast, it is not proud. [5] It does not dishonor others, it is not self-seeking, it is not easily angered, it keeps no record of wrongs.

JOURNEY #4

Dreams Found Through the Pursuit of a Soul Mate

Theme Focus:

Some people might not believe in the concept of soul mates. However, most all would admit that they dream of unconditional love. Each person's desires for romance or being married might vary as well, however their ultimate desire to be loved and to love is something that rings true through the very fabric of all of mankind. Our hearts are pulled with a strong gravitational pull towards the joy of love. Furthermore, God has clearly affirmed that there is no greater power or gift in this life than love. So, why are so many people (married or not) unhappy? Why are so many singles and divorced people full of discontent? My prayer is that through real world stories shared within this theme of the book (many from the depths of my own heart) that you will be encouraged to love your spouse more deeply, or will approach dating in a beautiful new way if you are single, as you continue to pursue dreams of a happy marriage, soul mate and/or family one day.

Chapter 14

A Very Common Modern Idol

An idol is anything that becomes an all-consuming pursuit in our life that surpasses our ability to see God's will. Some easy examples of this concept can be found in climbing the corporate ladder, attaining the dream home with the white picket fence and 2.3 kids, or finding your soul mate so your real life can begin. I'll share my life story about that later: striving to find a soul mate.

The concept of serendipitously finding your soul mate or the one true person that you were meant for is a very powerful desire. In no way do I desire to take that dream or possibility from your mind if you are a single person with that desire or if you are married. However, I desire to share with you an analogy about how the beautiful seeds of romantic hope and passion planted in the spring may never sprout, and may wither away in the fall, leaving the farmer without a harvest. It is a tough experience to face in a single year, yet the farmer can certainly find resilience and perseverance to weather winter's storms and prepare for the next spring. However, if years continue on with the same experience and the years turn into decades it can leave the farmer unknowingly blind or in a state of true disarray and hopelessness. The raw passions that existed in the early spring of planting are long lost giving way to bitterness and resentment that permeate.

Joe the Farmer's Story

I certainly am not a farmer in the physical sense. Heck, I'm not even gifted with my hands. Yet I myself lived the life of this analogized farmer. I suppose it makes the most sense for me to start with the early days when I worked at a chain of card stores during high school. I was pretty much the only male and worked with over forty women.

It was an interesting experience. I learned a lot about women that I didn't while growing up because of the strained dynamics in my family. I did find out that I enjoyed communicating in a deep and passionate way. My father, God rest his soul, used to say, "You should have been a girl." I know he jokingly was referring to my emotional and communicative sides that were not typically male. On my way to college, I left those ladies behind with them vowing that I would be one of the first of my class to be married. I remember standing from a distance while I had roses and custom poems delivered to each one of them that spoke about what they meant to me during that work experience. I headed off in my '77 Ford Granada to college and a big new world that seemed ripe to find my soul mate.

Through college I learned a lot and certainly didn't always make the wisest choices. I did however meet a very special person to me through the most unlikely of circumstances. A girl that expressed interest in me (one that I only saw as a friend) at that time introduced me to another gal that became my girlfriend and fiancé throughout the remainder of my college years. Though I will refrain from details, the engagement unexpectedly broke months before the altar, leaving me broken.

The Decade that Increased my Love Boat's Speed

Months became years as my 20s continued, and I was surely making unfair comparisons of other women I dated. I would rather find the right woman for six years than the wrong one for sixty. The compass of my heart was building momentum due north as I pressed on searching for my soul mate. She was becoming something that not only needed to equal the characteristics I valued in my fiancé, she needed to surpass it. I voraciously read dating, relationship, and self-help books. On their recommendation, I even created lists that measured dates against each other. Now I see clearly that this seemingly brilliant education I was soaking up was, in some cases, ruining opportunities with people that could have been good life partners.

It seemed like a noble passion. Slowly I saw my family and friends lose the ability to support and encourage me through my dating trials and tribulations. They believed I was too picky, and were probably right. I took pride in not settling. It became an idol. God has graciously answered my prayers which have thankfully re-directed my ship. I am still a captain of the sea of love that desires one day to be married and I can't say I am without silver in my mane. However, I now seek to drop my nets daily to harvest from the depths of the sea which is ripe with a multitude of relationships of both genders and varied ages that need tender love from me, not merely a few pearls that could be soul mates.

I pray that if you are single and desire to be married, that you would ask God to show you how to spread that passion within the world while you wait for the fulfillment of that dream. Don't let pressures from your peers, biological clocks, or emotions take control. Ask Him to help you to truly be ok with the potential of lifelong singleness. I say that not because I don't desire you to happily marry. I sincerely pray you do find that joy in a passionate relationship. I just believe if you can truly be ok with being single forever, that you are then ready to love the world more deeply while stepping fully into the purposes God has for your life, which might or might not include a happy marriage and family. I am embarrassed to say I have done this for longer than I can believe. The right person could come into your life tomorrow, so rather than focusing on finding that person why not pour out the love and passion within you to all those you interact with each day?

If you are a married person, I believe this applies to you as well. Don't allow climbing the corporate ladder, striving for financial freedom, building the dream home, or having children cloud your ability to realize the blessings found in each day. You can choose to be a blessing to those in your life. Rather than being self-focused on those big desires that can become our idols, I pray you would live your life striving to run down your dreams by living an outwardly focused life. I pray you would knock down any idols in your life this very day and ask God to show you how to love your spouse and those around you more and more. Live for the simple beauty found in the gift of life each day.

Point of Reflection or Action for Today:

1 Corinthians 16:14 (NIV)

[9] Do everything in love.

Chapter 15

A Church, Wedding Dress, and Ring Doesn't Always Mean Marriage

For most people, they would probably agree if you were talking about a church, a wedding dress, and rings that you were talking about a marriage. In most cases that might be true. However, this story built on personal vulnerability proves that there are truly two sides to any coin. Many people have had broken engagements or marriages. Even more sad, many people have gone through both (sometimes several times over) as they look back in the rearview mirror of their romantic past. The writing of this chapter was an essential last step in preparing my heart as a field ready for a new harvest. I know I can do so by grabbing the drenched towel that is the passion found in my past engagement while wringing out the wisdom of this season of my life.

A Denny's Enchantment through Unexpected Means

Like most stories, I suppose it is best to start where it all began: how we met. Though the first date between Bridget and I was to a local Denny's Restaurant, I would be remiss in not telling you about how we actually met. We met through the introduction of a mutual friend named Jen, who to this very day I hold dearly in my heart as someone that I feel was sent by God. What was remarkable in my mind was the fact that when Jen and I met, she conveyed romantic interest in me, and she was one of the first people in my young adult life to show me a poignant example of what true love is. She did so by introducing me to the woman that was: the first woman I ever fell madly in love with, the first person I was ever in a multi-year relationship with, and my first fiancé. Jen put aside her desires or romantic interest, and focused on loving two other people in an incredibly pure way. If she would have been selfish like so many others as they run down their dream of a happy marriage, then this story would have never happened.

I can remember the night Bridget and I met at that Denny's like it was yesterday. She truly captured my heart from "hello," like the movie Jerry McGuire." She was such a strikingly enchanting spirit like one I had never met before. What I found myself enamored with certainly went well beyond her clear, physical beauty. I remembered being intoxicated with her character, ambitions, personality, and so much more. I remembered being astounded by how I could see nothing wrong with her through the rose colored glasses I was wearing. Heck, I have never worn glasses besides sunglasses, so you would have thought I might have felt their weight hanging on my head that night, but I didn't. One rarely ever sees the reality when your heart becomes invested blindly. As we spoke for hours on end into the middle of the morning, munching on food we clearly didn't need, I remember hanging on her every word. She gladly returned the favor, and any fly on the wall that night was singing "love is in the air." I remember hugging her after the date, and never wanting to let go. I left that night sure that I was going to passionately pursue her with every fabric of my being. It was as if I was at the poker table, and I was going all in.

Following Your Heart

The concept of following your heart is a familiar one to so many people that are in passionate pursuit of their soul mate. I am sure you have heard the saying: "wearing your heart on your sleeve." Many times hindsight is 20/20, and if given the chance, one would make very different romantic decisions to spare themselves from the pain found in following one's heart. I am not here to promote the removal of raw passion from a healthy dating romance, but I am here to share an alternative, my friend!

I can remember the early days of dating Bridget for the pure euphoric bliss that enthralled both of us. I fondly remember us exchanging poems and little special affections of love as each month in our relationship passed. The amount of mutual thought, consideration, and compassion was certainly notable. I believe that is something that couples (including married ones) could be reminded of in regards to doing the little things in life. Each person might have different love languages and communication styles; however, everyone appreciates love and their loved one showing them that they continue to remain in the forefront of their mind regardless of it being weeks, months, years, or decades into the relationship.

Our relationship was so full of physical, emotional, and intellectual bonds. We had a magical connection in the main areas, ever before I knew there was a fourth dimension. My chapter on the power of the four corners can elaborate on that more. Looking back, I can say though that we made a common mistake that many couples do before marriage, and that is the concept of playing house. We lived together in sin as so many do today (because it truly seems almost socially expected nowadays). I am sure this was not supported by our parents; however, we thought it was wise and it was only a year from the wedding so we thought what could it hurt? We believed it was a wise thing to get to know one another in a whole new way so we could work out our differences before we officially began our new life together so to speak. Sadly, we learned the hard way, like so many do, by making that mistake. However, we were fortunate that it didn't leave behind the additional scars of divorce, and broken lives of children. So, I told you that I was going to present an alternative, both for those running down the dream of a soul mate, and those who are going after that very same dream again by pressing on through the pain of a divorce.

The alternative approach to following your heart is the powerful concept of leading your heart! I truly believe that this concept is not simply for singles, and I want that to be clearly stated upfront. It is a whole new way of re-engineering how you treat, honor, respect, and love someone of the opposite sex. And men, let me tell you something: the burden of leading your heart is the responsibility of the man in each and every relationship. If done well, a man cannot just lead his heart, but he can gracefully help a woman to guard hers. There is no magical formula here. Simply focus on getting to know the person in a deep way while being objective and not blurred by emotional or physical bonds. You both focus on getting to know the real person, instead of allowing euphoric emotions to cloud your judgment while you live out the adage that dating is meant to conceal what marriage later reveals. I have found that you can really get to know someone on a deeper level when you remove the romance blinders in the early stage. I believe that anything you start out well has a much better chance of ending well (like romance as you progress through engagement into a marriage). So I pray you can take that to heart if you are not married yet, as you look at your romantic dreams.

If you are married, I believe the call is now on both parties, however, clearly still on the man. I believe that each person truly has a life-long responsibility to choose to love the other person and to be faithful to them. That choice happens each and every day, when you remove yourself from temptations that can lead to inappropriate emotional and physical relationships, no matter what it costs you or how difficult it might be to do in the moment. You choose to show your spouse, yourself, and God that your ultimate romantic dream is truly found in loving them well all of the days of your life. That dream replaces the dream of running down the pursuit of your soul mate. Too many people recant their marriage vows like they were something they didn't say at all, and certainly not something they took seriously as they pronounced them to God and their guests on that special day. They don't feel in love anymore. Love is a choice and the mature couples that stand the test of time, realize that by leading their heart and choosing daily to love the other person no matter what (even when they seem unlovable) that they will come out stronger in the end, and will grow in abounding love.

The Butterfly Floats Away

I remember waking up one day to a sight I never thought I'd see. Bridget's engagement ring was on my dresser. It jilted my eyes from their early morning stupor. I remembered our conversation about how we could postpone the wedding. I told her if she was getting cold feet, feeling rushed or felt like we had things to work through, we could simply stay engaged for awhile. I was willing to do whatever it took to make things work. I was willing to move in with my grandparents again and allow her to have our apartment while I paid for it, and continued to passionately fight to see the three-year plan of my start-up business, Sharp Innovations, reach the success that my heart throbbed for. I told her that if she moved back home to Philadelphia after we already were playing house and living together, that we would surely fall apart. Though there was much I didn't realize at the time, including her getting physically involved with other men and perhaps other things I was never told, I believed that.

I was meant to allow the butterfly to float away and not disturb its flight path in that moment. She said she was living through me, and needed to find herself. She might have found herself into the arms of a past lover, though she positioned it to her parents and me as if at the time they were just friends who were going to move to another state to spread their wings a bit. So the butterfly floated on to Illinois. I believed that if we were meant to be, and she was truly the woman that I was meant to spend the rest of my life with, that the butterfly would find its way back to its home in PA. I knew it had to take its flight no matter how much it hurt. Though it left me standing in utter shock so painful that it felt as if it took literal months to muster the strength to lift my gapping jaw up off the floor that it drug across as I went through my daily motions trying to act as if things were ok.

Learning the Power in Trust

Trust is powerful. If any romantic relationship can stand firm on the foundation of trust, you have a lot to be thankful for and encouraged by as you walk through life together. Many people find complete trust to be something that they cannot easily give and sometimes ever truly offer to another person. I learned my lesson about trust days after my butterfly floated away. Though it was learned through actions that were not led by any malicious intention on my part, it was still painful. Though we broke up, we tried to still have a friendship with each other even if we rarely communicated in the months that would follow. She agreed to be my ride on my very first flight to the Strategic Coach® in Chicago that I now attend quarterly. She told me she never got my flight details, and since I was my own e-mail host through my business, I knew that the e-mail went out to her. It seemed strange, so I figured I'd re-send it to her and check to make sure she got the message. I was able to do that because I had access to her e-mail account because I used it many times when I traveled for business and needed internet access back when dial-up was normal (man do I feel old).

I saw the same e-mail address in her inbox tons of times in a row. Curiosity killed this cat, and I started by reading one message. As I began to realize who it was and what was being discussed (romantic rendezvous and such), I found my heart drawn towards reading the rest of them. Through the distrust I showed her that night, I believe I saw God providentially work to bring forth his purposes for my life many years before I'd ever grow to realize it fully. I definitely learned that even when you feel as if you cannot trust someone (including the person you see as your soul mate), you will find that you can always trust God in all things to create good from any dark moments or seasons we live through. He is the creator of trust, like all things in life!

The Coffee Shop that Forever Hides Rings

Fast forward ahead say like other nine or ten months to a Suburban Philadelphia Starbucks. Bridget and I met that day for the very last time as two unmarried people. I remember hearing from her via e-mail about her new engagement, and how she was coming to visit her family that weekend. I drove home that night with my new friend at the time, Andy, who became a kindred spirit. I spoke to her on my phone as I sat in my kitchen that night asking for her to meet me one more time at Starbucks near her parents. We could talk; I could seek closure and get my ring back, which I gave her when she decided to move home, thinking that we'd eventually be back together again. She agreed to my request, as I trembled so violently that I could barely speak coherently. Andy watched as I exposed my heart in an extremely raw way over the phone.

We had a conversation that was a lot shorter than I desired. She told me that she couldn't find the ring, because she misplaced it when she packed up her stuff and moved to Illinois. I didn't want the ring back simply for monetary recoup. I wanted it back because I felt like it brought negative karma to her new engagement and it simply seemed unfair for her to keep that special bond between us when I was seeking closure.

A Delayed Reaction from the Heart

Fast forward to a Saturday night around Valentine's Day. I contacted my friend Andy and told him I needed to see him and went over there in the middle of the night. I was plagued all night prior with emotions that overcame me in a crippling sort of way. I could not stop thinking about three things. Firstly, I was a passionate guy that would fight for anything that I believed in. Secondly, that I stood stunned and let the butterfly float away. Lastly, and perhaps most importantly I continued to mentally replay the e-mail she sent me that announced her new engagement. She literally told me that his proposal was nothing like mine, and that she always believed we were going to get back together. They pounded through my mind with such force that I felt like I was being swept away into some great emotional abyss. So, why did I do nothing about it when we met at that coffee shop? All I can do to answer it is tell you about the next part of our story.

My David and Goliath Story

Many people have heard the story in the Bible about the young shepherd boy, David, and the renowned warrior, Goliath. God used David to do the unthinkable and take down a mighty warrior, and eventually become the King of Israel. My response to the delayed reaction from my heart might not involve a battle field, a sling shot, or a warrior, though I definitely felt like I played the part of the young, courageous shepherd boy David.

I suppose I should start by explaining to you what Andy and I discussed at his apartment in the middle of the night. I told him about my heart's passionate response to the three forces that plagued my heart and mind as previously stated. I knew I needed closure, and it eluded me. I needed to be clear with Bridget, and I needed to tell her how I felt every moment since the butterfly took flight. I needed to ensure her that she understood the endless depths of my love for her, and even more importantly I needed to make sure that she really loved this other guy, and she truly wanted to marry him. I was worried she was doing it out of a sense of obligation or logical response to a couple lengthy relationships that fell apart for her (including ours months before the altar). I simply desired to get one hour with her again so I could honestly express myself the way I wished I did at that Starbucks. I desired to look her in the eyes and hear from her that she was truly making the best long-term decision for herself. So what does the modern day David do in a situation like that?

I knew that my Goliath was the seemingly insurmountable force that was her new life in Springfield, Illinois. She was engaged to this guy now for a of couple years. They had a house together, lived many states away, had pets together and a wedding on deck. To make matters worse, we communicated only a handful of times over roughly three years. Even from those that loved me most, and knew both of us and our relationship best, you would struggle to get a 5 percent success vote from them for what I was about to do. I bet David had an even worse vote from those around him back in his day, so 5 percent seemed just enough for this David to step to the plate. However, I knew what I came up with had to be the most intricate plan I had ever devised. I certainly wanted to minimize doing anything that created discomfort for her and even more so her fiancé. I figured directing all communication through her work was the least intrusive way to go about things from my very limited options.

I kept a massive amount of sentimental artifacts, pictures and the like from our relationship. I often thought that perhaps I should throw them away now that she was planning to marry another man so I could finally let go. However, I never did. I decided to do that finally by utilizing them all as contributing forces that could set off the largest firework display I could create. Now, I don't literally mean I blew them up my friend! I did however turn them all into hand crafted, and thematic artistry that was intended to express the passionate love that still swelled within me for her. I built six different gifts with a letter attached that tied into each day that built a word that we created that meant something special to both of us, even though other people would be left clueless. I built a mural of our lives, learned animation and produced a website about us for her, and various other efforts that sang the same love song. Each day different florists in the area would deliver them to her work and call me to confirm that she received the package intact. I realized that if her fiancé heard about it, that he would easily work to stop my effort if I sent them from the same place. My goal was to end on the sixth day landing at her work and asking her to lunch for one hour to share what was on my heart at the same place we met, a Denny's. I fondly remember so many of the women from the postal store clerks to the florists who were spurring me on in heartfelt encouragement despite the odds.

Unfortunately, I never got past the third day. It was my dream to get that one special hour with her. Despite the outcome, I truly believed that I would receive the closure I desired in failure, or that I would receive the blessing of winning her heart again through success. So it was an easy choice for me to do what seemed unthinkable. I got a delivery confirmation package of its own on the third day, and I remember sitting in my conference room dreading opening it after my team meeting was done. What I read next was easily the worst letter I had ever received. Knowing how much we both loved each other, it was like an out of body experience as I felt each dagger pierce my heart. I cannot be sure that she wrote the letter in conjunction with her new fiancé though it surely seemed like it, and I suppose it truly doesn't matter. What mattered was that she was firm about wanting to put a kibosh on the romantic performance that I was midstream in rolling out. She didn't realize that I simply only wanted one hour with her at Denny's at the time. She found out later in the letter that became my response. I remember calling all of the remaining florists telling them that they could re-use the frames and anything of value to them and could trash the rest. The sighs they gave on the phone were touching because they knew it was heart wrenching for me, though they never personally met me. Everybody loves a good love story where it works out in the end, though this one was not meant to be. It did help become part of the closure I sought. Also, it became a catalyst for a massive shift in my life full of new dreams (including my main dream of helping people live a life of deep seated meaning and purpose) that permeates throughout this entire book.

The point of this story is that God does not make mistakes, even if we do not like the outcome! I would have never grown, been reshaped or been able to evolve into the man that I needed to become, nor would I have had the unique life path and call to write this book if it didn't happen that way. I firmly believe it, and I am thankful that the flight never happened, though it took me many years to embrace it.

Burying the Hatchet in a Cornerstone

I found through the wave of new dreams, that one key was that I needed to give myself permission to let go of her so I could truly move on, and allow God to continue to work on my heart so I would be ready to be refined. As the years rolled on after this story, He started to change me and show me more about the man He desired me to become. He helped me to not focus anymore on comparing other women to Bridget. He did this by helping me to really learn what God wanted me to see when I looked at women and a romantic relationship with a woman through His eyes. He taught me to see romance again and to see it in a whole new way. One that would encourage me to be ready for the future He had planned for me, regardless of me being single forever or married. He helped me to learn why contentment in my life could be found through serving Him with the passion that was seen in my romance with Bridget. It helped me to shift my focus to serving God with my entire life, no matter the present or future circumstances. I am thankful that I learned what true love really is by having it come into my life and losing it. Many people I know lack assurance to know if they were every really passionately in love (even if they are married) because they never felt a similar magnitude of love lost. Though love lost is bitter sweet, it taught me so much and now I desire a great love with my relationship with God above all things. That has become a cornerstone where I buried the hatchet with Bridget as I walked forth into the realization and pursuit of all of the new dreams in my life!

Point of Reflection or Action for Today:

"Love is a force more formidable than any other. It is invisible—it cannot be seen or measured, yet it is powerful enough to transform you in a moment, and offer you more joy than any material possession could."

– Barbara de Angelis

Chapter 16

A Heart Prepared for True Love: The Dick Purnell Story

Dreams Profile with Dick Purnell

Internationally recognized speaker and author

Most people have either spent a notable amount of energy pursuing a spouse or have known others who have. My friend Dick Purnell is a man that can truly empathize with others who have desperately searched for a lasting love. Single for forty-two years, Dick is sensitive to the concerns of singles and married couples alike because of his own personal experience. Indeed, he was single for so long he has a lasting, genuine empathy for others who are walking that same path.

If you have never been married and you struggle with your singleness, this story is for you. If you have given up on the idea of finding your special someone, this story is for you. If you have had the unfortunate reality of going through a divorce and you still desire to find a lasting love, this story is for you.

It is my prayer that Dick's experiences would speak to you in a unique way, and give you a supercharged sense of hope and faith in regards to building a marriage that will last. If you are married, I pray that you might be inspired to encourage those singles around you with Dick's story.

An Unexpected Meeting

I met Dick Purnell at a singles' conference I attended at America's Keswick, a Christian retreat center in New Jersey. I had never even heard of him prior to that weekend. As I drove to the conference, I was simply looking forward to learning, growing, and being challenged as I reflected on my life and the dreams I was pursuing, and I welcomed the opportunity to meet new people. As the weekend progressed, however, Dick's story spoke to my own dating journey, and he inspired my public speaking and authoring dreams as I listened to his challenges within his career. It was greatly encouraging to see his new-found freedom and passion in his happy marriage and evolving career, and I was grateful for the opportunity to learn from what was communicated through his speaking series. Dick was definitely a man I was meant to meet as I considered my dreams for my own life.

Dick's Beginnings

Like many young men, Dick was very unsure of what direction his career should take. He wanted to be married, but he wondered when and how a marriage would ever find him as he walked through life with what often felt like more questions than answers.

Early in his career, Dick was asked to speak, but he was admittedly horrible at it—not a good indicator that you are destined to be a great public speaker! Regardless, he went to seminary and later stepped into an associate pastor role for four years. He also got his master's degree in counseling, although he didn't know how God would have him use it.

Walking forward in flexibility and faith, he eventually began working with Campus Crusade for Christ and watched exciting new doors open to become a public speaker.

A Career Molded by the Master Potter

As you seek to identify your purpose in life, you will face times of uncertainty and change. We all do. Dick learned that there is wisdom in continually experimenting by learning new things in a career. He has seen God open doors leading to a new future, despite apparent obstacles one may face.

His lack of training and skill in public speaking notwithstanding, Dick watched door after door open for him to come and speak. Instead of rejecting those opportunities because he "wasn't good at it," he was open to developing those skills. Looking back now, he is thankful he was open to God's molding of his career. Dick recounts how he saw God's handiwork as He changed him from a person that was an apparent speaking failure to a man that has inspired others across the world through public speaking and other forms of communication. He has absolute confidence in the strength and the gentleness of God's sovereign hands as He molds a person on His potter's wheel. Dick realizes that the key is remaining flexible to God's shaping.

A Heart Prepared for True Love

In the midst of a fruitful, developing career, Dick struggled with loneliness. He wondered why, after eighteen years of serving college students through Campus Crusade, he still wasn't married: his brothers had kids that were teenagers already! After dealing with waves of emotions and frustration at times, he eventually got to a place where he realized he needed a change in his perspective.

Dick made a conscious decision to pursue those things that God put in his heart—be it new dreams, directions, or passions. Yes, he desired a wife, but he would not give up his passionate pursuit of the career path he felt he was meant to pursue, despite input from the well-intentioned world around him that felt that the demands of traveling and ministry would make settling down unlikely. He knew that he was impacting the lives of many people while walking a path of purpose and meaning that transcended his desires for companionship and marriage.

As these convictions grew, his attitude about dating changed as well. He had dated a lot of people, but he realized he did not want to be "on the prowl" anymore. He wanted his life to be devoted to God instead of continuing to be discouraged by looking at the circumstances of his life through an "I need a girlfriend/spouse" filter, because he realized he was becoming critical of new women he met.

From a day-to-day standpoint, Dick continued to build relationships with women. At this point, however, he simply wanted to learn what they were like and what they desired most, and he desired to better understand the opposite sex instead of relying on assumptions accumulated during his youth. He also interviewed happily married couples to find out more about their stories, how they resolved conflict, and how he could learn from people that had already achieved the dream he sought. There is remarkable wisdom in looking to those who are already where we want to be and in seeking understanding from them on how they ended up there; and Dick simply focused on being humble and on passionately learning.

Not too many months later, Dick began dating a woman named Paula. Though there was much good in their relationship, they faced a point of major conflict, and Dick remembers a day of desperation in a hotel room when he was on his knees praying to God for wisdom. He read Habakkuk 3:17-19:

> [17] Though the fig tree does not bud
>   and there are no grapes on the vines,
>   though the olive crop fails
>   and the fields produce no food,
>   though there are no sheep in the pen
>   and no cattle in the stalls,
> [18] yet I will rejoice in the LORD,
>   I will be joyful in God my Savior.
> [19] The Sovereign LORD is my strength;
>   he makes my feet like the feet of a deer,
>   he enables me to tread on the heights.

Dick's perspective on his conflict with Paula shifted. To reap a bountiful harvest, one must prepare a field, plant seeds, and seek God's blessing upon its growth. As Dick considered the best way to see his field of dreams become an abundant harvest, he realized he needed to seek God for His plan above all else and be satisfied in that, even in times when it seemed like the harvest does not come.

He took refuge and encouragement from the Scripture he read that day. Shortly after that he spent the holidays with Paula and her family and they were able to seek God for help and successfully resolve their conflict. Nine months later they were married, and they have been happily married ever since!

Dream Reflections from the Heart

Today, Dick's ministry has evolved into one of reaching singles and married couples alike with the lessons that grew from his own struggles and pursuits, and he addresses audiences all over the world in person, on radio and TV. He is on the national speakers' team of the FamilyLife Marriage Conferences and he founded Single Life Resources, a division of Campus Crusade for Christ. Dick is the author of many articles and books, including the recent released Finding a Lasting Love.

As he looks back on decades that have encompassed his extended periods of being single, a flourishing marriage, and a career full of role change, he has a number of reflections to share. Our prayer is that these insights will become blessings to you and will serve as words of encouragement as you pursue your own dreams of marriage. If you are already married, perhaps these thoughts will help you and your spouse work towards becoming a couple that serves as a model of encouragement to the singles within your circles of influence.

- "When you have a life of purpose and passion, you become more attractive to others."

- "Live life fully, invest into relationships of all types, and always be open to personal learning and growth."

- "The timing with dreams is key—other things might need to be in place first, and you might even need to be learning how to handle rejection, initially." However, over time, God can bring your dream to life more clearly and powerfully than you ever envisioned.

- Sometimes the death of a dream can allow it to be reborn with refinement as we get our hearts right with God instead of focusing on what is popular or what others are doing in the pursuit of such success.

- "Focus on building your character—always! Don't be a self-pleaser (who) is self-centered and self-absorbed."

- "Learn how to deal with disadvantages and advantages." You need to live strong where you are (handling good and bad equally, regardless of your marital status or circumstances in life).

- The older he became, the more Dick realized the growing importance of strong relationships. So many people today trash their relationships or give up on them too easily when adversity, accountability, or challenge presents itself. It is really good for us to spend our life building and maintaining solid relationships of all kinds.

- "We need to be flexible in the hands of God!" Paula (Dick's wife) and he worked through some major issues during dating and it all brought them closer by the time they finally walked to the altar. He was willing to lose her to ensure he continued to follow God's best for his life and God brought them to a place of deep love only nine months later.

Dick saw his dating life as an ocean of emotions with crashing waves and exciting highs. He was reminded constantly that God is the God of highs and lows in our lives! He learned that both life as a single person and life as a married person can be full of adventure if we have an eternal perspective and trust God's leading. The Bible is full of stories of both single people and married people that God used in amazing ways.

When it comes to the dream of marriage, it is never is an unrealistic goal. Many times we just have unrealistic time expectations. Dick's forty-two years of patience proves that point. Many times the best things in life take time to age, like fine wine. His career direction and professional platform as a speaker and author would never exist today if he didn't go through that maturing process. His life affirms that God can take what seems to be your greatest weaknesses in life—like public speaking—and loves to turn them around so you can use them for the betterment of the world, and many times see your very dream become one of helping others around you successfully pursue the same very dream (in this case a happy and flourishing marriage).

Friend, I don't know where you are, or where you have been. However, I encourage you to embrace the above insights and hold on to the truth that God can help you see any dream realized, and that includes dreams of becoming married or growing your marriage to a deeper place than you ever dreamed of!

*More information available about Dick's ministry at www.dickpurnell.com.

Point of Reflection or Action for Today:

Matthew 6:31-33 (NIV)

[31] So do not worry, saying, 'What shall we eat?' or 'What shall we drink?' or 'What shall we wear?' [32] For the pagans run after all these things, and your heavenly Father knows that you need them. [33] But seek first his kingdom and his righteousness, and all these things will be given to you as well.

Chapter 17

The Passion Found in Leading Your Heart

Today's journey might seem to focus a lot on men, but to the women reading this, my passion is to inspire you to see into the hearts of men in a new way.

Men are certainly male by birth, however, they can learn to become true men through leading their heart. Furthermore, a man who leads his heart is empowered to guard a woman's heart and love her more deeply with a genuine agape love. This concept runs counter culture to a post-modern, self-centered, entitlement fueled mindset, so that isn't a surprise. My challenge to you today is to open your mind and heart to the potential of a completely new approach to your marriage or romantic relationship as you run down your romantic dreams in life.

The Wellspring of Life, Yet Deceitfully Wicked?

The heart is a funny thing when you think about it. It is said that it is the wellspring of life. The heart can be incredibly life-giving. Our hearts can become life-giving to others by reaching out to massively encourage them.

Considering all of these points as we look at life on this Earth, then can you see the irony in the fact that the heart is also deceitfully wicked? I have known many people that want to challenge that statement about the heart, though if we are honest with one another and we look at our lives we can see how we followed our heart in life and been hurt or hurt others. You might not be one that tends to wear your heart on your sleeve like I do, however I am sure you have seen emotions flow from your heart enough to see them spur you on to make poor decisions or actions. They made sense initially only to painfully realize later your error in decision making. For some, their heart has led them beyond their passions and seemingly respectable, initial agendas to extra-marital affairs, divorce, insurance fraud, embezzlement, or worse.

I want to be clear that despite the fact that through today's journey and this entire book I share much of my personal life experiences that echo the truth and reality of everyday life, I am no authority on love or the heart. Knowing that, I look to God for wisdom and truth in places such as Jeremiah 17:9-10:

> [9] The heart is deceitful above all things and beyond cure. Who can understand it?
>
> [10] "I the LORD search the heart and examine the mind, to reward each person according to their conduct, according to what their deeds deserve."

The Difference Between Leading and Following Your Heart

Let us move on beyond the doldrums of heart's deceit to look at two major paths people choose to take as it relates to matters of the heart. Most people including myself as I look back over my past, choose to follow their instincts and their heart as their default reaction to the winds of change in life. I, like many have chosen to wear my heart on my sleeve, figuratively speaking. Many can call it living a life of vigor and passion and see it as a great thing. I am not going to say there is never any wisdom in the passions within following your heart. What I am saying is that following your heart is a dangerous proposition unless it aligns with God's best for your life. So you might wonder, how do you know what God's best is?

There is no black and white answer for everyone since we have freewill and choice in life. However, it certainly starts with walking with God throughout your entire journey of life and first asking Him about the steps you want to take in life be it surrounding your dreams of marriage if single, preparing for a successful marriage if dating or enhancing your marriage if married. He can show each willing man how to "lead his heart." He will teach a man how to guard the heart and emotions of all women (not just his significant other or romantic interest) by seeking God constantly as he leads his heart instead of responding to how it pulls him emotionally. This is a tough thing and it requires an active, growing relationship with God. He will show the man how to put what is truly best for the woman before his or even her own desires if they are in conflict. More importantly, his actions and words will consistently speak to that accord. God will show him how to trust Him more and do the right thing, come what may. This man should come to God in prayer daily, meditate on His word found in the Bible, while reflecting on the rich truths about love and His love for us all as we take our questions to Him that effect the path of our romantic relationships.

It requires patience and self-control, because when you strike up a romantic spark, many times physicality erases the possibility of objectively learning about a person. Physical involvement could mean being blinded to areas of conflict that might be there or truths about the other person. That is where time comes in. There is no magic formula, though there is wisdom in spending four seasons or more with someone to really get to know them while maintaining sexual purity before you reach the marriage altar. You are both left then with the clear ability to see if you can both be open, honest, vulnerable, and transparent with one another without having your judgment clouded. If you are married, you should never stop this concept of learning about the one you love. If dating is when you get your high school diploma studying your significant other, then marriage should be when you continue on getting your bachelors, masters, and doctorate degrees as you continue to study and learn more about your spouse throughout a life of commitment and dedication to one another.

For me, one of my deepest, most passionate dreams in life has always been pursuing a marriage that would last a lifetime. It remains a passion and dream even as I write this chapter. I can tell you that God lit a fire in the heart of this bachelor that used to always walk blindly towards that dream with my heart on my sleeve. I honestly cannot tell you that I still don't find myself tempted at times to do that very same thing. However,

I am full of optimism, newfound passion, and hope because God has not only taught me the concept of leading my heart, he has helped me to live it out. It has affected my life in significant ways, and I continue to run down this dream in life for me realizing that like many dreams, God wants us to learn something even more than reaching a dream we set out for on our own initially to reach. Only He knows when and if this dream for me will be realized, though I am in awe of how He has taken my dreams and life in this area and continues to use it to inspire, encourage, and teach others through the reality of the changes seen within my own life.

Too Much, Too Soon, Too Fast

Let me share with you a story about how I re-learned the concept of the wisdom of time, four seasons, and leading your heart. We will call her Ruth out of respect for her privacy. When I met Ruth, I was kind of just going through life with a bit less of a focus on trying to find a wife than other times. I was enjoying meeting women and building friendships. Then we met randomly through friends of friends. It felt very organic and natural, and from the moment our first official date began, I felt like "she had me at hello." She seemed like the girl next door and more to me, and she told me early on that she felt I was the man of her dreams through a heartfelt journal she shared. I should have realized then that the draw of my heart was advancing the relationship more quickly than we were ready for.

Though I am not going to get into all of the details of our story, it is suffice to say that in nine or ten weeks her parents, her, and I were seriously talking about marriage and a wedding only four to five months later. It could have been alarming to many people, however I truly felt on the same page with her as if our hearts were tracking, and I was encouraged by how much her parents were trusting me and encouraging us. I tried to do all of the right things. I sought out pastors and other spiritual leaders on my personal advisory and accountability team to make sure the steps we were taking were wise, and we were not insanely rushing in over our heads. I was surprisingly met with validation to move forward, so I felt at peace.

Into our third month we were faced with unresolved conflict in the areas of conflict resolution styles and communication styles, among other things that I'll refrain from out of respect for her. Though I was never fully given clarity, she chose to break-up with me one Thanksgiving and all I remember is feeling annihilated by a tractor trailer I didn't see coming. It ran through my heart and I was spinning in my head trying to pick up the broken pieces. Despite my willingness to work on our issues, she chose to move on without resolving them. She wouldn't even respond to or believe that spiritual advisors could help us mediate our areas of conflict. Rationally, I wanted to fight for our love relationship because for the second time in my life I gave 100 percent of my heart to a woman that I loved. She told me I was the first man she ever loved, but was still unwilling to communicate or even seek reconciliation initially which was tough to swallow.

If I learned anything from my relationship with Ruth, it was to not let your goals and romantic dreams dictate the pace you set with someone you fall in love with. Take time to truly get to know one another, and lead your heart so you can ensure the other person has adequate time to deepen their trust and relational foundation with you. Do this, before you seriously discuss or pursue other stages of commitment including wedding discussions, engagement, and marriage. The wisdom of spending four seasons or more I re-learned painfully. Sometimes when we live out a lesson we have previously learned it becomes the only way it can go from head knowledge to heart knowledge. For me, I didn't want to hear or believe my pastor and others when they consistently told me that for Ruth and I it was simply too much, too soon, too fast as we looked back on the relationship. I know many times we don't want to hear voices of wisdom when they are spoken to us, though over time they settle within us so we can go beyond believing them to owning them. I have no clue what God has for either of our futures, yet I am full of a heart of gratitude (despite the obvious pain felt), because God has graciously taught me lessons in my own life that can benefit my continued pursuit of the dream of a happy marriage, as we well as the lives of others I have met.

There are many resources I have been fortunate to come across as I have learned more about the concept of leading your heart. First a book called: The Love Dare (www.thelovedare.com and the accompanying series of books and products) by Alex and Stephen Kendrick that accompanied the acclaimed movie: (Fireproof: www.fireproofthemovie.com), are full of rich beauty for marriages and singles. Another book by Dr. Jim Talley & Dr. Bobbie Reed: Too Close, Too Soon, is a great practical resource for singles or those in romantic dating relationships that are pursuing the marriage altar. Though I will not say that everything in that book could be a uniform application for our lives, there are many insights and points of practical life application in regards to levels of commitment and the progression of a healthy relationship in regards to social, physical, emotional, and sexual life.

Leading Your Heart

The last couple years of my life have been full of a sweet fragrance of change. Below is a poem that God put on my heart that I wanted to share with you. I pray that it strikes a chord in your heart today friend!

> The world wants us to believe that we have a new way to fulfill the desires of our heart,
>
> I watch the passionate pursuit in the eyes and the actions of so many singles,
>
> Marching on like soldiers going into a battle that they believe in fighting for,
>
> Men and women in nobility wearing their hearts on their sleeves believing that an aura of honor surrounds them,
>
> Love certainly is not a fight, but I heard a wise man say it is worth fighting for,
>
> They follow their hearts in the name of love doing what seems best in the moment,
>
> This powerful gift and force is something seemingly so rarely found, and so desperately desired,
>
> That they go all in like a surprising poker professional daring those around them,
>
> To find that many times that person they are interested in will match them and call their bluff,
>
> Blinded by the intoxication that consumes them through their rose colored glasses,
>
> Their heart becomes bound to another through emotional and physical bonds of whimsical, silver chords,
>
> As time continues on they pull harder on us,
>
> So many times I see our soldiers of love fall,

Only to see the painful burns of the silver chords remain,

Lingering as reminders of their battle led by following their heart,

God has a plan for us my friends and it is open for our acceptance each day,

Through friendship and genuine fellowship we are able to submit to His leadership as we should,
If we patiently wait and enjoy the blessing of each day He gives us together to really learn about others,

We honor Him by trusting that His ways are far greater than our ways as He has told us in His word,

We will see Him pour out revelation and encouragement that will go beyond what we expect,

His love will be lavished upon us as we honor Him through how we show each other love and respect,

As we continue life dating as singles let us do so in a way that shows God how much we trust and love him,

We will then see how a foundation of friendship encourages purity and purity encourages genuine agape love,

We build that foundation on the rock vs. sinking sand that the world's ideas and passions provide,

This love has the foundation to build a passionate love affair that goes on until we leave this Earth,

The three commitments that I have established I do so to step out in deeper faith before the Lord,

We need each other as brothers and sisters in Christ as we go through the journey of life,

Let us choose to be an overwhelming source of mutual encouragement and blessing to the opposite sex,

Not looking further than today for the treasure of the altar that so many run after passionately,

We are not even guaranteed life tomorrow,

Let us remember that and serve our creator well today, and if we wake tomorrow try to repeat that process,

I am focused on preparing my field for an abundant harvest,

When the Lord chooses to bring the rain I believe that it will wash
  over me like a pure shower of love,

Until then I am committed to leading my heart so I can continue to
  encourage and honor all women,

In the process ensuring that I guard their hearts as Jesus desires us
  to do,

I pray I might be used to teach others the blessing of leading your
  heart as my testimony continues...

Like we said at the onset of today's journey, men are certainly made male
by birth, however, they can learn to become true men through leading
their heart. Furthermore, a man who leads his heart is empowered to
guard a woman's heart and love her more deeply with a genuine agape
love. I have no clue what your romantic life looks like, if you are single,
married, divorced, widowed, or re-married. My prayer for the men reading
this is that you would look at your present love life regardless of your
marital status, and if you have never truly led your heart, that you would
dare to call out to God in prayer for Him to empower you to try this new
approach. You might just be surprised by what you find as a beautiful
result friend! For the women reading this, my prayer is that you might end
today with a better understanding in regards to the struggles men face as
it relates to guarding your heart while leading their own in a relationship.
Perhaps this can become a source of healthy discussion and newfound
passion towards relationship change for you both as you work together to
grow in love and run down your dreams in life together?

Point of Reflection or Action for Today:

"Immature love says: 'I love you because I need you.' Mature love says 'I
need you because I love you.'"

  – Erich Fromm

Chapter 18

The Power of
The 4 Corners

We all live by some sort of internal compass of sorts that drives us to see this world through our own unique eyes. We usually want to believe the way we view the world is correct. Our convictions about what people should and should not do in relationships might be well received by the world around us, yet there is a real danger found when we transfer these ideals we base our personal life decisions on, by allowing them to become the expectations we have of any significant other we pursue or are in romantic relationship with currently (for the married folks).

It does not take a person too long to realize that there are an endless supply of reasons (even if illogical) that drive other people's life decisions and choices. Turning our personal convictions into uniform expectations of others is dangerous because we are setting ourselves up for great hurt and disappointment. The world around you will let you down through applying such black and white expectations. One example could be how a person believes that everyone should contact a person back when they are in communication with them out of respect and courtesy.

That might seem very logical to many of us. However, many people don't see respect and courtesy as a daily commitment. They could have fear that holds them back in reaching out to you and being truly vulnerable and honest with you. They could be self-absorbed as many in this post-modern life sadly are. It could be that your marriage partner is fearful to tell you how they feel so they avoid responding and try and focus on talking about something different through a means of creative avoidance (or passive aggression). Whatever the case might be, my point is that if your personal expectations drive your life, you are setting up for failure and pain. However, if you are open to changing your perspective in how you love your spouse or pursue one through the dating process (for the singles out there), then you can prepare yourself for an extended season of beautiful life change.

I want to share with you a concept that I have taken to heart, and am thankful to have applied to my life. I have seen it grow and evolve over the years as I pursued the dreams in my life, none more important to me than the pursuit of a life partner that I could marry, love, and share my life with. My prayer is that I can share with you lessons I learned so you don't have to repeat the same heart wrenching mistakes during a season that I lived through. I believe that harnessing the power of the concept of the four corners can be applied to your life regardless of your marital status because each romantic relationship that shares a life bond with us, becomes either a beautiful, driving change agent, or a caustic force of repressive influence as we run down our dreams in life my friend. I desire the former for you and your dreams.

The Concept of the 4 Corners

The four corners are simply how much you value the importance of a romantic bonding with a significant other in the areas of: emotional, physical, spiritual, and intellectual bonds. You could use a pie or a football field as a good visual for the analogy of how you assess your personal view of the four corners in a romantic relationship. You could determine what percentage or how large the slice of pie would be for each area of romantic bonding, or for the sports minded you could determine how many of the hundred yards on the football field you would use to get down the field in an ideal way with four plays (each being one of the four corners of bonds stated above).

Regardless of the visual you use, you want to think of your view of the ideal relationship with your spouse or with your future spouse. Then you want to assess how much from 100 percent you would value each of the four corners in a relationship. Meaning how important is it in sharing a strong physical bond with them vs. an intellectual bond, etc. If you valued each type of romantic bond the same then they would all be 25 percent, however I find that is rarely ever true, and in many ways dangerously unwise.

A Common Romantic Reality: My Old 4 Corners

Though the old adage that it takes all types of people to make the world go around might be true, I believe there is a common thread between how many people view the four corners. I am sure you could make many generalized statements towards one gender or the other, as well as other life dynamics such as marital status. However, that is not my goal in sharing my story with you. I simply desire to lift out much of how I used to view the four corners as a single man. As many single men, I believe they would place the highest importance on the physical bonds in a romantic relationship. Looking back I can see how that view led to a path where bad choices became a future destination in my own life. Physical bonds definitely support a healthy, intimate, marriage relationship; however, in a dating context they may build a dangerous, false sense of security in the relationship. In a marriage, many times people that value this in an unhealthy way as compared to the other three corners see that they are much more susceptible to marriage infidelity. They also many times seek fulfillment of their expectations in this area outside of the marriage relationship, be it through pornography of some sort or through other inappropriate relationships.

Looking back in my story, I would say that physical and emotional bonds were most important to me, then followed by intellectual bonds and bringing up the rear far behind the others was spiritual bonds. For me, I would have seen it look something like 40 percent (physical), 30 percent (emotional), 25 percent (intellectual) and 5 percent (spiritual). Emotional bonds are clearly another important area of a healthy relationship, yet when you build a false sense of genuine intimacy upfront by not truly getting to know the other person before you invest in your emotions, many people can see all objectivity go out the window. I know that was true for me sadly as I had a lop-sided view of the four corners that were being grossly led by physical/emotional bonding. I was not able to many times fairly evaluate my ability to bond with a person intellectually because my desire for physical and emotional bonds simply urged me to put the cart before the horse. Oh and that other guy, Mr. spiritual bonds, well that was a personal thing at best and certainly not something to share with another person (at least that is how I viewed relationship dynamics for many years).

I can look back and realize that sadly because of my misaligned view of the four corners, I missed out on an opportunity to marry an amazing Christian woman named Heather many years back. She valued something much different that I was yet to learn (see below after I put on God's eyeglasses). It breaks my heart to be honest to tell you that I even called her "the Bible chucker." Looking back I can say that I simply was blind, and had misaligned values like many people do. I misunderstood simple, pure affection as a perceived awkward bonding style and lack of a deep enough connection to encourage me to continue to pursue her. I am happy to share with you that God taught me about His patience and He patiently opened my eyes so I could see true beauty in women. He also helped me to not continue to re-live painful mistakes like my decision with Heather forever, so it wasn't like some sort of "Ground Hog Day" daily replay of life we can't get passed.

A Shift: Putting on God's Eyeglasses

Many times, we cannot see what is true because we are not ready to ask for help. Many people do not want to see what is true about the relationship they are in or the one they are pursuing because they cannot see what God sees. God's ways are not like our ways. He is willing to show you a whole new way to view a romantic relationship if you are willing to put on his proverbial glasses. It requires vulnerability and willingness to challenge ourselves to be open to change.

Love through God's eyes is described in the Bible in 1 Corinthians 13:4-8a as someone who is: patient, kind, does not envy, does not boast, is not proud, is not rude, is not self-seeking (demands its own way), is not easily angered, keeps no record of wrongs, is never glad about evil, rejoices in truth, never gives up (always protects), never loses faith (always trusts), is always hopeful (positive), and endures all circumstances. In reality, much of Scripture talks about love through God's eyes. First Corinthians Chapter 13 is a great chapter in the New Testament of the Bible. If you haven't read it recently or never have, I would strongly encourage you to do so today.

So you might be wondering, what shifted in the way I viewed the four corners? Great question my friend! I can tell you that I see the wisdom in seeing a drastically different balance between those four areas of bonding. I see things more like this: 40 percent (spiritual), 20 percent (physical), 20 percent (emotional), and 20 percent (intellectual). Through that shift God showed me how building, maintaining, and investing into a relationship His way brings forth ultimate peace and long-lasting pleasure. I very much still value all four corners of a relationship. You can see that by the way I value the other three equally and in a notable way (percentage wise). I am confident God wants us to place value in all four corners!

The major game changer is that I focus on building, sharing, and engaging in such bonds after a meaningful spiritual bond is built. I understand that many people have greatly varying and in some cases opposing spiritual views as they go through their relationships. My encouragement if you fit in that category, is to dare to put God's glasses on so you can look at your marriage, relationship, or dating life in a whole new way. God's glasses are easily found through the pages of the Bible if you are daring enough to read it. The book of Song of Songs and Proverbs 31, in the old testament of the Bible, will help you understand God's views of a wife of noble character, and give men insight into how to love a woman well.

Growing and Abounding in Love

First of all, I think it is vital to keep in perspective one fact: we are not even guaranteed life tomorrow. So why don't we live with deep love today? This easily overlooked or avoided reality can affect how we approach life each day and how our ability to give and receive love occurs. If men can learn how deeply important unconditional love is to a woman, and reciprocally women can learn how deeply important unconditional respect is to a man, I believe that our relationships can soar to new heights. There is a wonderful website by Dr. Emerson Eggerichs called (www.loveandrespect.com) that I encourage you to visit for more on this concept. If you look at the list below and think about the closest relationships in your life I believe you might just see some room to grow and improve in giving and receiving love.

Furthermore, if you are willing to not only educate yourself about the love language(s) of the significant other in your life, but you truly invest in learning how to express love to them in that way (no matter how uncomfortable it is to you) then I believe you will love like never before. Also, I believe you will work together to pursue, reach, and inspire dreams in both of your lives. If you haven't read Gary Chapman's book, The 5 Love Languages, or taken the free on-line love languages test, I encourage you to do so at (www.5lovelanguages.com). You will learn more about each of the love languages: (words of affirmation, quality time, receiving gifts, physical touch, and acts of service) and how to give and receive love more deeply. Maybe it's even something that can deepen your conversation on date nights. Dare to love as you never have before!

8 Ways To Communicate Love Daily

(Things to Consider to Live Daily in a Loving Way)

1. We will express irritations and annoyances we have with one another in a loving, specific, and positive way, rather than holding them in or being negative in general. (Eph. 4:15; 1 Pet. 4:8; Rom. 14:13)

2. We will not exaggerate or attack the other person during the course of a disagreement. (Eph. 4:32; 5:1-2; 1 Pet. 3:8-11)

3. We will attempt to control the emotional level and intensity of arguments—i.e. No yelling, uncontrollable anger, or hurtful remarks (James 1:19-20; Prov. 14:29;15:1;25:15;29:11)

4. We will "never let the sun go down on our anger" or never run away from each other during an argument. (Eph. 4:26-27)

5. We will both try hard not to interrupt the other person when he/she is talking. (1 Cor. 13:4)

6. We will carefully listen when the other person is talking, rather than spending that time thinking up a defense. (James 1:19; Prov. 18:13)

7. We will not toss in past failures of the other person in the course of an argument.

8. When something is important enough for one person to discuss, it is also important for the other person. (Phil. 2:3-5)

Running Down Your Dreams by Harnessing the Power of the 4 Corners

Now there is no one size fits all formula here. My point to sharing this today is that I want you to stop for a moment and look at your marriage, your current relationship or how you approach dating and assess how you could grow and be open to change. While running down your dreams, the relationship with your significant other or spouse can either become a beautiful change agent or a caustic, negative life influence. I believe you can both work together to become the positive former option if you grasp the concept of the four corners and are willing to put God's eye glasses on. My dream of my future marriage going the distance all of the days of my life, remains clearer and more exciting than ever because of these lessons learned. I am encouraged today by the pursuit and achievement of so many dreams because I see things more clearly and differently.

Because we are imperfect, sinful people, we inevitably hurt each other when we are together for a long enough time. Sometimes we hurt each other intentionally and sometimes unintentionally, but either way, it takes massive amounts of mercy/grace to create and maintain a solid bond of love/unity. Much like the well known song, "Amazing Grace," I was blind but now I can see! I pray that you would desire to see your marriage or your future dating life through God's lenses and because of that would reap the power of the four corners to deepen your love and relationship with your significant other (now or in your future). That passion will supercharge the pursuit of your dreams in a passionate new way my friend!

Point of Reflection or Action for Today:

"The key to success is to keep growing in all areas of life—mental, emotional, spiritual, as well as physical."

– Julius Erving

Chapter 19

The Relationship Hall of Fame

As I look back on my journey through dating and my pursuit of the dream of meeting my wife, I can look back and remember stops where I was able to breathe in the fragrance of some of the most beautiful flowers you could ever imagine.

I will flow through these magical encounters as we go through my relationship hall of fame that I believe God used to show me what a true man is, and what his best is for my romantic relationship dreams. They have all reinforced a lesson that I am thankful to have learned early in life: *Truth is always true, even if everyone (including you) believes in falseness. So when will our false beliefs ever really become true?* Furthermore, these relationships have been a massive encouragement to me as I have pursued my marriage dream. It is my prayer that they will help you pick up the scent of the beautiful flowers around you right now as you reflect on those you know, as well as your dreams of deepening your marriage or of finding that someone special that will bring your marriage dreams to fruition!

A Foreshadowing of God's Best

Many years ago as I moved on from a broken engagement, I was graced by a glimpse of God's best before I could even understand it. I went out on a few dates with a woman named Heather. She brought warmth, love, and encouragement with her presence. I very much enjoyed my time with her; however, at the time things seemed to be awkward from a physical (or practical) level as I viewed our relationship. It is funny how one can let little superficial things, like an awkward first kiss, erode relationships of amazing value. I say that because Heather was a passionate follower of Jesus Christ, and I did not even know who He was at that time sadly. Because of that, my focus was on the wrong things as I evaluated the four corners of relationships (physical, emotional, intellectual, and spiritual bonds). God has been very clear in the Bible that a Christian should not be unequally yoked or marry someone who is not a Christian (see 2 Cor. 6:14). Consequently, there was never a shared peace about pursuing a further relationship at that time. I realize now we could have very well made an amazing couple in marriage.

Since we dated, there have been many special moments shared through encouragement or unexpected gifts. Eventually, we agreed that the greatest wisdom was for a friendship to remain at a distance as we both wanted to honor and encourage the growth of her marriage. There was a richness to the season in life we shared, and her gift to me was one that foreshadowed God's best for my future. It will forever remain etched in my heart. I look back now and thank God for seeing a picture of God's best in a real and tangible way, even if I wasn't ready at the time to grasp it. It made me better prepared for my future life as a single, Christian man that desperately sought God to walk to the altar with my future wife in a way that matched God's best for that dream of mine.

Today is a Gift. Untie the Ribbons!

So my dating journey continued on as I pursued my dream of a happy marriage. It brought me to a woman named Elaine who became another milestone on the pursuit path of my dream. Little did I know how much more God would show and bring me through her. Elaine encouraged me in my early walk with Jesus even though we didn't date for very long. She did so by being an awe-inspiring example of strength, dignity, character, and respect. Though I made a decision to not continue to date her because of our age difference and my concerns towards having children in the future, I was clearly impressed by her. I say that because she is clearly one who loves the Lord with all of her heart, soul, mind, and strength (see Mark 12:30) and it is a reality in her daily life (not merely her words).

Since our time together, we have seen that men and women can truly grow in a pure, healthy friendship even when there was a romantic interest from the onset. That remains an encouragement to me this day. Little would I know that our future would hold for us deep spiritual discussions, prayer, and mutual encouragement. Never in a million years would I have realized that God had purposes for Elaine and I meeting well beyond our individual dreams of pursuing a soul mate and marriage. I am pleased to share that God took my dream and my relationship with Elaine, and spread it to bring for an array of insights for you in this book as I focus on encouraging you to run down your dreams in life! I remember to this day fondly when Elaine told me her view about daily life: "Life is a gift, so untie the ribbons." Looking back on her childhood, she could have easily not be here this day. She faced nineteen simultaneous medical issues during her late teenage years, and her initial physician was amazed she was even alive by the time he diagnosed what was wrong. Thankfully God showed her mercy and had a continued purpose for her future, one full of dreams for her to fulfill. Because of those experiences she has a special appreciation for life today that is inspiring. She has an amazing outlook on life. It is one that boldly pursues dreams in life, none more meaningful than honoring God with her body and life even if it means that she delays or forgoes her dream of finding her soul mate. She loves God most.

The Girl Next Door: A Wife of Noble Character

I am confident that most people have heard of the concept of or experienced (the girl next door) in their lives. Little did I realize I would encounter it in the most inspiring and literal way possible with a wonderful woman named Eve. I knew her for quite some time. We attended the same Bible study at my local church for many months before we ever dated. I couldn't fight my draw towards her. She taught me so much. She helped me to better understand how firsts in life are beautiful. I was honored to be the first person that she seriously dated. She helped me to understand the great wisdom in purity and how that relates to building a healthy relationship in preparation for hope of a future marriage. I learned how boundaries and slowness have beauty. Though we might not have made it to the altar and ended up just as friends, I see our time as full of sweetness. I think we both just realized that our differences were too great for the long-term.

I am eternally grateful for my time with her when we dated. It helped me to understand more of what a man truly was, and how apart from God's grace that I would never be able to fully be the man that women truly deserve. She helped my perspective to profoundly shift. In so many ways, she taught me what a wife of noble character is (see Prov. 31), and why that is the sort of woman that I want to marry. After our relationship ended, she bought the house across the street from me. Through that I have found God encourage me to be an encouragement to her. I look forward to the day when she becomes the wife of noble character that I know she is. You never know what you can learn from the girl or guy next door!

A Letter of Profound Significance and Encouragement

Anyone would love to get a letter that touches their heart, and blesses them with massive encouragement; that is a no-brainer. Today I want to share with you one such letter that will forever stand out in the timeline of my life. I was in the midst of an overwhelming life (we have all been there before haven't we)? It was a busy life personally and professionally. One in which people were introducing women to me all at the same time, and I didn't feel like I knew which way was up that summer. A sweet woman named Mary rose to the top. Again, God brought yet another woman that could further paint the portrait of His heart so I could better understand His love for me, and what He desired for me as I reflected on my dream of building a marriage that could stand the test of time (in a world that values that less than ever). Mary's inner beauty spoke to me in a notable way. She definitely counts all things to be less significant (even dreams) compared to the surpassing greatness of knowing Jesus Christ as her personal Lord while living for his glory (see Phil. 3:8).

Though my time with Mary was like a taste of a finely aged wine, there was a letter that came from her father that will forever be logged in my memory banks. It came right around the time we decided to keep our relationship a friendship instead of pursuing a long-term, romantic relationship. His letter to me is one that I'll never forget and will always cherish. He encouraged me to continue to walk out my dream of pursuing my wife in a way that brought God glory. Fortunately, I was able to lead my relationship with his daughter well (by guarding her heart and respecting purity). That in part, compelled her father to send me a letter that showed his respect and admiration for the way I approached his daughter. I am grateful that her dad did the unexpected to encourage a single man that continued to pursue such a powerfully, personal dream of marriage. Though it was difficult, to yet again feel as if I was not supposed to pursue another one of God's truly beautiful woman that reflected His inner character. His letter to me reinforced that he wanted to meet me one day though we lived hours apart. God showed His faithfulness yet again by creating a unique opportunity for us to meet, since Mary and I remained friends. It was a blessing to meet her father, and be able to share a moment of deep sentimental value and tenderness between two men in a world that seems to discourage men being tender. God continues to bless us with a great friendship, and I recognize our futures remain in His hands.

This season of my life confirmed that leading your heart is so key for men. I believe all women deserve a man that can lead well (now more than ever). A man can do this best by deploying the love triangle strategy. It is one in which God is at the top of the triangle, and both people encourage one another to independently pursue God with their lives for the best outcome for the relationship (even if that doesn't mean fulfillment of a marriage dream). This is something that is so key not just for dating, but for leading first in a healthy marriage as well. Lastly, I would like to encourage you to read a book called: The Love Dare. It does a great job to help a couple be outward focused within their romantic relationship, and certainly encourages men to learn to lead well. If you haven't read this special literary work, then I greatly encourage you to do just that as you continue to pursue your dream of a marriage, a lasting love and/or a deeper connection with your spouse!

The Lady Who Got Half of My Cross

I walk around each day with a special cross on my neck. There are two names interwoven on each part of the back of the cross (Esther and Robert). They are my grandmother and father respectively, and symbolize so much of the man that I am. They help the world that gets to know me better understand where many of my dreams were launched from. My grandmother is the only one who remains as I write this chapter, so I want to focus on this special lady who got half of my cross. So much of who she is has given me greater clarity about what a wife of noble character looks like, on the back-end of things. For those earlier in a marriage or those desiring one day to be married, her outlook on relationships and life continues to be a blessing to the world that knows her as God continues to give her extended life on Earth.

She has been an encouragement to so many, that my prayer is that her life would encourage yours and the pursuit of your dreams. She was one of twelve children to a couple who built a love that lasted for many decades (something almost non-existent today). As she looks back over her life in the midst of her tenth decade, she realized a few nuggets of wisdom that related to her dreams and life purpose. Perseverance is the key to so much in her eyes. She realized that you need to persevere in love so that when you have done the will of God you will receive what He has promised you in life (see Heb. 10:36). Looking back she is confident that God's plan many times could be different and turn out better than what we expect (despite our best laid plans). She affirms you have to fight any temptations to grow depressed or weary as you walk through the seasons of life that seem not to make any sense logically. She firmly believes, when someone is down you should work to help them up. It is a passionate calling for her that became the fulfillment of a dream that I believe God's heart has for all of us.

She encourages us to be open to His plans and to seek Him with our dreams because He has the most qualified answers. People call her a dreamer. She believes life is a dream and God works in mysterious ways. We should enjoy the ride, and value relationships deeply. Furthermore, she has a steel trap memory, and it is amazing how she is able to reflect gratitude to the world in abundance. It is even more remarkable today in a world that is so fast-paced and self-centered. She has been my teacher of outward focused living, and for that I am eternally grateful. She is like a record that never stops playing your favorite love song. Her essence is one of passion for caring for others first, and it is an endearing quality that has impacted my life forever. She has spread that gift in a contagious way to many more than me (what a life legacy to leave behind one day)!

The Wisdom of an Accountability Team

Though much I have shared with you today was about special women (and their contributions) toward the pursuit of my dream of finding my bride, I can say that both genders have significant parts to play within the "Relationship Hall of Fame" that God has so carefully assembled for me as I walk through life. I am forever in debt to several men of faith and leadership (Michael, Dan, Steve, Judd, and my Pastors) that become my accountability team. By way of Michael I found that you never know what you can find at a chance meeting at a diner. Through a random lunch, God shaped an amazing friendship that continues to grow roots deep within my life. Dan became a new father to me through a season where my earthly father's time on earth ended. He has been special to me and has been able to bring forth wisdom that my ears needed to hear. Steve has been a pillar of love and strength from the land down under. God used him in part to bring me into the saving knowledge of God's gift of salvation. He has challenged me and helped me to live the rest of my life in a passionate way. Now I desire to forever know more about God and His purposes for my life (my biggest life dream of all) that I will be running down until my last breath.

Many men I find like to be in control, and make their own decisions in life. They certainly don't want to be vulnerable, transparent, or accountable to others many times. Often men simply do not like to get that close to others to share their emotions in a truthful way. God helped me to see that it was an essential part of preparing me to be ready one day for Mrs. Joseph Sharp. Iron sharpens iron, so does one man to another (see Prov. 27:17). To the men reading this, do you have people in your life that are speaking into your life in ways that bring forth consistent honesty, transparency, vulnerability, and accountability? If not, who do you know that you could reach out to have a conversation with today? Give God the ball, and let him show you what he is capable of men!

Lastly, what I seek to share with you most today is how people stand out in our lives and truly become appointments God has planned for us. They become a founding spark toward where we are meant to go in life many times even before we realize it. All we need to do is remain open, and ask God to give us eyes to see and hearts to embrace those special, life-changing encounters as we run down our dreams!

Point of Reflection or Action for Today:

If you are single:
Today I encourage you to re-read the Scriptures shared throughout this theme of the book, as well as the entire 13th chapter of 1 Corinthians in the Bible. Then, reach out to someone you know that is married and whom has made a significant deposit into your life in the past (be it teaching you something, helping you through relationship dynamics, or simply being there for you in times of need). Seek to encourage them and express the love and sincere appreciation you have for them (and their contribution in your life).

If you are married or in an exclusive dating relationship:
Today I encourage you to look at your spouse or significant other and chose to do something unexpected for them to reinforce your love.

14. A Very Common Modern Idol

- Sharing your passions in life for the betterment of the world while you wait on a soul mate is a great counter to the peer pressure of the world that encourages focusing on yourself first.

- Life is too short to waste it. Don't allow getting married or having children stop your primary focus on being a blessing for others each day.

15. A Church, Wedding Dress, and Ring Doesn't Always Mean Marriage

- There is as much power in losing love as there is in finding it, as we pursue the dream of marriage.

- Many times a love relationship that comes crashing down is just what we need so we can walk forward to become the man or woman that God truly planned us to be.

16. A Heart Prepared for True Love: The Dick Purnell Story

- When it comes to the dream of marriage, it is never an unrealistic goal, many times we just have unrealistic timelines.

- God can take what seems to be your greatest weaknesses and use them for the betterment of the world for the very same dream you are pursuing.

17. The Passion Found in Leading Your Heart

- Men are male by birth, yet they can learn to become true men through leading their heart.

- A man who leads his heart is empowered to guard a woman's heart and love her more deeply with an agape love.

18. The Power of the 4 Corners

- A relationship with God many times will drastically shift what you value in a romantic relationship.

- Understanding the concept of the four corners can profoundly impact how you approach/engage your current romantic relationship or your dreams of one in the future.

19. The Relationship Hall of Fame

- There are certain people that God puts in our lives that we need to fully recognize to help us realize our future dreams.

- God's picture of a healthy love relationship and marriage is far different than what most of us realize on our own.

Running Down Your Dreams—Taking Action!

For singles, those divorced or widowed:

Who do you deeply respect that you can you reach out to get perspective from whom has a long-standing healthy marriage? They might be able to help you see something you cannot see today, and could help propel you on towards your romantic dreams. Many times if we look to someone who is at the very place we want to be in life, and are willing to learn from them, God can do great things in our lives. Write about it in the space below, assign a go-date for you to take action, and journal about what your next action should be to make progress towards the dream.

For married people:

If you are married, what commitment can you renew with your spouse and/or who do you know who is currently single who you can reach out to today to help in their pursuits of love? Write about it in the space below, assign a go-date for you to take action, and journal about what your next action should be to make progress towards the dream.

My Dream's Name: _____

My Go Date: _____

Dreams Journal

For more free resources to help encourage you in your pursuit of dreams found through marriage, love and the pursuit of a soul mate, please visit:
www.livewithpurposecoaching.com.

"Sometimes our candle goes out, but is blown into flame by an encounter with another human being."

– Albert Schwitzer

JOURNEY #5

Dreams Found Through Powerful Relationships

Theme Focus:

Some people change your life forever. Sometimes we don't recognize or admit it upfront, and because of that we might not make reciprocal investments back into their lives. I would clearly not be the person I am today without some very powerful relationships in my life. Many of the dreams I have reached at an early age in life, would have not been possible without them. Moreover, so many of my newest dreams couldn't have been born without their contributions and investments into my life. For that I remain full of gratitude and thankfulness that I will attempt to pay forward throughout the days of life I am still given. My prayer is that through real world stories from powerful relationships within my own life path that you will be challenged to look at your own life and define who they are in your world. From there, I pray that you will have a growing sense of clarity and desire to cultivate deeper bonds with them and reflect a heart of thankfulness as you pursue, share, and discuss your dreams with them!

Chapter 20

The People God Places In Your Life So He Can Refine You

I am sure if we are honest with ourselves we all have people that are in close relationship with us that disappoint us regularly. They are difficult to handle because of their volatile emotions or simple ability to create discouragement for us because of their overall negative outlook on life. Perhaps nobody will come to mind that you see regularly or is in your immediate family. If that is true, then consider yourself blessed. For many people, including myself, that simply isn't the case. I could complain to you about each aspect of the close, yet not so ideal relationships that I have had to deal with throughout my lifetime, but there is no fruitfulness in complaining in my opinion. However, there is much fruit in looking at each of them from a reverse engineering sort of perspective. Our human brains (even the most complex ones intellectually speaking) are quite limited when compared to God's sovereign view of humanity that encompasses the entire past, present, and future reality of our daily lives. Each relationship exists for a purpose. It is our choice to allow our minds and hearts the openness to access the truth that lies there for us to recognize as each day of our life goes through God's refining fire. He desires more for us than we could ever dream up on our own. Perhaps some personal stories can shed more light into how that refining fire works, so you might see the connections that exist between your dreams and the relationships within your own world this very day.

The Power in Becoming a Caregiver

I was definitely asked to grow up before my time by many people's standards. In hindsight that might have prepared me for my future. Growing up I faced all sorts of adversity. Poverty, emotional, physical, and sexual abuse, just to name a few, were certainly massive hurdles for a young man to jump over and continue on track in a straight path. However, the forces I was faced with didn't hold the real power. People that I was in close relationship with were the force that truly impacted my life path, more than the events as I grew up and strived to pursue my dreams. I say that because if they were simply tough events that happened to me and I never had to interact with the people involved later in life, then it might have been a different story. That certainly was not true because they remain in my life and in my case most of who I am referencing today were family and the closest friends I have ever had. Since I am not one that would take any sense of peace or pride in renouncing my relationship with any family member or friend, I found myself in a real conundrum as my life has evolved.

My father passed away one June due to a battle with cancer, and he left behind two sons and a wife. My father was truly the cornerstone of the family unit. He certainly didn't choose to leave the planet when he did. That is God's choice alone for each of us unless we do something horrifically selfish like taking our own life. Even in those cases God still ultimately knows that we were going to do it (and why) as he watches all of mankind over each generation. As you might expect, my father's exit shook up my entire family. This was true even more so because it was only about a month between his cancer diagnosis to the day he died. On top of that my mother has faced a mental illness her entire life, and my father really took care of many aspects of her life to support her because of her condition.

Since then, we found an assisted living home for my mother to live in near me. Growing up and going through life in my more recent years with my mother hasn't always been easy. Mom flipping over furniture, running outside screaming randomly, or blaring ambulances at our house at 7 a.m. when the school bus was coming to pick-up my brother or I during one of my mom's episodes became common practice. Many times it was like walking around land minds at home growing up in the family I did. Today, I might not have to deal with those exact same childhood challenges or all of the day to day decisions like cooking her meals, and doing her laundry. However, I did need to take on many new roles that further defined my relationship with my mother. I now find myself taking her to most if not all of her appointments, am the provider of an allowance for her spending money, payee of all of her bills, overall life decision maker as her power of attorney, and manager of anything in her life that really falls outside of what an assisted living home can provide.

I do this gladly as her son to love her, honor God, and my earthly father (God rest his soul). That doesn't mean it is always easy though. There are so many times that I wish I had help or that I could change my mother's condition so she could be truly free of the internal oppression that she faces in her daily life. As a single man, many times I wish I could as her son come to her for advice and have deep and meaningful communication with her though that is normally all but impossible, nor do I feel it is a fair expectation to place upon her. All of these factors can easily create a pressure cooker in your heart, mind, and spirit as your life advances if you allow your expectations and your response to your circumstances in life to dictate how you live. I can look at all these life stage changes with the relationship with my mother and can clearly see how God's refining fire has been poured out on me like metal on an anvil that is being pounded on and refined under fire by the blacksmith. My mother's life, needs, limitations, and mental condition continue to bring me blessings that have allowed me to grow as a man in ways that most people might never grow.

I have also been very fortunate to have had so many extended years of life with my grandparents on my mother's side of the family. Since I moved to Lancaster for college, they have been only ten minutes from me. I can remember how supportive they were for me as I grew up. I can remember so many times they were the reason I got my only new clothes for school or had an ability to go somewhere for summer vacation. I headed off to college and actually had the privilege of living with them and my older brother for two years. Since then I moved several times and eventually launched my entrepreneurial career, graduated, and found my own home.

My relationship with my grandparents, unlike so many young people in this increasingly self-centered world, actually deepened and grew in beautifully, profound ways as they lived through their 80s and 90s. I have been their power of attorney as well, and do everything I can do for them like my mother including doing all of their purchasing of groceries, etc. I have helped them put into place a cleaning/daily living assistance company that also helped me and the neighbors' efforts of caring for them, while respecting their desires to remain in their own home vs. going into an assisted living or elderly care home. Even though that might not be the most wise choice in others' eyes, I am fortunate to share in this adjoined life path the way I am as I continue to run down my dreams. I say none of this to promote myself. I simply want to paint the picture that I have been faced with roles in many ways to offer parental support to my grandparents and mother in my 20s and 30s. Through that continued experience as I write this story I can see how God lavished His process of refinement upon me through it all. He has given me uniquely renewed perspectives in life that you can't put a price tag on. I believe that they can only be used in amazing ways for my future family if that is in His plans for me.

Family Feuds That Wage War Against Your Soul

Never let grudges affect the pursuit of your dreams. Everyone wants their closest relationships to be positive, loving, and healthy. I've seen firsthand that many are not that fortunate. Let me share a story with you about how a grudge can damage relationships for generations (names have been changed to respect these individuals' privacy).

John has a grudge against his brother, Mark. For years, they fought for a reason unknown to their family. Luke, John's son, prays that his father's perspective will change and that John and Mark make up. Luke's vision for reconciliation is driven by his Christian faith.

Mark and John were close for most of Luke and his brother, Matthew's childhood. Mark pampered Luke and Matthew when their father financially couldn't, bringing Luke to Disneyworld and the like. But in the last decade of John's life, something went wrong. Mark and John started a feud that wasn't clearly defined and meaningless.

The brothers didn't speak to each other for a full seven years, and their growing hatred for each other affected the boys. Luke didn't understand why Uncle Mark didn't communicate with his family, but came to accept it as reality and became complacent about the issue. Matthew, meanwhile, took his father's grudge personally, and purposefully wrote Uncle Mark out of his life.

John died suddenly. While he was dying, he asked his sons not to tell Uncle Mark. After he passed away, however, the brothers decided to contact Uncle Mark and let him know his brother was dead. Uncle Mark came to the funeral. During the eulogy, Luke pleaded with his family to mend broken bridges and reconcile with each other. For the next couple of months, it seemed like maybe bridges had been mended. Matthew got married, and the family appeared to be at peace with one another. Eventually, however, Matthew remembered the grudge towards his uncle, and decided to continue to harbor it.

The grudge grew. Matthew resented his Uncle Mark for helping lead Luke to Christianity. To this day, Matthew continues adding stones to the scale that weigh his opinion of his Uncle Mark. But while Matthew's grudge deepened, Luke's desire for reconciliation grew.

Matthew's attitude continued to grow more bitter, to the point where he was practically unapproachable to people that didn't hold his precise view on things. His resentment for his uncle continues to grow. Furthermore, his resentment has turned into bitterness that severely cripples his relationship with his brother. It also creates a poor relational example for his young children to witness, as well as an added burden for his wife to balance in regards to family communication as she continues to walk with others within the family on the proverbial, broken, egg shells day to day. To this day, the now one-sided feud is a point of bitter sorrow for Luke and his Uncle Mark. Luke continues to pray for a heart change for Matthew and reconciliation for him and their uncle.

He desires to love him every way he knows how despite what restrictions Matthew places on their interaction or that of his family which he also adores. God refines Luke as he runs after his dreams, including his dream for Matthew's future to be ultimately one of peace that can only be found through God's Holy Spirit and a relationship with Jesus Christ.

I say all this to show you that feuds don't just affect the person you're feuding with. They affect everyone around you. And although, if you're caught in the middle of a grudge, it may seem meaningless, I assure you that even if we can't see it, God puts certain people into our lives for distinct purposes. Even feuds can teach us how to love each other and forgive. Life is too short for grudges to get in the way!

Unexpected Seasons of Change Found in the Closest Relationships

Life is full of seasons. It is one of the reasons why life is so rich and interesting. We might go through seasons of suffering and prosperity, though they both add to our life no doubt. One friend marched into my life unexpectedly in the midst of mutual broken engagements and two very similar life paths. It didn't take us long to form a bond and friendship like neither of us experienced before and through that process we became best friends for about a decade. We faced so many things together: being his best man and the only friend to attend his wedding in Scotland, tough relationships in each of our lives, and even working for the same company. He was a great listener. Our lives continued to change. We both sought to define our lives, though what my friend might not have realized was that I was asking God to change me from the inside out. His ability to listen to me and care for me grew to frustration and disinterest. One day he said that he thought that perhaps his ability to listen to me might have become an emotional crutch for me and I believe that was pretty true in hindsight, I just wish I didn't have to learn the way I did. I felt like the wind had gotten knocked out of me.

Over the first five years or so as a Christian, my life and our relationship changed. We both became prepared for a massively different season of our lives and sadly that began with the removal of our relationship. One fall Sunday we watched our favorite NFL football team (which I proudly admit to be The Philadelphia Eagles!) I was in the kitchen at halftime making him food as I regularly did. He told me point blank that he wasn't sure if he could be my friend anymore mostly because of how much God had become a central voice in my life. He also felt like he couldn't handle the emotional weight I was putting on him anymore, and our relationship conversations had become a crutch. It came as such a shock to me that it truly rocked my world and turned my life upside down emotionally speaking. We have spoken and seen each other a few times since then, however, it was far from what it used to be. Eventually, he affirmed that he never wanted to hear from me ever again. He will always be loved, and I will forever pray for a new season of growth for us as renewed friends that goes beyond mere reconciliation.

Letting Go of the Past

I have found that letting go of your past many times can be the key in transforming your life as you walk into your future and pursue your dreams. Unfortunately, this could mean letting go of people that want to be let go of (even if they are dear to you), or that are holding you back from pursuing God's best for your life. It is a hard truth to swallow at times, yet I have seen massive wisdom in not only applying this principal, but holding true to it within my own life.

My prayer for you now is that you would passionately think about your dreams in life, and as you pursue them you wouldn't simply see the doors open and close. I pray that you would seek God fervently so He can reveal to you the why behind each door that moves by His hands in your life. There is so much to learn about the doors that close, open, and re-open in your life. Nothing is wasted by our Almighty Creator. Never forget that as you continue to travel through your life to the destiny that God continues to fashion for you; He pours out his refining fire of unending patience, ultimate forgiveness. and redeeming love.

Point of Reflection or Action for Today:

Matthew 18:21-22 (NIV)

[21] Then Peter came to Jesus and asked, "Lord, how many times shall I forgive my brother or sister who sins against me? Up to seven times?" [22] Jesus answered, "I tell you, not seven times, but seventy-seven times.[a]

Chapter 21

A Good Coach is Always Coachable: The Founders of my Yellow Brick Road

If I have learned anything key about chasing down dreams over the years, it's been how important it is to build powerful relationships. Take The Wizard of Oz for example. As Dorothy sought to find her way home to Kansas, she faced the daunting task of making her way along the unknown yellow brick road. Why did she push forward? Supposedly, a wizard at the far-off end of the road could fulfill her dream of returning home. Dorothy was not alone on her path to the meet the wizard. She ran into her new friends: the Scarecrow, Tin man, and the Cowardly Lion. They all came together to help Dorothy pursue her dream, while they pursued dreams of their own.

Though, I have so many other coaches in my life that have contributed to my life in significant ways, let me introduce you to Ed, Gina, and Adrienne. Even though I am a business and life coach today for many successful people, I am reminded daily of my need to continue to have coaches in my own life. As I commit my life to focus on living a life of purpose and coaching/inspiring the world around me to do the same, I am reminded of a few "big picture" nuggets of wisdom.

First, you need to be open to acquiring new skills. Allowing yourself to plateau in life will dry up the fuel needed to achieve your dreams. Furthermore, not all learning is equal. Incremental, on-going education fuels life-long learning and encourages a life full of the pursuit of dreams. Additionally, surrounding yourself with people who will constantly push, challenge, and encourage you will keep you humble while spurring you on with greater velocity as you pursue your dreams. May the story of my relationships with Ed, Gina, and Adrienne bring you to a place of greater clarity and confidence as you consider your own dreams.

Dreams Profile with Ed Staub

President of Staub & Associates, Sales/ Management Coach, Entrepreneur, and Ministry Leader

I met Ed only three years into my entrepreneurial career. Thankfully, I was not naïve enough to believe that I had all of the answers. I might have already shown signs of sales success, but I knew I had lots to learn. I ran into Ed after he was well into his career as an elite and well respected coach with Sandler Training. I remember sitting in Ed's training class one winter and being challenged to pursue a completely new way to think about, sell, and run my business. I focus on sharing the knowledge I learned from Ed with others I coach, and I continue to implement Ed's process in my own endeavors with great success. Many years later, my team and I still benefit from ongoing education classes that Ed's company, Staub & Associates, offers. As our relationship deepens, he continues to help me grow. I'm so grateful that we share a like-minded focus on using our careers to inspire others and to serve God. We are also fortunate to share in a biweekly prayer group with other business owners who all share a similar life passion.

For twenty years, Ed was a top sales producer in the trucking industry and happily married to his wife, Tibby. His career gained more prestige when he started the Preston Trucking Institute. One February day, he saw an advertisement in the newspaper with a blaring headline: "1-800-UNHAPPY." It resonated in his heart even though he was successful and working for a great company. In the midst of an economic recession, Ed decided to step out in faith and visit David Sandler, the creator of the Sandler selling system. After that meeting, Ed told his wife that he was "100 percent confident he needed to move on to become a franchise owner of Sandler"...and leave behind his lucrative role and perks at Preston. Despite any initial setbacks he faced, he never doubted he did the right thing to follow his dream. Now after decades with Sandler, Ed has never been more passionate about his career and life.

Now, Ed is president and founder of Staub & Associates, a certified affiliate of Sandler Training. Ed has an extensive background of more than four decades in sales, management, and training in the trucking and training industries. His company develops a team of coaches to provide their clients (business owners, sales managers, sales professionals, non-selling professionals, and customer service reps) with necessary selling, leadership, and communication skills needed to develop new business and more effectively serve existing customers.

Ed prioritizes modeling Christ in the workplace. He serves in a leadership position at New Life For Girls, a national Christian-based drug abuse & alcohol rehabilitation organization. He and his wife co-chair the marriage and family committee at their church. Ed and Tibby have enjoyed over forty years of marriage, and have three children and seven beautiful grandchildren.

Serious Training for Serious People and Insights Beyond

When reflecting on people and the pursuit of their dreams, Ed and I agree that what he brings to the table as a coach is only a fit for people that seek serious training because they're serious about reaching their dreams. Furthermore, he believes God has given him a platform in two main areas of life. First, Ed feels his business is a platform to help people build better relationships in a world that seems to increasingly devalue the benefit of strong personal connections. Second, he believes God has given him a passion to help see marriages and families thrive. Through their extended career and ministry efforts, Ed and his wife help encourage people to build or rebuild marriages that stand the test of time. During my years around Ed, I found the following insights to be the ones that best relate to how Ed has pursued his dreams in life and how he helped others to do the same:

- "Relationships suffer because people are always looking for a quick fix." When it comes to true growth and the development of powerful relationships, there are no quick fixes in life that last.

- "Everything in life begins and ends with relationships." You need to establish relationships that are powerful and not based upon the superficial, like "what can this person do for me."

- "Begin with the end in mind as you go through life." Ed focuses on waking up and living daily in a way that pleases God, rather than being anxious about the circumstances in his life (including his personal battle with multiple sclerosis). He does so by living in a passionate way that is focused on becoming all God planned him to be, pressing on each day in seeking God for wisdom and direction to impact the lives of others.

- Ed firmly believes that to leave a legacy behind in life, you need to live one out first. How you live matters.

- The Bible has been a life-changing influence over Ed's dreams, career, and life. He believes his life continues to grow in regards to passion and purpose as he continues to spend regular time reading his Bible each day, meditating and praying to God. Three verses that have impacted him most have been Philippians 4:6-8, Romans 12:1-2, and Proverbs 3:5-6.

*More information is available at getano.sandler.com.

Dreams Profile with Gina Pellegrini

President of Pellegrini Team Consulting,
Author, Speaker, Entrepreneurial Coach, and
Entrepreneur

In my second year as an entrepreneur, I met Gina through my participation
in The Strategic Coach Program®. She became my first serious business
coach, though I had been absorbing the coaching resources of Strategic
Coach's founder, Dan Sullivan, for some time. Gina quickly took a shine to
me. She was easy to learn from and approachable. For nearly eight years,
I visited her each quarter in Chicago or Santa Monica. She was with me
through the creation of many of my businesses, and remains an integral
person who helps me travel down my yellow brick road in life.

During my interview with her, Gina recounted how she met me as a
twenty-one-year-old. She described me as under-experienced as an
entrepreneur, but over-experienced in life. She felt I was clear about my
mission and purpose in life (perhaps more than I thought, to be honest).
She sees stories like mine as an encouragement that many young people
can become successful while taking action as educated risk takers. She saw
characteristics in me that she believes have helped me to be a good student
in life, as well as a successful entrepreneur and coach: I was well-rounded,
giving, spiritual, people-oriented, positive, and respectful. Gina and I agree
that my ability to coach and help others chase down their dreams is partly
because of my pure willingness to be coached.

Gina owns Pellegrini Team Consulting, a Minneapolis-based firm
specializing in team building and leadership development. Gina works with
business owners to streamline systems, increase productivity, strengthen
accountability, and improve communication. With her help, employers
become better leaders, and more involved in the company vision, decision-
making, and growth.

Gina hosts two teleconferences series: The Revenue Resource, a
program designed to sharpen the phone skills of marketing assistants,

and The Ultimate Team, a group series on effective leadership and team performance. Her products include Let Go and Lead!, The Appointment Scheduler, The Wisdom of Teamwork, The Power of Two, and The Personnel Package. Gina has been featured in various trade magazines and is constantly receiving invitations to serve as a keynote speaker for leadership conferences.

Before starting her business, Gina was an administrative and marketing assistant for a top financial producer in Chicago. She has drawn on that experience to design successful teamwork programs for clients throughout the United States and Canada. Gina has been affiliated with The Strategic Coach Program® for more than sixteen years and is an Associate Coach. She has a passion to help create a center for teenage girls that don't have the funds or support they need to go to college. This is an outworking of her dream to help those who feel they don't have a purpose in life, by supporting, inspiring, and empowering them.

Insights from the Creator of the Power of Two

When reflecting on people, developing powerful relationships, and pursuing dreams, Gina and I agree that there is truly a unique power in each relationship. Two people in synch can clearly transcend the efforts of any individual. During my years around Gina, I found the following insights to be the ones that best relate to how Gina has pursued her dreams in life and how she helped others to do the same:

- She never thought she would have her own business. However, someone else saw something in her when she didn't and encouraged her. Just nine months later she started her business (without savings), and she has been passionately running her business for over twenty years!
- "Many times people don't set goals because they are afraid to fail." Setting goals actually helps us to mark real progress as we move towards achieving them. There are no unrealistic goals or dreams in one's life, only unrealistic timelines.
- "Sometimes you need to go for big dreams that scare you!"
- Gina constantly and pro-actively seeks out people who can help to make her a better person.
- "Good coaches don't always help you feel comfortable, but they help you constantly grow and expand."

- "You need to adjust to each person and help them as the individual that they are. Each person has a unique personality, needs, and passions to be harnessed."

*More information is available at www.pellegriniteam.com.

Dreams Profile with Adrienne Duffy

Co-Founder of Big Futures, Inc., an internationally acclaimed speaker, author, facilitator, coach, and entrepreneur

I met Adrienne after about nine years as an entrepreneur. Like Gina, I met her through my participation in The Strategic Coach Program®. Like Gina, she had a unique style that made her an effective coach for entrepreneurs. My years with Adrienne have been inspiring as we have both walked into new seasons in our respective lives. Much like how Dorothy was meant to meet the cowardly lion as she, the scarecrow, and the tin man traveled down the yellow brick road, I was meant to meet Adrienne. I might have met her as I approached a decade of being surrounded by coaches, but it's been a blessing to continue on in my journey with her by my side.

Adrienne noted how I'm always on a mission, and it's always about more than money (which differs from many others she has met). She felt a key ingredient to the pursuit of my dreams is that I always attempt to expend energy with integrity, while holding fast to a commitment full of strong determination to evolve, grow, and succeed.

Adrienne, co-founder of Big Futures Inc., is an internationally acclaimed speaker, facilitator, and coach. Along with her husband, Patrick James Duffy, she's the architect of The Moon Project®, an innovative leadership coaching and organizational development program designed to help individuals and corporate teams achieve their vision and goals in order to reach their "Moon!"

Through The Moon Project®, Adrienne provides organizational development strategies and leadership coaching to business leaders, entrepreneurs, couples, and families from diverse industries and backgrounds. Adrienne is also responsible for leading workshops for hundreds of entrepreneurs each quarter through her long-term alliance with The Strategic Coach. Adrienne continues to develop and implement leading-edge learning materials designed to help focus and enhance vision, strategy, planning, and results.

Adrienne began her adult life as a highly successful musician and performed with the Civic Orchestra of Chicago. She earned a Bachelor of Arts in music performance from Northwestern University and completed post-graduate studies in Europe under noted flute masters James Galway and Jean Pierre Rampal. Recognizing that her ability to evoke peak performances from her students and herself had applications beyond the music industry, she moved the focus of her attention to assisting individuals and teams within organizations.

Adrienne co-produced The Moon Project® Transformentary™ film which was recognized with an AMPIA nomination for Best Motivational Production. The year Adrienne and I met, the second film in The Moon Project series, Above and Beyond, Exploring the Power of Inspiration in Action was released. In addition to her involvement in producing The Moon Project® film series and learning programs, Adrienne composed the original music for the films. Adrienne is co-author of the book Pathway to Freedom. This book provides a roadmap for individuals and organizations who choose to be entrepreneurial in spirit and in action.

Residing in Canada, Adrienne, Patrick, and their daughter Clara imagine and live their family and individual moon projects with love and inspiration. Her biggest dream is to be the best possible parent she can be, along with the inspiring career dreams she pursues. Furthermore, she is also building a retreat property for off-site groups for the Moon Project. She wants to help others find peace, do planning, and create vision to launch into a bigger future.

Insights Gleaned from Going Above and Beyond:

When reflecting on her unique life path, people, developing powerful relationships, and the pursuit dreams, Adrienne and I agree that there is something remarkable about inspiration in action. During my years around Adrienne, and through my interview with her for this book, I found the following insights to be the ones that best relate to how she has pursued her dreams in life and how she helped others to do the same:

- "You need to really show up every day to effectively achieve goals and run down your dreams."
- You always need to have something in life that encourages a bigger and brighter future as you run down your dreams.
- "You always need to have something in your future where you can create unique value in the world as you seek to live a life of increasing meaning and purpose."
- "There are always opportunities for 'coachable moments' at any time regardless of your role at the time. Life can show up to coach you anywhere."
- "When the student is truly ready to learn, the teacher will appear in your life to teach you."
- To reach seemingly impossible goals, you have to really own the dream (not just think of it)—like her dream to study under the #1 flutist in the world.
- You need to have a community of support to drive you constantly towards a bigger and brighter future.

*More information is available at www.moonproject.ca.

As God uses people in my life like Ed, Gina, and Adrienne to continue to coach me, I continue to be reminded that anyone who is pursuing a dream in life can benefit from ongoing coaching. Take it from someone that has become a successful business and life coach, that everyone—including coaches—needs coaches. My life affirms that any good coach is first a good student!

Point of Reflection or Action for Today:

Proverbs 15:22 (NIV)
22 Plans fail for lack of counsel, but with many advisers they succeed.

Chapter 22

The Dancer from Boston Who Pulled an All-Nighter

Dreams can be found or crystallized through powerful relationships. A woman came into my life at a time where God was preparing my heart to handle immense tragedy as well as become ready to see my life begin to be transformed in ways I never thought of previously. It was late December, and I was floating on a cruise ship getting ready to ring in the New Year. One person I met captivated me and become a character that will always standout in my life. I fondly remember the year or so that we held a close friendship, despite the fact that we sadly have no personal contact or relationship today. This chapter is focused on inspiring you, as well as to honor and pay tribute to her contribution to my dreams.

The Beauty Behind Why She Pulled The All-Nighter

I should start off by explaining to you that Gretchen had, and I am sure still has, a very giving heart. We left that cruise glad to have met, and not sure if a long-term romantic relationship would develop or not. We saw each other several times that year despite the distance between Boston and Lancaster. We had numerous phone conversations and exchanged many e-mails and letters. During the spring after our cruise, my family found out that my father had lung and bone cancer that was in stage four. In less than a month his life came to an abrupt end. The five days or so that my family had to prepare all the details of my father's funeral (since nothing was planned in advance), was an overwhelming time. I tried to pull my head together and lead my family through this time of pain, though much of it was truly a blur as I look back now in the rearview mirror. I did my best to tell as many friends and family as I could about the viewing and funeral services in the midst of the sea of other high priority details that needed my attention. Honestly, I had no clue who would actually come.

Gretchen did not tell me she was coming. Heck, I honestly don't even remember how much notice she got about the services; maybe 24-48 hours, if that. She knew I was overwhelmed, hurting, and in need. She also cared about me deeply, though what was next to come was even more overwhelming (in a good way). I stood in the funeral parlor greeting guests and trying to hold back my emotions as people steadily came in. Then Gretchen walked in. I was blown away that she was there, but the full effect didn't hit me until I realized what she did. With limited notice and conflict with her full-time teaching job, she chose to drive all night long from Boston to Lancaster, PA, to show up for the morning services.

The primary principal I am trying to share with you here as you look at your dreams of today or your future is: *Do the unexpected for others to show them love by making meaningful, life-altering deposits in their lives, no matter what it costs.* Gretchen was coming no matter what. Convenience mattered little to her next to love and sacrifice. Her presence totally changed the complexion of that day for me through her act of kindness and love. It is a lost art in relationships and communication in our increasingly impersonal, technological world. Maybe she did it as an act of unconditional love for me that I wasn't able to fully reciprocate at that time, maybe not. If you become intentional about living a life path that is based upon a commitment of making consistent decisions that focus on doing the unexpected for others, then I believe that you will reap a harvest of blessing and new dreams as you shift your life focus off of yourself. Too many people dwell on problems instead of focusing on becoming a doer of unexpected beauty in the lives around us. It can easily become your legacy in life, my friend, if you will make this new commitment.

From Wallflower to Finding
New Inspiration to Grow in Life

As we look at the pursuit of our dreams we find many times that new inspiration and dreams are found along the way. Gretchen was an experienced dancer and teacher. I didn't even know how to spell the word rhythm, let alone find it. I always felt awkward in dance settings so I was your proverbial dance wallflower.

It is very easy to stay within our comfort zones instead of stretching ourselves in new ways. It wasn't until I met Gretchen, that I saw the possibility to stretch in the area of dance. She was graceful, patient, and a great teacher. Since then I have spent considerably more time dancing, and discovered a new passion for it, including a new dream of taking ballroom dancing lessons.

I want to encourage you to never underestimate how many new doors you can open up for the dreams of others. Gretchen was able to plant, grow, and inspire a series of dreams through her willingness to do the unexpected in a loving and compassionate way. You can open up doors to dreams in people's lives that perhaps you will never see personally, through doing the unexpected with love and compassion leading your life. Those three things are a great formula for planting, finding, creating, growing, and inspiring dreams!

Letterhead for this Book

In addition to pulling the all-nighter and doing the unexpected at the funeral, she went further to create for me a notepad of customized letterhead for this book years before it ever became a reality. She wanted to encourage and inspire me to pursue the dream to share from my heart with you and all who read this book. She has helped me to pay it forward by re-focusing this book to become all about making meaningful deposits in your life, while more clearly showing you how to pursue your dreams (or see for the first time new dreams born in your life). Who knows, maybe I'll go a step further one day to show her my gratitude and locate her so I can send her a copy of the book on the very letterhead that she so thoughtfully made for me.

God brings us together with people so we can learn from each other.

Despite how any relationship might end or how long the season shared might be, I want to encourage you to look for what you can learn and give. Look for what God is trying to teach you so you can grow from the relationship. Dreams become realized if you are open to receive the wisdom that God seeks to impart to you through each relationship or season. I hope you can apply these lessons to your life through Gretchen's example to me. I pray you would desire to become a change agent for the world and the dreams of others by committing to a life of doing the unexpected through pure love for others.

Point of Reflection or Action for Today:

"Some people come into our lives and leave footprints on our hearts and we are never ever the same."

– Flavia Weed

Chapter 23

It All Began With "G'Day Mate!" The Steve Charman Story

Dreams Profile with Steven Charman

CEO of Intelligent Developments Pty, Ltd., Spiritual Ministry Leader, and Entrepreneur

Through my relationship with Steve, I have learned to never doubt how you can forever change and be changed by a simple willingness to open your heart to initiate a conversation with a stranger. Furthermore, I am convinced now that if you open yourself up to truly wanting to know more about God, He will deliver and take your dreams to new heights each and every day. Many times He will use amazing and unexpected relationships like the one Steve and I share. Furthermore, He will continue to take you to new levels of spiritual understanding and glory.

Rays of Sunshine Like No Other

We met one day as a bus pulled out of a hotel in Las Vegas. I joined a tour group in the middle of the trip. I remember Steve's first words to me: "G'Day Mate!" He went out of his way get to know me better. It only took us minutes to realize how much we had in common.

Ironically, we ran similar businesses, mine in Pennsylvania and his in Australia. Also, we both were still going through the heartbreak of significant romantic relationships that ended. There are many other things that created our initial bond, but it's important to note the sunshine that radiated from Steve that you simply couldn't miss. At the time, I didn't fully comprehend where it came from. Initially, I contributed it to his extremely generous personality. I grew to realize over time that something was really different about Steve. Early on, we had many discussions about the meaning of life, God, and our spiritual views as we traveled the globe together. We wasted no time talking about things that truly mattered. I was typically open to discussing any topic; however, like most non-Christians I had my own views about how God fit into my life. There was much I didn't know about Jesus and the Bible. Over the course of about two years, God used Steve as one of the key people that eventually led me to a personal relationship with Jesus Christ. God brings certain people together for a reason, even if we see it as chance. God has used my relationship with Steve to help both of us realize that people who grow closer to God don't do so as "lone rangers." There is spiritual strength in togetherness.

A Career Directed by the Hands of God

I was blessed to watch Steve's career path be directed by the hands of God. Paying attention to his journey can pay dividends for you in the pursuit of your dreams. Steve's father was a role model as a business owner, and that helped Steve to have courage to take action with his career dreams. He sold computers as an entrepreneur throughout college. Then, he landed two big gigs with major corporations. Working with fast-paced media start-ups NineMSN and InfoChoice, Steven gained extensive exposure to the inner workings of highly successful and high-traffic web businesses. Steven worked in numerous product teams to deliver innovative web sites and web systems to these businesses, and bucked against the 9-5 routine.

After the dot com boom and subsequent bust, it became clear that successful online businesses need more than just good technology. Smart businesses take a holistic approach to people, process, and technology. Steve stepped out in faith to launch Intelligent Developments. Since inception, Intelligent Developments has grown to offer complete customized solutions to take business systems to new levels of efficiency and profitability. As company founder and CEO, Steve has developed a passion for engaging people, process, and the latest Microsoft technology to address common issues faced by business, and to release businesses to new levels of performance and scalability. However, he definitively states that the most meaningful aspect is what God taught him about business and his purpose in life through his career journey. Here are some of the highlights that Steve shared me with me:

- God taught Steve more about his true identity and how God made him. He learned that he truly has a calling to be a leader. Interestingly enough, God prepared him for that role before Steve even realized it.

- He learned to mesh his talents and passions into what he calls "the blessing zone," instead of simply making a lot of money and hating what he was doing. He's learned firsthand that that money cannot bring fulfillment that lasts.

- Through going after what you are meant to do, you can come face to face with failure as you put it all on the line. However there is real growth in that process, versus simply living a life focused on security through complacency. Going for what God's best is for you is, many times, so much more than we can even dream of.

- He learned that walking into what you believe is a calling from God is tough. "Stepping out in faith takes courage, but it's so worth it." As noted in the book of Proverbs, hope deferred makes the heart bitter, but longing fulfilled is the true tree of life (Prov. 13:12).

Hope Deferred and Longing Fulfilled

Many times, we might be faced with a hope or dream that needs to be deferred so we can be prepared to reap the full harvest that God has planned for us. When that happens, He can help our longing to be fulfilled in ways we could never dream on our own. At one point in Steve's business, his trusted advisors had some strong concerns in regards to the future of the company. Steve's response was born of prayer and pure faith. Steve believed in God's supernatural power, through faith, to do the impossible and lead his business into a new season of prosperity. For Steve, God did just that, and allowed the world around him to better realize God's active power and work in our lives. He isn't the God of the past, or a God who randomly hears our cries. He is a God that cares about details in our lives, even when things seem hopeless in regards to our dreams.

Another dream Steve had was a dream of racing Formula Ford cars and, correspondingly, co-sponsoring one through his business. It might have been very expensive and even frivolous in the eyes of other small business owners during times of economic struggle, but God is an extravagant, loving God! He is not a stingy old man in the sky that wants us to embrace a poverty mentality. He does want us to be content with little or much, yes. However, if God doesn't clearly ask you to lay down a dream, then why lay it down forever? Steve's life and the pursuit of his dream to race was born through this very same mentality.

Today he sees his purpose in life to have godly influence in the hard places he encounters in the world. He desires to influence people in a positive way through his business career and leadership roles in which he serves. He yearns to help transform lives from emptiness to prosperity, while helping people encounter the goodness of God. He wants the goodness of God to be released over all the earth. God is so much bigger and better than we typically give Him credit for. Steve wants to empower others to understand what true freedom looks like through the Holy Spirit of God.

A Exciting New Season:
Encounters with the Holy Spirit

God continues to take Steve and me through new seasons in life, and I continue to be left in awe of our Creator. Admittedly, I didn't really understand prophecy or churches that focused on the prophetic and saw healing on a regular basis. I thought there was just a lot of crazy stuff going on and potentially much that is false or not truly representative of God. The concept of prophecy seemed to be something that only existed back in the times of people like Moses in the Old Testament of the Bible. Man, was I wrong! There was so much for me to learn about what the Holy Spirit of God was doing while I was simply walking through life seemingly unaware of the spiritual realm. I began to be encounter unexpected dreams and prophetic words of knowledge as my journey with my Australian friend, and with Christ, continued.

So what is a word of knowledge? To quote Randy Clarke, "A word of knowledge is a supernatural revelation of information that is given by the Holy Spirit. It is not something that the person who gets the word knows by their own senses, rather it is supernaturally revealed by the Holy Spirit." You can't see someone walking down the street with a cast on their leg and say that God tells you that you perceive that they have something wrong with their leg. Something like that would be ridiculous! However, you could get a word of knowledge that God wants to heal someone's leg. A word of knowledge has to be supernaturally revealed in order to be a gift of the Spirit. Something that is known by natural intuition cannot be revealed by the Spirit. That is because you perceived it from your five senses. It has to be something that you are totally unaware of in order to be a true word of knowledge. Let me tell you about some of my first encounters with such spiritual awakenings in life.

During one of my visits to Sydney to visit Steve, I was confronted with experiencing a miraculous healing. While attending his church, DaySpring Church of Sydney, I asked Steve and another man, Daniel, to pray for healing of my foot that had shooting pains with every step. These men fully believed in God's desire and ability to heal me on the spot. After the first couple prayers it felt marginally better; however, they didn't stop believing in the Holy Spirit. They continued to pray and then, I kid you not, I was jogging around the church and the pain was gone after feeling a warmth overspread my foot during their last prayer! They definitely helped to debunk my previously skeptical views towards prophetic healing, because I experienced it firsthand. I realized that it wasn't something that was only a past biblical phenomena, it was something that was really happening throughout the world each day through genuine faith and the power of the Holy Spirit!

During that same month, I was in Fiji and Sydney. I found myself having different and very vivid dreams every night for about ten consecutive days. Generally, I sleep deeply and don't remember any of my dreams. However, one night after I had a group of people from Steve's church leadership pray for me, I had another dream encounter. I woke up around 5 a.m. with the strangest and most vivid dreams and words of knowledge, spoken in the dream from a past employee that I hadn't communicated with for years. It seemed so crazy! I sat in that bed writing down everything that was revealed in that dream by my past employee. Among other things, I received a message that explained a path I never saw before to allow for the company to become employee-owned while making unique strides to leave office leasing for ownership (which would grow tangible assets for my team over time). It was very much a dream that affirmed outward focused thinking and blessing those around me in a new and exciting way. God chose someone that would have some connection to the information shared so I would believe it, and yet ensure it was someone from so long ago that it wouldn't seem like it was something I ate the night before that was creating some wacky dreams. I ran across to Steve's bedroom and told him what was happening and all he could do was laugh, smile, and praise God. It was a morning I'll never forget! But wait—it gets better!

Days later, Steve and I both continued on to spend a holiday traveling in Thailand. Nothing was more beautiful that an encounter I had with a waitress named Nui. With my healing at DaySpring Church and the words of knowledge received fresh in my mind, God stretched my faith yet again!

The night prior, I sensed that this woman had back problems, though like many people, I did nothing. The next day I felt led to ask her if she truly had back pain. She said she did. I asked her if I could pray for her healing right then. Despite our language barriers, Steve and I prayed for her and she was miraculously healed on the spot. She told us she felt a good bit better after the first prayer, so we prayed a second time believing for full healing and that is what happened! I was blown away to see how the Holy Spirit worked in response to the power of praying for healing in the name of our Lord Jesus Christ and believing that healing could occur right there. It certainly had nothing to do with anything Steve or I possessed. He confirmed He is truly a living and active God in our daily lives.

If I was honest, I still wasn't fully convinced that she was healed and that God did what we saw with our own eyes. Over lunch, I wrestled over that doubt in a discussion with Steve. Throughout the week, I was buying coconuts that the waiters would cut up so you could drink right from them. Nui was so blown away by her healing encounter with God that she, later, bought me a coconut to drink as a gift. They make so little money over there—I was very touched by what she did. It was a very touching confirmation for me about what God did for her in response to prayer and faithfulness as we stepped out in faith to do what God put on my heart to do, despite any hesitations, doubts or fears I could have had at that time. I can still remember her running to the shuttle as we left Thailand to give us a goodbye hug and affirm that her back was feeling great, days after we prayed together!

Unfortunately, so many people (including Christians) don't understand the Holy Spirit's work is real and alive today. People have received documented words of knowledge from God through sensing them, reading them, seeing them, thinking them, saying them, dreaming them, and physically experiencing them. There are many great spiritual advisors and resources out there, like Randy Clark of Global Awakening, who have written books and presented message series on this very subject. I encourage you to explore a deeper understanding of who God's Holy Spirit truly is. It is our belief that God's spirit can open up doors for you in your life that you would have never realized existed. You can see your life purpose become super-charged and launch forward as you embrace encounters with the reality of the spiritual realm that is active on Earth this very day. God is bigger than we will ever fully grasp, and He wants us to spend our lives being mentored by His Spirit. The Holy Spirit can help, not only in your dreams becoming realized, but also in helping you not take steps in the wrong direction, or miss the true callings (and dreams) that God has for you if you seek Him.

There is so much pure beauty in the powerful relationships that God forges in our lives. My prayer is that you would grow to have eyes to truly see what He's doing in your life. Never doubt how you can forever change and be changed by the willingness to open your heart to initiate a conversation with a stranger, like Steve did for me. My entire life has been altered, in part, because of his actions. I truly believe you would never be reading this book, if God didn't bring us together. If you open yourself up to truly wanting to know more about God, He truly will deliver and take your dreams to new heights.

I believe that God brings us together in life with certain people, even if temporarily, to teach each other meaningful life lessons. Sometimes this includes bringing both people together to grow and change simultaneously as God's sovereignty is orchestrated throughout. Who can you reach out to in the name of love?

*For additional information about Steve, visit www.intelligentdevelopments.net.

Point of Reflection or Action for Today:

Who can you be the life altering game changer for in the midst of your day today, by taking the first step to reach out to a stranger like Steve did for me?

Top Insights Summary from

20. The People God Places In Your Life so He Can Refine You

- Reaching your dreams in life is fueled by embracing people who are placed into your life for a reason or season, be it difficult or encouraging.

- Many times we can learn the most about ourselves and the path we are walking towards our dreams through the most difficult relationships or the ones that need us most in our inner circle.

21. A Good Coach is Always Coachable: The Founders of my Yellow Brick Road

- Be open to acquiring new skills forever.

- Incremental, on-going education fuels life-long learning and a life full of dreams.

- Surrounding yourself with people that will push, challenge and encourage you forever helps keep you humble and spurs you on with great velocity as you pursue your dreams.

22. The Dancer from Boston Who Pulled an All-Nighter

- When you have vision to see the remarkable or unexpected actions you can do for those you love, do them.

- God brings people together for a season to encourage the pursuit of your dreams and to help us learn lessons to breakthrough our fears.

23. It All Began With "Good Day Mate!" The Steve Charman Story

- Never doubt how you can forever change and be changed by the willingness to open your heart to initiate a conversation with a stranger.

- If you open yourself up to truly wanting to know more about God, He will deliver and take your dreams to new heights all of your days on this planet.

Running Down Your Dreams—Taking Action!

What one relationship can you further develop that will cause you to grow the most? You can do so by being intentional about pursuing them and seeking to spend more quality time with them this year! I also encourage you to look for ways to give of yourself, so you can make investments in their life as well. Nothing is insignificant if it comes from a pure heart. Everyone has something to offer. Write about it in the space below, assign a goal date to the dream of advancing a powerful relationship, and journal about what your next action should be to make progress towards your dream(s) that you might want to share with them.

My Dream's Name: _____

My Go Date: _____

Dreams Journal

For more free resources to help encourage you in your pursuit of dreams found through the development and cultivation of powerful relationships, please visit: www.livewithpurposecoaching.com.

Proverbs 3:5-6 (NIV)

[5] Trust in the LORD with all your heart and lean not on your own understanding; [6] in all your ways submit to him, and he will make your paths straight.[a]

JOURNEY #6

Dreams Found Through the Lack of Money

Theme Focus:

Most of us weren't handed wealth. Perhaps you are in a place of financial desperation as we speak. Perhaps things are so bad that you see no way to pursue any of the dreams that remain locked away in your heart because of your lack of financial resources. Maybe you have made many poor decisions with your money and you have gotten yourself into such a jam that you are simply too exhausted and confused to know what next steps you should take to pursue your dreams. Many people are simply lacking needed financial intelligence or guidance from those who are in a stronger financial position. Learning from these types of people can help you begin to make financial progress within your life so you can pursue your dreams. My prayer is that through insights from financial gurus and real world stories, your emotional gas tank will be filled and help you to walk forward with greater confidence as you run down your dreams!

Chapter 24

Financial Wisdom You Can Bank Your Dreams On

The lack of true financial intelligence in the upcoming generation is astounding. I believe this is largely due to the lack of importance that educational systems in countries like the United States place upon it. We need to look at helping them develop street smarts, real world life skills as well as many other areas of character and life development. Some of these include conflict resolution, interpersonal communication skills, pre-marital relationship education, and spiritual life understanding. Instead, our society encourages over-saturated education in areas like technology, while the areas of life that could raise up a generation of leaders remains underdeveloped.

I believe poverty teaches more than hitting the lottery, receiving a massive inheritance or signing a seven plus figure deal (like many of our athletes and celebrities do). There is certainly much to benefit from the academic world and a good education. However, my goal in this chapter is to talk about some fundamental financial boundaries that I believe can challenge you to re-wire your approach to your financial life. I believe they could allow you to determine if the dreams you are pursuing now really are the ones you want to see become your legacy in life. If not, then I pray that these stories will shake the foundation your dreams stand on now, so much so that they would alter your life path towards new directions of passion so you can re-write your legacy beginning today.

The Janitorial Master Mind

My father was a janitor for roughly the last twenty-five years of his life. It may not have been his dream job, but what he learned and taught me and everyone around him was amazing. In terms of street smarts, this man was truly a janitorial master mind! I believe our upcoming generation could learn much from him and the other wily, old-school voices of wisdom that still remain today. I am sure you know others like him. As I share this story with you, my encouragement to you is if you do know someone please go spend more time with them, to make an investment into your life by further investing in the relationship with them. Seek them out and learn from them.

Let me share some of the highlights that might help you in the pursuit of your dreams. My father seemed to make a penny and a dollar go further than the average person. He was able support a family of four in a very steady and noble way even though he made extremely humble earnings. He was able to do more than the typical coupon cutters and the bargain Betty's of the world (whom I do respect). Here is the cliff notes version of what I learned:

1. **Teach a child to earn something they want, do not give it to them** (even if you could). My father might not have been able to provide many of the things my brother and I wanted, but he would encourage things like matching each dollar your child earns towards the goal or dream they have. He taught me how to develop a strong work ethic and that has affected my adult life and future aspirations.

2. **Teach a child the beauty found in understanding the difference between a want and a need.** My father taught me that we didn't need new clothes, or anything else that the other children had, to become someone of value or success.

3. **Spend from the money you have, period.** Too many people want to shower their children with the life that they didn't have

growing up, even if it increases their debt. In doing so, they many times encourage a self-absorbed, lazy attitude of entitlement that will affect their child's future in massively negative ways.

4. **Learn to appreciate what you have.** Too many people are not thankful for the simple things they have every day (shelter, clothing, and food). They are our true essentials in life, not what type of house we live in, what toys we have, the name brands we wear or the type of food we indulge in.

5. **Pay yourself first.** He might have wanted to teach burying a part of your paycheck in a box in the backyard as a rule, but the lesson behind his old-school ideas were brilliant and correlate with the financial masterminds of any generation. Make sure you and your children take a part of what you earn every month and put it in a place of safe keeping for your future. This money should be earmarked for the dreams in your life, even if it forces you to forgo some creature comforts or toys you might want in the here and now.

These lessons actually helped me start my first four businesses and purchase my first car that didn't require a team of mechanics and Maaco coming to my rescue!

The Best 5k I Ever Spent

How you spend every single dollar you have makes all the difference as you run down your dreams. Five thousand dollars is not a huge amount for launching a new business. However, $5,000 for most college students is a considerable amount of money if they actually earned it themselves. The seed money I accumulated as a college student went to launch my first majorly successful company, Sharp Innovations, Inc. The money was earned through playing with some stock market investment in technology stocks during the dot.com explosion.

I was a twenty-year-old college student who was very wet behind the ears. I heard chirpings of the doubters in my life all the time, even that of close family members like my father. Many of them meant well, and wanted to see me take on a stable job with a good company that could provide for my future. I believe other people simply stated their doubts because of their own feelings of fear and inadequacy that would hold them back from stepping out in faith to dare to become an entrepreneur.

I look back with a smile spanning wider than the Golden Gate bridge, because I did step out in faith. I had belief in my unique abilities and gifting that God stored in me as a unique creation made in His image. I can say this even before I fully realized how God was at work in my life. These abilities and gifts became realized as I stepped out in faith to give birth to that business that has been a successful, stable blessing for my team and I for more than a decade. My encouragement to you is that you should not allow financial limitations, age, or even negative input from your friends and loved ones stop you from running after the dreams that swell in your heart.

If you can take your passion, and seek God for wisdom, discernment, and direction with your dream, I believe the outcome is less important. What matters more is that you believe in your dream. You believe in what others believe is impossible or improbable. So whatever your dreams are, I challenge and encourage you to run them down!

You Can't Serve Both God and Money

Gretchen has notable success in the real estate industry. Brandon has amazing success in a completely different industry. They are both striving towards massive career and financial goals with relentless pursuit. I have even heard statements like "I want to conquer the world," which I could appreciate and laugh about. For roughly the first eight years of my entrepreneurial life, I spent my career focused in a similar way. I had a goal of starting ten or more companies in ten or more industries before I died. I had big goals and aspirations and had no problem focusing my life passion on them wholeheartedly. I am thankful now that I can tell you that God changed my focus to become more outwardly focused!

I don't believe Gretchen and Brandon are pursuing their dreams in a way that can allow their hearts to ever be fully satisfied, nor quench their thirst for financial success or reaching a place where they feel they "made it." I believe they are both learning the same life lessons without realizing it, despite their success: *you cannot serve both God and money*. Now for people who don't believe in God or the validity of what is clearly stated in the

Bible, I suppose much of what is said here could fall on deaf ears. My prayer is that you would see the application for your life.

Many people allow money to drive their life actions, decisions, career, relationships, and priorities. I know plenty of people professionally and personally that strive after money with relentless pursuit because they want to give a life to their children that they never had. Money is not all bad. There are certainly many noble and beautiful philanthropic, charitable, and humanitarian causes that wealth can support. Money can fuel an economy and revitalize a nation. However, the *love of money* can also be the root of all kinds of evil.

The Bible says this in multiple places, so God must have thought it was important for us! In the gospel of Matthew and Luke, God states: "No one can serve two masters. Either he will hate the one and love the other, or he will be devoted to the one and despise the other. You cannot serve both God and Money." In running down my dreams, I have seen that this is so very true. Any time I noticed that the pursuit of money was driving the decisions I made, I never felt at peace, nor did I want to hear anything about God or what He had to say. Conversely, my life changed in a spectacular way when I was willing to give over the dreams I had in my heart to God (which included being financially successful as an entrepreneur and leader). I truly desired to see His dreams for my life. He did, and they are far greater than mine!

I have seen the most prosperous days of my life after I shifted my focus to God rather than money. I realize He has given me the courage, opportunity, blessing, and life to start the businesses I have (as well as live in the time and nation I do). I have peace knowing that God is in control of everything, and if He would choose to take my business(es) from me to shift my life in a different direction (even if less successful financially), I would know that I would still live a life of peace and contentment that many others never experience because they are pursuing money in an unhealthy way. If my future holds less financial freedom or billions of dollars earned, that is up to God to sort out. He knows that my heart's desire is to use whatever provision He brings into my life to benefit others in increasing measure for His glory. I leave the results in His hands. He did create heaven and earth and everything we know, so those hands seem more capable than mine anyways!

Questions To Ask Yourself When Building Your Legacy

Here are some questions that I would like to end our journey with today as you think about the dreams you are pursuing now, those you will pursue in your future, and the sort of legacy you truly desire to leave behind. It might be helpful to journal your thoughts and pray over them, after considering the following:

1. What's worth keeping track of daily?

2. What's worth always measuring?

3. What's worth saving and/or preserving?

4. What's worth investing in?

5. What's worth remembering permanently?

6. What's worth sacrificing for?

7. What's worth fighting for?

8. What's worth dying for?

9. What's worth always doing?

Remember, we come into this world with nothing and leave with nothing. My desire for you is to live a life of deep seeded meaning and purpose that is led by a legacy that will richly outlive any amount of wealth or success you ever build. If you know someone you care about that you feel is overly consumed by the pursuit of success and wealth, my hope is that this chapter might have provided encouragement to you to pay it forward and challenge them through a loving discussion. I pray your legacy becomes one that allows people to passionately remember you for the love and meaningful deposits you made in the lives of the world around you more than anything else.

Point of Reflection or Action for Today:

Matthew 6:24 (NIV)

[24] No one can serve two masters. Either he will hate the one and love the other, or he will be devoted to the one and despise the other. You cannot serve both God and Money.

Chapter 25

The Financial Intelligence & Stewardship Tango: Insights from True Financial Gurus

There are so many conflicting opinions of how to best handle money (even more so in tough financial times), that it can be tough to discern wisdom from falsehood. I have found that one of the best ways to reach your dreams is through listening to sound principles from those who have already walked through similar struggles and learned from real life situations. The focus of this chapter is to help you take steps forward in your finances with greater confidence and hope, while avoiding the financial pitfalls that have dashed the dreams of so many. You will have the opportunity to join in a "group dance" today and learn or perhaps relearn some dance steps within financial intelligence. Let's talk about what I call the "stewardship tango" that can teach you a whole new way to approach financial flow.

I am delighted to share with you the stories of five men for whom I have deep respect regarding financial matters. When it comes to money and the pursuit of dreams, our primary role in life should be one of a financial steward. Furthermore, the path to true contentment in life can be found through basic financial intelligence while you run down your dreams. As you consider any financial struggles you might be facing now, or you ponder the next steps you should take in life as it relates to the use of your finances, I pray that you would leave today's journey inspired to grow.

Dreams Profile with Ronald Bare

CFP®, and President of
Bare Financial Services, Inc.,

Understanding Financial Stewardship and Financial Maturity

I met Ron through one of his employees, Jeremy, who became a business/life coaching client of mine. After helping Jeremy to grow, Ron decided that hiring me to work as a coach for his entire company was a good move. It has been a blessing to partner together with him over the last couple years as he continues to help his clients grow in their understanding of financial stewardship and financial maturity. He has seen first-hand how many people need basic financial education. He has personally learned and is passionate about helping people truly understand financial stewardship.

Ron really impresses me with the integrity and God-centered approach he brings to his practice. He uniquely blends white collar know-how with blue collar work-ethic. This rather ambiguous combination is strongly echoed when you enter Ron's office that sits on the land of his family's farmhouse. Below are some of the most memorable insights I have gleaned in my time with Ron:

- Focus on developing a "big picture," or clear vision, of how your money can be a tool to accomplish God's purposes. Learning a scriptural approach towards finances helps us understand the purpose of money and empowers us to take action towards the desires within our hearts.

- There are over 2,000 Scriptures in the Bible that share God's heart about money. Learning a scriptural approach toward finances helps us understand money and empowers us to take action towards our futures.

- He helps clients understand the core principles of Kingdom Advisors (a well known program that teaches about financial stewardship and biblically based financial planning) in a practical way such as:

  - Consistently spend less than you earn.

  - Avoid and minimize the use of debt.

  - Build flexibility into plans for unexpected times.

  - Set long-term goals while being flexible to God's leading.

  - Live an intentionally generous life (with all of your resources, not just money).

- "Stewardship is about using money for God-given goals. It is important to live it out, not just think about the concepts." Ironically, many times down economies or the lack of money sparks greater interest in stewardship discussions with clients.

- Ron helps clients understand that we don't truly own our money; rather, it is all from the hand of God. He empowers people to move from a hoarding or security mentality to a giving mentality that changes lives for the better.

- "True contentment has everything to do with our relationship with God." However, a proper biblical worldview on finances can enhance our contentment as we use the tool of wealth to accomplish the desires God gives us in accomplishing His kingdom's purposes.

- In tough financial times, it is important to look at what you can do to grow, change and educate yourself, even if you are in a period of waiting. Your career/vocation should be used as a part of your legacy, not seen as separate from your personal life.

- You need to be intentional and specific about goal planning. You need to be willing to follow where God is leading you in terms of the use of your finances. Be willing to delay gratification and position yourself to truly realize your dreams by being faithful in stewarding the wealth God has given you.

*More information available at www.barefinancial.com.

Dreams Profile with David Weidman

CFP®, and Senior Financial Planner for
Ameriprise Financial Services, Inc.

A Link Between the Mind of an Entrepreneur & the Heart of a Social Worker

I met Dave through the introduction of another man I introduce you to in this chapter, my CFO, Tom Hopta. Dave impressed us both because of his ability to lead people towards financial success through the tough lessons learned from past economic recessions. Dave brings the mentality that is a true calm within any storm, and I have been fortunate to walk through a recession with him already on a personal level. Dave merges deep financial markets experience with a mind of an entrepreneur and the heart of a social worker. I have found that to be an encouragement in an industry that puts pressure on advisors to only look out for their own interest. Below are some of the most memorable insights I have gleaned from my time with Dave:

- Money will never make you happy or content in any sustainable way. Regardless of where you are financially speaking, you need to see an internal shift in how you view money from a self-centered approach to a God-centered approach.

- "The best financial advisors learn how to operate with the mind of a successful entrepreneur, while leading with the heart of a social worker, to best advise others in financial matters."

- Asking God to help you lead your heart during financial turmoil and tough times is essential. Understanding that God still exists in the midst of any bad moment can help people view the lack of money with a greater sense of optimism and hope.

- Commitment is key when it comes to giving and financial stewardship. It should be a belief that permeates your heart and life so you don't compromise on your commitments during times when you are more lacking financially. Giving back is an essential part of building a lasting legacy in life that will outlive you!

- You need to remain faithful in your prayer life. Only God can truly help you get where you want to go. Even the best financial advisors ultimately need to ask God for guidance for both themselves and others in the pursuit of their dreams.

*More information available at www.davidpweidman.com.

Dreams Profile with Tom Hopta

Senior V.P. & CFO with Sharp Innovations, Inc., Financial Stewardship Coach for Live With Purpose Coaching, Property Manager for Destiny River Properties

Financial Stewardship Within Your Means

I met Tom during my last year of college at Millersville University when I was doing on-campus recruiting for my company, Sharp Innovations, Inc. Tom has become more than a financial life line or trusted advisor. He truly is my first go-to-person when I have financial questions. There is simply something special about working with Tom fulltime within all three businesses that we run together this day: Sharp Innovations, Live with Purpose Coaching, and Destiny River Properties.

Tom is someone who walks throughout his day seemingly breathing in numbers and financial information more than air itself. He stays plugged into the top experts in the field and is one of the best financial analyzers and negotiators I have ever known. He also echoes the reality that life (which includes your financial goals) should be about financial stewardship within your means. Whether God has blessed you with more than or less than average income, each one of us has a financial responsibility in managing the resources we are blessed with. It is God who owns the material things in life—He simply places us as caretakers of them. Tom promotes obtaining experiences in life, versus tangible assets. "Things" get old, break, depreciate, or become outdated. Experiences last us a lifetime and have great effect on others we influence. Just imagine: on your death bed, will you wish you bought another new car or spent more time with your loved ones?

Tom has a passion for helping people minimize inefficient use of money. Below are some of the most memorable insights I have gleaned in my time with Tom:

- Focus on people first. Serve others first and lead with a servant's heart as you pursue your dreams in life.

- Sadly, statistics show that the percentage of giving from the poor is more than the wealthy. We need to reverse that trend.

- Placing tremendous faith in God, no matter how tough things get financially, is only accomplished if you do not see yourself as the victim of difficult circumstances in life. There is always someone in the world that has it worse than you.

- Do not spend money on things that do not honor God. Money is not the only gift you can give to others. Your time is extremely valuable.

- Don't invest in things that depreciate, invest in things that appreciate. This sounds simple, but many people overlook this during their lifetime purchasing habits, and it severely challenges their financial future.

- He encourages young adults to steer clear of peer pressure that focuses on leveraging credit cards or buying fancy cars with larger payments. Start small, and pay only with the money you have, not with money you think you have.

- It is important for you to serve God by extending your gifts to take care of others.

- Past generations have lived through recessions, depressions, and major wars. Their advice is a blessing when applied to your life. Don't try to "keep up with the Joneses." It's not a race when you are not in control. God is!

- Don't buy on impulse. If you are debating whether to buy something, consider the cost of the item and what it will be worth to you five years from now. Most of what you think is a need is actually a want.

- Never co-sign for a loan under any circumstance. It will affect your financial health. If you must co-sign, make sure to take out a life insurance policy on the person you are co-signing for and require they make you the beneficiary of the policy. Pay for the policy yourself and have them pay you as a part of the co-sign agreement.

- Don't let your bills pile up and just forget about them. They won't fix themselves. Plan for the future a little at a time so that you can live today.

- Lastly, trust your gut. If a financial professional recommends something and it does not feel right, then it probably isn't.

- Tom recommends some resources for further growth in financial education: Bottom Line Personal magazine, Kiplinger's Magazine, and The Automatic Millionaire by David Bach.

*More information available at www.sharpinnovations.com.

Dreams Profile with Steve Gift

CPA, CFP®, President of Gift & Associates, LLC., and Managing Member of numerous supporting businesses

Avoiding the Entitlement Trap by Focusing on Things that Matter

I met Steve when he acquired the firm that had previously helped my businesses with taxes and accounting. Since then, I have been fortunate to work with Steve in a coaching and consulting capacity and focus on strategic growth and advancement for his future companies.

Through that intimate time together, I have grown to appreciate the breadth of financial wisdom he has amassed over the past decades. Steve brings an approach that helps others avoid the common entitlement trap of today's culture by focusing on things that matter. Below are some of the most memorable insights I have gleaned in my time with Steve:

- "If you have an entitlement attitude, it will encourage you to use bad debts like lines of credit to simply 'keep up with the Joneses' in life," while you compound negatives in your financial life from which you may never recover.

- It is important for you to build a financial strategy that has transitional wisdom to benefit others (one that goes beyond your own life) regardless of it being your personal finances or businesses you own or manage. While you pursue your dreams in life, it is important that you continue to make it a focal point in life to serve others, no matter what your financial picture looks like.

- "It is important to care about the financial future of the upcoming generations as we make our financial decisions now in life." What we do now has generational effect.

- Steve's recommended reading includes Life's Greatest Lessons: 20 Things that Matter by Howell Urban.

*More information is available at www.giftassoc.com.

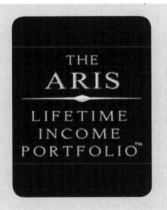

Dreams Profile with Paul Spurlock

CRPC & President of Advanced Retirement Income Solutions, LLC

Going Beyond Following Traditional Wisdom

I met Paul through my life/business coaching efforts through Live With Purpose Coaching. I was fortunate to walk alongside Paul as his company was exploding in remarkable ways. His company was exploding because of his faithfulness to honoring God with his career, and because he truly has unique expertise in customized mathematical income planning. He has helped people throughout the U.S. accomplish what they never thought possible. If you are one that wants to seek new financial perspectives while holding fast to tested financial wisdom, Paul is certainly a great man with whom to connect.

Through our time together, I have gotten to know what is truly on Paul's heart, and how that is driving his career as he passionately serves his clients. He sees his business as a true means to fund and advance the kingdom of God and what God is doing on earth. He continues to strategize for ways to distribute Bibles and spiritual resources to the world in need, fund the planting of new churches, and support missionaries. He also is passionate about helping the less fortunate right in his backyard, while never forgetting where he came from during his seasons of life when he was lacking money. Below are some of the most memorable insights I have gleaned from my time with Paul:

- Money is a tool to accomplish godly purposes. Paul's obedience to God's word in the Bible and letting go so God could lead his life have been keys to his achievement of financial success.

- God prepares us for our futures through trials in life while developing our character whether we recognize it or not. See James 1:2-5.

- Your career and financial dreams should be first and foremost about serving and blessing others as you run down your dreams. Helping people that are down and out financially really matters. He knows this by personally living through times of financial strain and massive abundance.

- Fight to never let financial dreams or success go to your head and corrupt your mind.

- God challenges us to tithe and see what He will do with our faithfulness. The amount of giving isn't important. Start anywhere you have to and build up from there incrementally by stretching your faith annually.

- What is important is that we are faithful stewards of our money if we have abundance or are lacking financially. If we are faithful with little, God is more likely to entrust us to manage more. See Malachi 3:10.

- It is essential to diligently seek God's will for your life and then carry it out regardless of how that impacts your finances or stretches you.

- Many times, Paul discourages clients to go after 401K and IRA maxing because they are fully taxed on the back-ends. He encourages and specializes in finding tax-free investments versus tax-deferred investments.

- Don't simply take someone else's word about financial matters. Investigate ideas and find common threads to validate true wisdom versus falseness before you take action.

- Paul's recommended reading includes: The Infinite Banking Concept by R. Nelson Nash, Blind Faith by Ed Winslow and Visioneering by Andy Stanley.

*More information available at www.arisplanning.com.

If you don't have advisors or feel like you are not getting the advice you should as you dance throughout life, I encourage you to reach out to any of the gurus that I have assembled for our financial intelligence and stewardship tango lesson today. When it comes to money and the pursuit of dreams, your primary role should be one of a giver, regardless of financial abundance or the lack thereof. The path to true contentment in life can be found through basic financial intelligence and seeking God's wisdom in the Bible while you run down your dreams. I pray that you are blessed today as you reflect on the insights shared, your finances, and the dreams you are pursing most passionately!

Point of Reflection or Action for Today:

Matthew 6:19-21 (NIV)

Treasures in Heaven

[19] "Do not store up for yourselves treasures on earth, where moth and rust destroy, and where thieves break in and steal. [20] But store up for yourselves treasures in heaven, where moth and rust do not destroy, and where thieves do not break in and steal. [21] For where your treasure is, there your heart will be also.

Chapter 26

Creative Financial Vision Ability

No matter what your dream is, there is a good chance it will require a financial investment to pull it off. Many times, it will require more than that. It will require some of what I call Creative Financial Vision Ability (unless of course you are independently wealthy). If you are weak at being creative with getting the most out of your dollars, perhaps you know others that are gifted in this area that could help mentor you? No matter what your situation is, you will undoubtedly be faced with financial challenges as you run down your dreams.

Creative Financial Vision Ability has nothing to do with how much money you have now, nor what level of education you have. This concept has a lot to do with having a keen ability to find unique solutions others do not see at the surface, as well as relentlessly pursuing a way to succeed until you find it. It is about looking at the mountains in front and realizing that they have a fixed existence. You can walk around them, climb over them, fly over them or come up with some other unconventional means to get on the other side. It just requires determination, patience, perseverance, the ability to delay gratification at times, and holding onto true faith and creativity at all costs.

My prayer is that during our journey today that the insights shared will encourage you to have a new sense of vision in regards to see how you can overcome any obstacle that might be standing in the way of reaching your current dreams. There are always solutions if you are willing to stay committed to relentlessly pursuing truly creative ways to get past your obstacles!

Tips for Maximizing Your Budget

If you don't have a personal budget or budget for your dream idea, venture or business, then you need to create one! Don't try to take shortcuts unless you like chancing your dreams. I have seen too many people's dreams quickly dashed because they did poor or no financial planning or budgeting prior to the start. It is an invaluable process that is essential to help you know if you are truly ready to take your first steps yet or not.

People who are committed to living within their means will have a greater opportunity to break past financial limitations and capitalize on their dreams. You need to have a budget to know what your means truly are vs. estimating and running on hope. Below are some of the best ideas and approaches that I have implemented to stretch my dollar and walk forward with the empowerment of creative financial vision. I condone nothing that is unethical or illegal, however you can do many creative, unconventional moves to run down your dreams, such as:

1. Break past fear, and have money mentors. Build a personal advisory team and spend time with them, even if you have to offer your time to help them in ways that make sense to get face time with them. The purpose is to build constant financial progress, education, and support as a life-long commitment. It will pay you increasing dividends over time.

2. You should pay off or pay down debts as a pre-launch strategy to your dream while building a solid dream or business plan upfront. Make sure you get a critique from others more successful than you, and don't be afraid to pitch your plans and ideas to local banks. I have found more than favorable results in certain situations. If you don't try, you will definitely not get financial support.

3. Focus on intelligent use of credit cards and/or a line of credit. I say intelligent, because many people get themselves into major trouble in this area. I recommend getting a line of credit when you can get a good limit and rate, and only use it when you must or are capitalizing on new dreams and opportunities. I used it to buy out another firm, and to get through down financial times. However, I got it upfront before I needed it when I could establish a solid line of credit at a great rate. I also use credit cards for everything personally and businesswise that I can, though I pay off everything monthly. I simply use credit cards for ease of tracking and use the reward benefits they provide,

not to make irresponsible purchases. Don't use credit cards when you can't pay them off each month. The line of credit rates will in almost all cases be much better.

4. <u>Focus on build banking relationships early (many times even before you need them that much).</u> Try and build quality connections with more than one financial institution and maintain relationships with your contacts. In several cases I was able to pull off things that at face value seemed against the bank's policy because of my personal relationships.

5. <u>Build a residual income strategy before you walk forward into a dream business.</u> Most businesses can create re-occurring income (even if it is unconventional in the respective industry) if you are willing to think outside of the box. Many times customers would rather pay in drastically smaller amounts, and if you can automate it to collect through credit cards or checking debit, even better. Most of my businesses over the years have had a strong focus on this concept, and it is one of the main reasons we made it through recessions and tough times.

6. <u>Build a cash flow farm solution.</u> Many people are surprised to know that I have been paid upfront for a very high percentage of the goods and services I have sold within my businesses (even when the competition will not do it and prospects question you). If you give your customers payment options (including monthly payment strategies and use up-front discounts), you will find that your clients will front-load the cash flow for your business while allowing you to be much more stable financially when new sales slump (and in most businesses they will at times).

7. <u>Work a part-time job or arrange a temporary living solution for six to twelve months.</u> Maybe you can live with friends or family. In college I worked for my apartment complex as a security guard and got free rent in the year prior to launching Sharp Innovations, Inc. It allowed me to operate the business and manage my personal finances within very limited means.

8. <u>Start your business or dream venture by living within absolute needs only</u> (and do a major financial expenses cut assessment first). Most things are wants, not true needs. Basic food, clothes, and shelter are needs, not all of the other stuff that countries like America promote to the public. If you have limited means, pay yourself bare bones to get

started. My employees made more than I did for the first two years I ran Sharp Innovations.

9. <u>Home-equity leveraging.</u> If you own a home or other property and have built equity, you can map-out a multi-year payoff, pre-planning strategy like I did when I started 9 Local, Inc. in case it fails. The concept is you have a plan upfront how you will leverage the equity within your property and pay off your dream's seed money you needed upfront over a period of years. Yes you will pay more interest-wise, but it will allow you to maximize your risk, while knowing if you earmark your funds in a safe account like a money market that you can then setup automated transfers each month as a part of your plan to pay off the debt if you fail like I did ultimately with 9 Local. It allows you to not be stuck in terms of not remaining financially flexible and creative in response to the initial failure. This is important if there is a secondary dream that you want to run down. Also, it allows you to take other monies you might get like tax returns or other unexpected means each year and pay down the debt faster (while you realize that you have the funds needed to pay off the home equity loan upfront if needed). The key to this whole concept is being able to get a loan when a decent interest rate is available.

10. <u>Pre-existing businesses—always look at how you can create a bigger future for the greatest number of people around you</u>, even if you need to go through downsizing or staffing changes with tenured staff. Many times you might have senior staff or key people exit the business to rectify financial challenges. However, you can create greater opportunity in trade for more people by re-assessing each of their compensations. It is a great strategy if you are diversifying your business, starting another one and/or getting involved in the pursuit of other dreams or ventures outside of your core business (be it independently or with others).

Building Your Autonomy Funds

Another great concept about creative financial vision is that you can plan to save, spend, and use your money in very unique ways that resonate deeply within your heart and spirit. I was taught the concept of building Autonomy Funds through my affiliation as a student at The Strategic Coach®. An autonomy fund is a conceptual fund that gives you power to do something or provides the power to be free from something. The overall concept is that you build conceptual funds for how you would use the money you earn or would earn through the success found within the realization of your dreams. I find by doing this, that it creates deeper drive and incentive for the dreamer to take action and pursue their dreams. Without a deep-seated purpose and driving influence (or reasons why you are running down the dream), I find many people simply never get out of the gate successfully. When it comes to financial limitations and dreams, I believe there are no unrealistic dreams, just unrealistic time expectations. Below are some of the funds I have created over the years as I have done my own personal planning and worked with my financial advisors. Many of the funds I have now, take a part of my current earnings that get auto-transferred (either monthly, quarterly, or annually) and send them into a separate bank account that is building interest. Then I spend only what exists within each respective account. Your list of funds could be different of course; however, here are some examples of some of mine that might help you become inspired to create your own for your dreams.

- *Free Days Fund* – earmarked for annual travel and missionary travel planning.

- *Emergency Reserve or Security Fund* – earmarked in case I would hit unexpected financial turmoil or long-term illness beyond my long-term disability coverage. It varies but I would definitely start with at least three to six months of your earnings, and build up from there.

- *Dream Home Fund* – monthly transfer from my earnings done over many years that allowed me to build a nest egg for my future dream home when I get married.

- *Charity/Tithing Fund* – monthly transfer that I focus on growing annually that ensures money is taken off the top from my earnings and is held in a safe, interest baring account for end-year charitable, giving distributions as well as donations throughout the year.

- *Family Trip Celebration Fund* – building a fund to take extended family on a Disney cruise to fulfill a shared dream.

- *Unique Opportunities Fund* – building a side account that is flex money that can allow you or your family to capitalize on unique opportunities or investments that might come up.

- *Heath & Well-Being Fund* – it has allowed me to take discretionary money and invest in personal training classes, exercise programs/resources, nutritional products, massage therapy and the like. I believe that the better steward we are of our body, the easier it is for us to run down our dreams in life.

- *Family Support Fund* – building a fund to allow for financial management of elderly family or others that are in need of my assistance.

- *Creativity and Education Fund* – building a flex account that has allowed me to hire a multitude of coaches, go to seminars, conferences, and purchase knowledge products to continue to expand my knowledge base in new areas of passion.

- *The Friendship Fund* – I have built a fund that has allowed me to take a percentage of my earnings and earmark it for special family surprises, to bless others I meet throughout my travels or to help those within my church as needs arise that touch my heart in a personal way.

- *Children's Futures Fund* – though I do not currently have children, I have made certain investment strategies like real estate I own through Destiny River Properties or through other investments with my financial advisors that are future-focused.

- *Youth Community Fund* – building a flex account to be available to help in unique ways within the community or to invest into the youth in the community be it through programs like Big Brothers/Sisters or other mentoring opportunities. One of my dreams is to become a mentor and launch an organization that inspires, trains, and empowers the young entrepreneurs within my community to go places beyond where I have gone.

Like I said, your dream could be a dream vacation or a unique concept that has personal meaning for you or your family. It does not have to be a business. I had a coaching client through my Live with Purpose Coaching business that planned a summer road trip dream with his wife where they rented an RV and were going to travel around to national parks, live off the land, and do odd jobs, while making a multitude of new friends and sharing the love of God with strangers each day. That is their unique dream and fund they came to call the "The Love Your Neighbor Tour." It required financial assessment and creative planning like I shared with you today. As you can see in my list of conceptual autonomy funds, many of mine allow me to maximize life experience through planning, boundaries, and creativity.

If you make it a life commitment, you and your family can work inside of a budget and have amazing experiences. I plan vacations and missionary work each year that allow me to learn, grow, and rejuvenate myself. I work within a budget through each and every year. You can start very small like I did, and then build it up as your means change, and carry over any unused monies annually. If I did not do it, I might have had a bigger nest egg for the future. However you run down your dreams and see new ones in life, it is more exciting to go after them than wait for a day that might never come for you to capitalize on because your sole focus is on saving.

So as you look at your dreams and strive to reach them, I challenge you to deploy some of the creative financial vision strategies I have mentioned today. Remember, people who are committed to living within their means will have a greater opportunity to break past financial limitations and capitalize on their dreams. Furthermore, when it comes to financial limitations and our dreams, there are no unrealistic dreams, just unrealistic time expectations.

Many times, all you need is to force yourself to have creative vision to see how you can overcome any obstacle in your way. There are always solutions if you are willing to relentlessly pursue truly creative ways to get past them my friend! Life is an incubator for dreams for those that build and implement creative financial vision strategies, and incrementally build on them. God brings the right teachers and opportunities to you in the due time, if you walk out in faith believing that He will bring the rain as you take care of planting and preparing your field of dreams.

Point of Reflection or Action for Today:

What is your dream? Can you create an autonomy fund name for it today and begin to assess your specific financial needs?

JOURNEY #6 Dreams Found Through the Lack of Money

24. **Financial Wisdom You Can Bank Your Dreams On**
   - Money is NOT the root of all evil, the love of money is.
   - You can't serve both God and money as you pursue your dreams in life.
   - Build your legacy in life as you pursue your dreams by using your wealth to focus on making meaningful deposits in the lives of others in increased fashion.

25. **The Financial Intelligence and Stewardship Tango: Insights from True Financial Gurus**
   - When it comes to money and our dreams, our primary role should be one of a financial steward.
   - True contentment and basic financial intelligence can help you reach your dreams.

26. **Creative Financial Vision Ability**
   - People who are committed to living within their means will have a greater opportunity to break past financial limitations and capitalize on their dreams.
   - When it comes to financial limitations and our dreams, there are no unrealistic dreams, just unrealistic time expectations.
   - Force yourself to have vision to see how you can overcome any obstacle. There are always solutions if you are willing to relentlessly pursue truly creative ways to get past them.

Running Down Your Dreams—Taking Action!

<u>For those who are in a difficult financial position
or face a lack of money:</u>

Who do you know that is financially free or inspires you because of their financial intelligence? What could your next action be to reach out to them today to discuss your dreams? They could become the game changing catalyst to helping you approach your dreams with a new sense of direction and hope. There are no unrealistic dreams, only unrealistic timelines. Never allow a lack of financial resources to cripple your belief that your dream is possible. Mountains might stand in your way, you just need to figure out how to get past them. Write about it in the space below, assign a go-date for you to take action, and journal about what your next action should be to make progress towards the dream.

<u>For those who are currently in a strong financial position:</u>

Who do you know that is down on their luck, who has a dream but simply lacks the financial intelligence, guidance, and resources to achieve it? You could become someone that blesses their life through the sharing of your most precious resource (your time). I encourage you to pray and ask God to help show you whom needs you the most right now so you might take action because of your gratitude for the many financial blessings you enjoy now. Write about it in the space below, assign a go-date for you to take action, and journal about what your next action should be to make progress towards helping them with their dream(s).

My Dream's Name: _____

My Go Date: _____

Dreams Journal

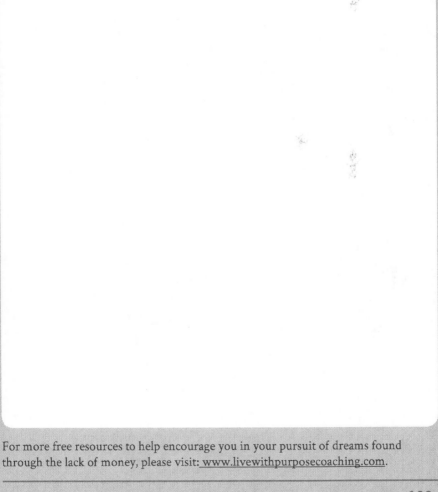

For more free resources to help encourage you in your pursuit of dreams found through the lack of money, please visit: www.livewithpurposecoaching.com.

"Failure is simply the opportunity to begin more intelligently."

– Henry Ford

JOURNEY #7

Dreams Found Through Failure

Theme Focus:

Failure can be one of our greatest teachers and sources of growth in life. For many dreams we pursue in life, we must be willing to grow to achieve them, even if it means growing through failure. My prayer is that through some truly powerful real world stories, that you will be encouraged to learn a new way to view and approach failure in your life. I believe you will have a new lease on life as you move forward toward running down your dreams!

Chapter 27

Why I Love People that Don't Buy From Me!

There can be excitement, optimism, and intrigue about people that don't buy from you as your pursue your dreams! Though I could easily provide more stories from my own life, I will focus on two powerful examples to paint this picture.

My Key Master

An unexpected person held a key to a very important door in my life. One fall, I was conducting a meeting with a prospect named Jim in my first, modest office space. The early days of me needing to sell enough each month just to pay the bills for my employees was really not much if at all in the rearview mirror so to speak. It was certainly a time of humble beginnings that collided with the excitement of my entrepreneurial passion and the dot.com explosion all as a magical trifecta of sorts. After I went through the typical consultation with Jim, we determined at the end of the conversation that though he was impressed with me and my business, he just didn't feel he was at the right point strategically to be ready to develop a website for his business. So at that point, he became a rejection in the sales world and a dead prospect for me.

Jim told me that he was so impressed with me that he wanted to give me a tip. His advice was that he felt that I was a natural fit for an organization called The Strategic Coach®. It was an entrepreneurial development and mastery program for business owners with vision. They had minimum requirements of earnings of $100,000 per year to join their entry level program, and well let's just say my personal earnings were well south of that. I researched their company and listened to some of their knowledge products, and the more I listened to it the more it spoke to my heart. The concept of not having your business run your life was like a gong clanging in my head. I was working eighty to one hundred hours per week. I arguably watched my ex-fiancé walk out of my life because she wasn't willing to fully support my three-year vision that I did achieve on schedule looking back. This program spoke of working smarter, taking more time off, finding more freedom, and making more money. These are concepts that don't take long for entrepreneurs to get excited about. I spoke to a sales representative named Tammy who was very helpful. She was able to get me qualified in the program on the fact that the company as a sole proprietorship earned more than $100,000 in revenue at the time I believe. Perhaps she figured out another way to get me through the matrix, only she truly knows.

After that time, I poured myself into learning and became one of the youngest people that ever joined their program. I sat in a room with people two to three times my age who almost didn't know what to say to me. They all made exponentially more than me and I felt like Donald Trump doing business travel and staying in nice establishments when I still had such a humble business, living arrangement and earnings. I was extremely thankful for the blessing the experience provided though. I became known as the student who never stopping working all the way through the flight home. I am surprised I didn't get carpel tunnel with how much nonstop writing I did! To me it wasn't work though it was just my passion colliding with the work ethic my father taught me. Many other businesses owners were there to be catered to or even unsure why they were there. I was clearly there to grow and soak up everything God had for me to find in that place. I truly believe I am a student for life and they see me as a "lifer." My early coach, Gina, even encouraged me to pursue a conversation with their organization to become a coach because of what she saw in me. At first mention I was only like twenty-one or twenty-two and I didn't feel qualified. Later, as I approached thirty, I did a more aggressive follow-through effort and found out though I might have relevant gifting, that they just were not hiring additional coaches at that time. From there, I moved on and became a business/life coach on my own. So how ironic is this entire story that all started with a man I see as my key master, that told me no in the process of trying to sell my website services to him. He opened my mind to a world I never would have considered at that time, and from there I became defined largely by the key that he gave me. Ever since I have been looking back with a smile, as I remain just truly blown away by how God worked through that meeting to alter my life path in a profound way. Walking into that day, it was just another meeting where I might have been trying to sell something for a one to two thousand dollar project to benefit my firm. If my meeting with Jim would have gone through simply as a sale and just been that, I would have lost so much. As I reflect and write this story, you couldn't have paid me a million dollars back then for the beauty I found in the next decade and beyond through the NO that Jim gave me. Thank you Jim for being my key master, even if you never realized you served that role. I truly believe God brought us together for a reason and for that I'll remain eternally grateful.

A Day Without Expectations

Life has a way of flying by as we go through our daily motions. Many times the roles we have in life and our circumstances seem to dictate our decisions, actions, and attitude. They are built around expectations we have each day in what we are seeking to do, how we want our day to go, and what we expect of others including God (though it goes unspoken many times). I wanted to talk to you about one beautiful day where I lived without expectations.

Joel didn't buy from me. He contacted me about four years after launching Sharp Innovations to talk about his start-up architectural firm that he wanted to build a website for. For whatever reason, he chose to not work with me despite my efforts. At the time, it just seemed like another failure. The game changed a couple years later when we re-connected to discuss a potential partnership with his second business. I held a lot of skepticism about us being able to partner together well because of the way our past communications were handled, though my management team agreed it made sense for me to venture into a meeting with him to kick the tires. My expectations were towards likely failure. I distinctly remember waking up that day asking God for guidance and to help me be open minded for whatever that meeting (and the day) might hold. Being eternally faithful as God is, He did just that for me.

So I showed up that day a few minutes late; I had been held up with another client. I talked to his attractive office manager, Kate, while I waited for Joel to meet with me. I had a very intriguing conversation with her where we realized we had an initial connection through a series of mutual friends, church, and spiritual life in general. I should add this was important to me because I was a single Christian man desiring to meet the right woman to share life with. I didn't go to Joel's office that day looking for romance. I approached that day through prayer and a proper outlook. It would have been very easy for me to have never had that conversation while staying in business mode vs. being present with her. I could have missed the moment that presented itself.

Continuing on with the story, Joel and I finally did have that meeting, and it went extremely well. We found we shared a deepening faith in Jesus Christ as fellow Christians. We shared our personal stories and testimonies about what God did in our lives to show us who He was and what He desired for our lives. I saw Joel re-live vivid past memories through our discussion and we spurred each other on with a righteous passion as our conversation continued. The final blessing was that shortly after our meeting. Joel became a life and business coaching client for me, which certainly hadn't been on my agenda. It was an entire day of new life lessons from God.

Stop Planning Your Life!

I remained open minded as to what God could do and show me through that meeting. It reminded me of a powerful lesson that I try to apply to each day I live. Planning is not a bad thing; however, doing everything in moderation in life is a key concept. If we stop trying to control each day, and instead open ourselves to the beauty that God can show us through answered prayers or doors He opens and closes, I believe we can counter the trend of simply going through the motions. Each day can be full of unexpected blessing. I am not saying it will be all roses, but when we surrender control of our dreams to God daily as we should, we can grow a zeal for life daily that allows us to wake up wondering just what He has in store for us that day.

If we live focused fully on the future or even dwell in the past, and allow it to control how we approach relationships and opportunities each day, it can become a negative. I pray that you would ask God to show you how you can learn from the failures in your life so he can show you a new way of living each day. I pray that new dreams would be born or current ones become clearer for you as He empowers you to become more present.

Point of Reflection or Action for Today:

"A pessimist sees the difficulty in every opportunity; an optimist sees the opportunity in every difficulty."

– Winston Churchill

Chapter 28

A Glorious Response to Failure: The Hawthorne Family—Fiji Story

**Dreams Profile
with Mike Hawthorne**

Entrepreneur, Visionary, and Fijian Missionary

Each day it is another opportunity to bask in the beauty found in the unknowns. Even if you are walking through today going through the motions, you never know what your day truly holds or who you might meet. That is an exciting reality that I can personally attest to through this amazing story that is about embracing failure in a glorious way.

I was headed on a trip abroad to visit several countries. My journey first took me to do short-term missionary work in Fiji, a land I didn't initially know a lot about, or figured I'd ever end up serving in.

Early into my trip, I was fortunate to meet Mike Hawthorne and his family. I was quickly enamored by this entrepreneurial visionary who shared a lot of common ground with me. However, what was most engaging was the unexpected life transformation for his family of eight that took them to Fiji to become long-term missionaries. My prayer is that you will be challenged and touched by their story as you reflect upon your purpose in life and the pursuit of your dreams.

Success, Failure and the Golden Handcuffs

Long before he ended up in Fiji, Mike lived in Colorado. He was a successful medical sales professional for thirteen years. He had everything he wanted—a wonderful wife who homeschooled their six kids, a ranch, multiple properties, fancy cars, horses, and more. He had the proverbial white-picket-fence-American-dream-come-true story.

Despite having, by all appearances, a wildly successful and happy life, Mike found himself in bondage to what he called the "golden handcuffs." He realized that his previously gained success was forcing him to live and maintain a lifestyle well beyond his family's needs. He was focusing on the wrong things in life, and he found himself tied down as he reflected on pursuit of a different life or career shift, all because of the expenses and expectations that existed in the lifestyle to which they had become accustomed.

Mike wanted to make a career shift. He lacked fulfillment in medical sales and found himself drawn more and more towards being an entrepreneur. He started his first of two companies. After a couple years of successful growth, they were faced with serious adversity. They hired contractors who mismanaged their funds and left Mike's business in a comprising legal situation. After a protracted battle, the business failed and needed to be legally dissolved.

Next, Mike and his partner launched a new real estate and construction firm with a unique spin on industry systematization standards, aimed at developing more efficient building projects in Wyoming and Colorado. Their second business became a successful business as well: then recession hit. Over time, he realized in his heart that even in the good times, continuing to lead this business was not what he was meant to do. He wasn't ever full of peace and passion despite times of success, and he knew it wasn't God's best for his career. He needed a life change. He decided to step down as CFO so the business didn't need to pay him, which would help the financials of their struggling business. Moreover, he wanted to do something with his life for God.

Sell Everything and Follow Me—All the way to Fiji

Like many people, Mike tried to control his circumstances, even though so much was out of his hands—like the legal issues when his company didn't do anything wrong, yet they were stuck fighting a battle against a company with deep pockets. His business failures filled him with doubt and compelled him to wonder why he left a good career to pursue his entrepreneurial visions.

Mike began to reach out to God like never before. "I learned a lot of things: notably that sacrifice doesn't mean as much when you are giving to others from an overabundance of money." He realized that nothing is more precious and powerful than the investment of your time to benefit the lives of others. Even if he could write big checks, he found himself wrestling with how he spent his time.

Until then, he was spending a few minutes here and there with God as he went through life. "If you spend five minutes with your child or your wife each day, how much will you really impact them, build a relationship with them, or really know them? The greater the love for a person, the more you should desire to spend time with them, right?" Mike went from spending a random five minutes with God here or there to an extended period of time where he was spending an hour or more a day with God. He became desperately focused on drawing closer to God. It became a passion for him to spend more time with God—through prayer, reading his word daily, and making those things a life priority—despite how a busy career seemed to fight against doing just that each day.

It changed him. In reflection, Mike is confident that there is no magical formula for a growing relationship with God. He could have easily spent more time than an hour per day with God, though the exact amount of time was not the main issue. For him it is more about investing deeply in his relationship with God and making that a life priority. He enjoys seeing how that has altered and changed his life for the better.

Even though his two businesses initially succeeded, he was ultimately faced with failure because he had lost passion in his life and career, and he knew he needed to embrace the winds of change. His wife had always wanted to be a long-term missionary. He had done some short-term missionary work and was providing financial support for missionaries around the globe, yet Mike never saw himself picking up and moving for any sort of long-term missionary work—but that was his idea, not God's. God's idea was for him to get rid of everything and follow Jesus Christ with his life, just as Jesus directed the wealthy man in Luke 18:21-23. Mike was confronted in his spirit to go way out of his comfort zone and do just that.

The family looked at many countries in which they could serve, including the Philippines and Romania. Mike didn't even know where Fiji was on a map, initially, but through a series of amazing events it became clear that it was where his family was suppose to go. Doing the unthinkable, his family gave away many of their possessions and sold the rest—the ranch, the horses, the equipment, the cars, the properties... everything except his saddle. ("I figured a man needs to keep his saddle!") They headed down to Fiji without much more than some tools and furniture they purchased from the proceeds of selling their assets. He didn't realize it at the time, but Mike looks back and can see how his family's original focus on accumulating money provided a road block for a deepening of their faith. It very easily becomes a sense of security and allows you to trust in your provisions versus in God for your provision.

Ironically, the big company that he was in the previous legal battle with went under, and he was released from any on-going issues just as he was embracing his new life calling into long-term missionary work in Fiji. This was one of many signs that God was affirming this major life change that was completely uprooting their family.

Beyond the Beauty of Fiji

Fiji is a beautiful place, there is no doubt about that. However, the Hawthornes would face much adversity and be tested in ways that overshadowed the beauty that exists in the country. Beginning life in Fiji was to be a major shock for a family who was used to living a luxurious life and was now instead living in a run-down, temporary facility without electricity or even hot water. They were presented with other new daily situations like killing rats. It took two hours one way to get to the grocery store, four hours to get to a dentist, and they were happy if they could actually find what they needed.

The Hawthorne's ultimate goal was to build a "Mission Home" in Fiji which could be used to house short-term missionaries and allow them to make on-going deposits in the lives of the island locals by serving them and showing hospitality to them. However, Mike and his family had to deal with a cyclone that brought massive devastation to the area and posed substantial delays and challenges towards the new home they were building. A second family (his old business partner) was also with them and was building a second house, and both families faced health issues. Some grew so severe that the other family was forced to leave the country for additional medical attention for their daughter.

Life has definitely changed for their family, but they have a very new way of seeing the world. They are focused on being content in all things and on leading a much more pure, simple life.

Future Unknown, Mission Focused on a Bigger Future for Others

On my trip to Fiji where I met the Hawthornes, I was at The Mission at Natuvu Creek. Natuvu Creek's ministry is focused on offering free medical services to the surrounding islands. They do a lot of this through donations, the on-going funding of the founders, and through willing medical professionals from around the globe who have true servants' hearts and volunteer their time during short-term trips.

When I met them, the Hawthornes were nine months into what had become a one-year home building project. Their dreams go well beyond the pre-established medical ministries at Natuvu Creek. They want to use their property to house other people who want to come and serve in other missionary capacities around the islands, be it in education, labor projects, or other areas of on-going need.

Once it is completed, they plan on living in their new home indefinitely. However, Mike knows there is much that God has yet to reveal. They could easily see that a day might come wherein they would leave their home behind at the service of the growing ministry efforts of Natuvu Creek, and they would start over again somewhere else, trusting God to provide for their daily needs. Mike is also starting a new outreach ministry in Fiji called Adventure Outreach Ministries. This ministry will host mission teams who want to serve the people of Fiji on short-term mission trips.

Mike wanted to leave you with some details that he felt God shared with him, as you reflect on your future and the dreams you are pursuing in life. "To trust God as you pursue your dreams in life, you need to not be fearful. You also need to be content in all things and truly trust God." Mike recognized how we can so easily get caught up in the material things in life (even more so in America—a performance-based, affluent society that feels the need to show something for themselves). If you can reevaluate your goals and experiences in life through God's eyes, that becomes evidence of faith in action. God used failure to redirect Mike's life in a remarkable way.

Fiji was, for their family, the point of renewed life that countered a season of outward success that was choking his heart. Mike found himself waking up more excited—even though he didn't have hot water or electricity and was killing rats for his young children—than he was going to a cushy office back in a posh U.S. setting each day. Surprised? He went home daily walking on this twenty-minute journey on a rocky road with true peace and warmth, despite the fact that much of the world could view him as being in a position of some level of poverty. People are on his heart now more than ever and he is able to focus consistent, concentrated life energy on relationships and serving others, and it is becoming contagious for him and his family!

Don't simply stay within what you know in life. Don't let your fears hold you back from doing what might seem, at face value, to be the impossible. If you are willing to give up everything you have for God's glory, He will create a path of new dreams that will lead you to a special legacy in life. Ask God to give you ears to hear Him and eyes to see the path He wants you to walk as you focus on running down your dreams.

*For more information on Adventure Outreach and Natuvu Creek ministries, to get involved as a missionary or to make donations to help either organization in Fiji please visit: http://www.missionatnatuvucreek.org. You can contact Mike and his family at mike@adventureoutreachministries.org.

Point of Reflection or Action for Today:

Luke 18:21-23 (NIV)

[21] "All these I have kept since I was a boy," he said. [22] When Jesus heard this, he said to him, "You still lack one thing. Sell everything you have and give to the poor, and you will have treasure in heaven. Then come, follow me." [23]When he heard this, he became very sad, because he was a man of great wealth.

Chapter 29

Beauty Built from the Midst of Failure: The MBC Story

Dreams Profile with Pastor Steve Cornell

Senior Pastor of Millersville Bible Church, author, nationally recognized public speaker on spiritual life, and expert on the Eighteen-Year Factor

Many young adults struggle determining what they're meant to do with their lives. Some people spend their entire lives struggling to answer that sometimes elusive question. Perhaps you are currently facing failure through the loss of employment, or you lack satisfaction with your current career track. If you or someone you know are grappling with these types of issues or are working towards bouncing back from failure, then this story is for you! My friend, Pastor Steve Cornell, is a man that knows very well what it takes to respond to failure and fear with courage and faith.

A Meeting that Changed my View of Church

I once viewed church as a place for stained glass where you were meant to fear God and be left kind of confused and in awe. After meeting Pastor Steve, God used him, in part, to break that mental stigma I had towards church. First of all, I never saw a church that had basketball nets and multi-purposed facilities. My views of what church was were also polluted by the input of the world around me. I am embarrassed to say that those vague societal inferences held more weight than my own personal experiences. Furthermore, from the very first day we met, Pastor Steve offered honesty, vulnerability, and transparency from the pulpit. These qualities are respected by the world, but it's easy to hold judgments and skepticism and assume that they don't exist in the church.

Pastor Steve was thrust into spending the formative years of his life with a rough crowd on the streets of Philadelphia. God has used that experience to help him preach in a consistent and effective way to broken people who desperately need to understand their purposes in life. Seekers find those answers while having powerful encounters with God. I am ecstatic to share with you that I am one of those people. I found my purpose in life because the Holy Spirit drove me to find a local church, though at the time it simply seemed like an annoying voice in my head that wouldn't let me go until I took action. Friend, I truly believe if it wasn't for a powerful encounter with God, followed by finding a wonderful home church led by a man of courage and character, this book would have never become a reality.

Against the Odds

The story of Millersville Bible Church (MBC) begins at the conclusion of a former congregation who faced the painful reality of their imminent demise. At the end, they decided that they valued the work of God in this university town more than their identity as a congregation. After serving the Millersville community for twenty-one years, the Evangelical Mennonite congregation had steadily dwindled, until only seven members remained. Finding it impossible to move forward, this small group implemented a series of decisions that were as unlikely as they were courageous. First, they recognized the need for a vibrant evangelical witness in the community. Second, they understood the strategic value of their location near the campus of Millersville University. Third, they determined that if the church were to move forward, they would need to relinquish ownership of the church and seek new leadership with fresh vision and energy.

A Beautiful Response: The Heart of a Willing Servant

Pastor Steve had an internal battle between fear and faith. Fresh out of seminary, he was scared by the reality of trying to save a dying church. He didn't want his first role as a senior pastor to become a failure. However, what drove his decision more was the fact that he knew his response to being confronted with failure could not be led by small faith. Perhaps it stemmed from his survival of the tough streets of Philadelphia. No matter what, his response to failure and fear became one of beauty.

One April, God honored Pastor Steve's faith and called he and his wife, Becky, to take on the seemingly impossible task of leading the newly formed Millersville Bible Church. Together, the aging congregation and the inexperienced young couple confronted the odds that God is so fond of overcoming. Slowly, the work began to grow as God opened doors into the community and the university. By their second year, the congregation had grown to more than eighty, fifty of whom were university students. The excitement was balanced with the challenges of growth, not the least of which was the strain of limited financial resources combined with a woefully inadequate building. Pastor Steve had to be involved in outside employment for the first four years of the work. Along with financial pressures, Steve & Becky were greatly tested as they started a family and a church at the same time. But God proved His faithfulness, blessing Steve's commitment to preaching the Word and the congregation's willingness to share the burdens of the young ministry. They focused their energies not only on the community, but also on the unique needs of college students—a blend that marks the ministry to the present.

The First Twenty-Five Years of Flourishing Growth and Discipleship

Today, that original congregation of seven exceeds 500. The small, dilapidated original church witnessed the addition of office space next door, and then succumbed to the wrecking ball to make room for a more suitable meeting space to accommodate the thriving student ministry. Thirteen years after Pastor Steve's start, the congregation purchased a building and thirteen acres of land. After a year of extensive remodeling, the congregation moved into its present worship and educational facilities. As with any healthy church, the history of growth is chronicled by the development of effective leadership. The church that began with a young pastor who had to work a second job has witnessed the steady addition of elders, pastors, and ministry leaders to serve the needs of the active congregation. Six elders bear the primary responsibility for shepherding the flock; four full-time pastors minister to the diverse needs of the congregation; and the various ministries are led by a small army of dedicated staff and volunteers.

The MBC story is clearly one of a "Twenty-Five-Year Transformation." This concept describes one's commitment to truly embracing a life of change over a twenty-five-year span. This process allows a person to change their way of thinking so they can see the next twenty-five years of their life with more opportunity, passion, and excitement than any twenty-five years of the past, regardless of one's history or age. I am proud to tell you that not only did God bless the faithful seven who believed in a brighter future and their new pastor, but that it has gone places I believe those first congregants never would have believed. The simple fact that this church that I have been privileged to attend for several years now has grown and expanded into new facilities without debt isn't what is most important. The fact that God has given courage, unique spiritual gifting, and a desire for Pastor Steve to remain passionately engaged in his role throughout the past twenty-five years (when many peer leaders don't make it five years these days) is something that's of particular note. He is actually more excited about the potential within the next "Twenty-Five-Year Transformation," and that is what is most beautiful. Moreover, it is the reason why I share this story with you now, as we look at the potential found in your dreams. It has a lot to do with faith, courage, belief in what you can't see, and willingness to passionately pursue something for an extended period of time. Even doing so when our society encourages us, sadly, to leave our spouse, quit our job, and to get our needs met by that "greener grass" or to leave other significant relationships without necessary thought and reflection.

A Vision of the Next Twenty-five Years
in Our Post-Modern World

The post-modern era is one that prides itself in personal style versus faith. It values spiritualism and the ability for humans to choose their own path, while holding limitless tolerance for the belief of anything. I do acknowledge that there is power and beauty in free will and in the choices each individual makes. The danger, however, is found when you walk into a "Twenty-Five-Year Transformation" in your life without standing on strong convictions that drive and guide your life. You attempt to walk into a future that is always brighter than your past. However, murkiness takes over when you can't define what you truly believe. This leads to a disconnect between the passion needed to sustain you in order to reach your dreams. You can either live in a way that accommodates the mindset of the post-modern era (by agreeing to not stand firm on what you believe in a way that defines your life/future), or you can passionately live in a way that offers a courageous and inspiring alternative way to live life as you walk through your next twenty-five-year journey. If you do the latter, I believe the dreams found in your "Twenty-Five-Year Transformation" will be fueled by a fire that will never burn out and will sustain you throughout that quarter century life journey, just like it did for Pastor Steve.

A Pastor's Life Transformed:
Becoming an Expert on the Eighteen-Year Factor

Each person has a unique path in life that they are meant to travel. They hold an exclusive contribution that only they can make. As we walk forward in life we are given the opportunity to amass knowledge and wisdom in areas through the pursuit of dreams, personal life experiences or hardships. Many times, we would never predict the areas of life that we would grow to specialize in as the decades pass in our life. God takes pleasure in helping us to become sources of strength, wisdom, and inspiration for the world around us through the greatest weaknesses, pain or hardships that we face. For Pastor Steve, it was the redemption of life as a troubled youth that God used for His glory. He took him from the backstreets of Philadelphia as a downtrodden teenager, to become a highly respected pastor, counselor, spiritual advisor, and expert in the area of how a person's first eighteen years and upbringing has affected their lives in a profound way (he calls it the "Eighteen-Year Factor"). He is in the midst of publishing a book on this very topic, and is asked to write and speak on this subject quite often. Every person he has interviewed on this topic has had a powerful story to share about how the first eighteen years of their life affected them in significant ways, both good and bad.

He would be first to admit that this wisdom and knowledge has come from the hands of God alone. Here are some of the best insights Pastor Steve has learned during his "Twenty-Five-Year Transformation" and through his role as an expert on the Eighteen-Year Factor:

- God taps into our lives in a splendid way through the toughest challenges in our lives.

- "People, many times, only see the fruit in their life when successful, while ignoring the root causes of issues and failure." They ignore the core issues that continue to hold them back from effectively pursuing their dreams. God can show them and redeem those root issues.

- He learned that wisdom has to have knowledge to function, but wisdom is the ability to put knowledge into action.

- "Be honest about your expectations before God, and focus on things that matter most. Always focus on relationships and caring about other people first."

- "When people accept they failed, they must be presented with hope or the ghost of that failure will eat them up." Hope can see what can be in light of what is (while living in reality). Give someone hope, but be honest and don't help them live in unreality.

- "Sometimes when people are helping others shed the chains of past failure, they encourage others to live in such a way that doesn't try anything new." (Many times they never reach their full potential because of that protectionist/perfectionist approach to life.)

- Failure and fear always go together. "In a culture with tons of insurances and safeguards, we want to insulate ourselves from fear (including retirement)." If you allow fear of risk to control your mind's ability to venture out into the unknown, you will most likely not become all you can become for God's glory.

- He didn't make growing MBC his comparative reality with his peer churches. Instead, he focused on discipleship and growing each person.

- Recognize the significant people in your life. The willingness of Pastor Steve's wife, Becky, to follow him anywhere and truly live as a wife of noble character is one of the primary reasons the couple is where they're at in life. Also, many of the elders have had great longevity of service over the twenty-five years. Pastor Steve attributes their unity in purpose as being a core foundation for the church's growth.

- "Every verse in the Bible is for 'perspective formation.' Scripture will refine your life if you immerse yourself in it daily."

- Staying committed to a central purpose in life for a sustained period of time allows you the greatest opportunity to see God reveal new dreams in your life through areas of wisdom and specialization that you grew into.

Pastor Steve realized that the failure of MBC that he walked into as a twenty-four-year-old seminary graduate was actually a life-changing blessing in disguise. The failure of that old Mennonite church gave birth to great opportunities for him. This was true because he had the courage and faith to respond to the opportunity of the pastoral role despite his obvious initial fears and doubts. He was able to do so, primarily, because he possessed the heart of a willing servant and remained humble from the beginning.

God chooses to put His treasure in fragile vessels (normal people) and then He goes to work in our lives with His all-surpassing power (see 2 Cor. 4:7). Age is irrelevant when it comes to God's ability to create and help you pursue new dreams as you face any past failures or fears. Pastor Steve fondly recounted a story when he recently officiated a wedding between an eighty-three and ninety-year-old! They were courageous to seize life again and pursue new dreams. They did so despite any past setbacks, hardships, or failures they faced. Their courage inspired every single person in the room that day in a glorious way and Pastor Steve felt it certainly brought a smile to God.

Friend, I don't know where you are, or what failures you might be facing. However, I encourage you to embrace the above insights and hold on to the truth that God can help you see any dream realized. That includes any dream you have that aligns with God's will. God delights in transforming a person's life, and turning little into much!

*More information about MBC and Pastor Steve's ministry available at millersvillebiblechurch.org (notably his blog).

Point of Reflection or Action for Today:

Hebrews 6:10 (NIV)
[10] God is not unjust; he will not forget your work and the love you have shown him as you have helped his people and continue to help them.

Chapter 30

A Life Path Not Defined by Doubters

One of the greatest reasons for people failing to effectively run down their dreams is who they listen to. Simply put, they allow the wrong people to consistently speak into their life in ways that they never should. They present their dreams to those around them, and are faced with quite a bit of apprehension and resistance to seriously running after them. They tell them it is fun to think about such ideas, but to actually take action on them, that is a different story. Many times, these poisoning arrows that kill our dreams are shot by well intentioned family members or friends. That is a reason why so many dreamers take to heart what these voices say in opposition to taking committed action on their dream. Unfortunately, most times these people are simply projecting their own fears, weaknesses, or shortcomings on the person with the dream. The person with the dream could have significantly greater resolve, determination, and unique abilities to actually be successful. Many people never take action on their dreams, because their life direction comes from listening to the doubters and negative voices from within their sphere of influence. My prayer today is that I present solutions to help you take action, and not live a life that is driven by doubters as you further reflect on the dreams deepest in your heart.

Going Through the Motions

I love the song "The Motions" by Matthew West. It describes going through the motions instead of embracing the fullness and opportunity found in each day. They see a few days become a few weeks, then months, then years and even decades before they realize their whole life became a passive existence in which they were going through the bare minimum efforts each day just dealing with their responsibilities in life. They realize that they are bored in their career, their marriage is stale, they never made time for hobbies they once had passion for and many of the relationships they view as their closest are shallow or less than optimally fulfilling. Worst than that, they look back on life regretting so many dreams that they gave up on or never believed in enough to take action on and they still plague them this very day.

Managing Who Speaks Into Your Life: Your Personal Board of Advisors

One surefire way to ensure you don't live a life that is simply going through the motions is to evaluate who you listen to when it comes to your dreams. It is critical that you choose the right people to speak in your life, while always remaining open to new people that God appoints. It is dangerous to stay status quo with who you allow into your inner-circle in life. You should never close that door. Also, I encourage you to surround yourself with people that encourage seeking solutions to problems while offering consistent and constructive input. They will help you reach your dreams.

Some existing relationships diminish your confidence. It could be friendships that do not evolve and perhaps always seem threatened vs. inspired by your dreams. Moreover, there is power on not holding on to a relationship that doesn't want to walk with you into your growing future. Sometimes these decisions are tough, and perhaps the best solution is to maintain the relationship while decreasing the amount of time spent with them. You can do this while being mindful of certain areas of life that you try not to get into much with them.

Now, I am definitely not saying that you should cut out all relationships that are not your cheerleaders. I am also not saying for you to quit on lifelong commitments like a marriage if your spouse raises opposition to the pursuit of some of your dreams. You should always factor in such life commitments you made into all important decisions you make. If you are single, then perhaps you can consider this principal when choosing a mate. I am simply saying that if you allow certain people that focus most on the past, obstacles, negatives, and fears to consistently speak into your life as it relates to pursuing your dreams, you will not only see your dreams dashed, you will find that you have no energy to dream or pursue dreams.

One practical solution is for you to go through the process of picking your personal board of advisors. To do this, reflect on the people you respect the most, and the ones that inspire you most to reach your dreams in different areas of life. Look to people who embody the type of life you are pursuing in terms of character and accomplishment. You do not need to officially tell them that they are on your board of advisors. You should, however, tap into their strengths and wisdom in an ongoing fashion. They might be in different areas of specialty. One could be your mentor in finances, one could be a career mentor and so forth. These people can help you live a life fueled by passions and a constantly brighter future.

You can start by pouring into their lives and serving them out of love and genuine friendship through your quality time, love, and help. In doing so, you can ensure your outward focus builds deeper roots with each of them. I also believe it is wise to go through the process each year of assessing who is on your personal board, who should stay, who should go, and who should be added if applicable. Life changes in dynamic ways many times over a span of a year, so it is appropriate to re-evaluate things. For me, I do so at the end of a calendar year when I create my resolutions.

Lions, Pits, and Snowy Days, Oh My...

The Bible is full of so many rich, practical life examples that we can learn from this very day as we go after our dreams. I love the story of Benaiah. One day he did the seemingly illogical by chasing after a lion into a pit on a snowy day and killing it after taking a flying leap of faith (see 2 Sam. 23:20-21). The reason why I mention his exploit is because he brings out the concept of being a lion chaser. It remains as applicable today as ever when we think about our dreams and how to pursue them. Lion chasers take the challenge and go for it despite the odds. They see their big moments as opportunities to change their lives forever. For Benaiah, it was a step towards eventual military greatness by becoming the go-to-guy for

King David of Israel. Benaiah didn't allow the doubters to stop him from doing what he was appointed to do. Mark Batterson is the Senior Pastor of National Community Church in Washington, D.C. He is a modern day definition of a lion chaser, and he is a pastor! He authored the book In a Pit With a Lion on a Snowy Day. Below are some of the applicable highlights that encourage us to not listen to the doubters, but rather live our lives as lion chasers in regards to the pursuit of our dreams!

- God is in the business of strategically positioning us in the right place at the right time. But the right place often seems like the wrong place, and the right time often seems like the wrong time (p. 19).

- Impossible odds set the stage for amazing miracles (p. 39).

- The more we grow, the bigger God should get. And the bigger God gets, the smaller our lions become (p. 39).

- Opportunities often look like insurmountable obstacles (p. 78).

- Lion chasers are humble enough to let God call the shots and brave enough to follow where He leads (p. 99).

- Faith is embracing uncertainty (p. 100).

- One courageous choice may be the only thing between you and your dream becoming a reality (p. 123).

- The goal of faith is not the elimination of risk (p. 123).

- The willingness to fail is a prerequisite of success (p. 142).

- Our destiny is determined by whether or not we seize the God-ordained opportunities presented to us (p. 145).

- Part of spiritual maturity is caring less and less about what people think of you and more and more about what God thinks of you (p. 165).

Where the Rubber Meets the Road:
My Path Not Driven by Doubters

I have found that sometimes even a down economy can bring great opportunity. When I started Sharp Innovations, Inc., it was in the midst of the dot.com explosion and I am sure timing was a key to my success. At the time, though, my family and many friends told me not to do it, and go for a safe job. They said I was too young, and it was too risky. Fortunately for me, I write this today after well over a decade of success with that firm. Furthermore, when I stepped out in faith roughly a decade later to follow what God put on my heart in terms of writing this book, public speaking and a new role as a business and life coach, I found myself smack dab in a depressed market. It was ironic; a beautifully timed occurrence because more people than ever needed advice, counsel, and coaching.

My point is that you can look at any economic climate and seek the opportunities for success with your dreams. To find opportunities, you may need to do some things differently. You will need to look honestly at what new demands are being presented so you can come up with new ways to address them for the benefit of the world around you. If you own or work within a business already, then first and foremost, look at how you can make changes in how your business operates and in what new solutions, services, or values you can create to help an increased number of people. For me, I have seen about 50 percent of my coaching clientele come from clients initially within Sharp Innovations because of the personal relationships I already had with them. I offered a new capability that matched a true unique ability, passion, and dream of mine to meet a need in a changing world. I started by creating value in offering business/life coaching articles and videos through my blog. If you don't make it about you and first look at how you can create a bigger future with more opportunity for your prospects, clients, key team members and the world around you, then you are focusing your energy best in any economic climate. In doing so, you might just be pleasantly surprised by the fruit of your labors!

Any Good Board of Advisors Needs a Chairman

I want to leave you today with a few reminders as you ponder your dreams and the potential for failure which could be holding you back right now from stepping out in faith. Sadly, many people never act on their dreams because their direction in life comes from listening to the doubters and negative voices from within their sphere of influence, who maybe are afraid to do what they are daring to do.

You need to evaluate who you listen to when it comes to your dreams. Surround yourself with people that encourage seeking solutions to problems while offering consistent, constructive, and encouraging input. They will help you reach your dreams. There is power in existing relationships that diminish your confidence. There is also power in not holding on to a relationship that's holding you back from your future. Lastly, your relationship with God is one that you should stand firm on. Let Him be the chairman on your board of advisors! Too many people make their decision about God and their relationship with Him based upon the lukewarm spiritual beliefs that surround them today. God wants us to live an abundant life (John 10:10). If you were wrong about Jesus Christ or your personal relationship with God in any way, based upon your spiritual convictions and decisions, when would you want to know about it? My answer would be absolutely today, but that's just me. Fortunately, God is very accessible through prayer and can help you assess your dreams and the people you let speak into your life better than anyone else. For those that love God and bring their dreams before Him, He will also help doors to open and close so the right people surround you as you run down your dreams.

Friend, my prayer for you today is this: don't let doubters lead the path for your life. You only live once my friend. I can promise that during your last hours of life on this planet, that you will not look back on life and regret the dreams that you went for and failed at nearly as much as those dreams that were never realized because you never made an attempt.

Point of Reflection or Action for Today:

"A person without a dream never had a dream come true."

– Andy Andrews

27. Why I Love People that Don't Buy From Me!

- Some people need to close one door in our life, so they can help us open a new one.

- Being present and seriously embracing the gifts within each day can take you further than your future or past many times.

28. A Glorious Response to Failure: The Hawthorne Family Story

- Living life in a way that is led by putting your spiritual faith in God into action, can take you to exciting new dreams and remarkable destinations despite any failure you face in life.

- If you are willing to give up everything you have for God's glory, He will create a path of new dreams that will lead you to a special legacy in life.

29. Beauty Built from the Midst of Failure: The MBC Story

- Failure many times gives birth to our greatest opportunities in life when we have the courage and faith to respond to them.

- From the heart of a willing servant, God delights in transforming a person's life, and turning little into much.

30. A Life Path Not Defined By Doubters

- Many people never take action on their dreams because their life direction comes from listening to the doubters and negative voices from within their sphere of influence who are afraid to do what they are daring to do.

- You need to evaluate who you listen to when it comes to your dreams. Surrounding yourself with future-based people that encourage seeking solutions to problems and offer consistent, constructive, yet positive input will help you reach your dreams.

- There is power in exiting relationships that don't build your confidence when possible. There is also power in not holding on to a relationship that doesn't want to walk with you into your future.

Running Down Your Dreams—Taking Action!

What was your most devastating failure you have faced in your life to date? What was your response? What did or can you learn from it as you reflect on your current dreams? Why and how did it happen? My goal is not for you to dwell on the failure itself. There is power in journaling about such experiences, so you can seek to glean new insights that you might not have fully realized to date. Write about it in the space below, assign a go-date for you to take action to respond to the failure in a positive way (if current) or to respond positively through your greatest lessons learned as you reflect on your current dreams. Perhaps you even know someone else that is experiencing a similar failure in life? Perhaps you can share your story and insights with them and help them respond in a positive way? Journal about what your next action should be to make progress towards your current dreams or in helping someone else through your wisdom gleaned.

My Dream's Name: _____

My Go Date: _____

Dreams Journal

For more free resources to help encourage you in your pursuit of dreams found through failure, please visit: www.livewithpurposecoaching.com.

FATHER

ROBERT
JOHN Sr.
NOV. 3, 1940
JUNE 10, 2004

SHARP

44

JOURNEY #8

Dreams Found Through Death & Illness

Theme Focus:

Death and illness are never pleasant or easy to handle. But much like failure, death and illness can become some of our greatest teachers. I firmly believe everything in life happens for a reason as God's divine intervention works in our lives. Being faced with our own mortality seems to have the ability to change how we live. Many times it helps us to have a personal encounter with God Himself. I have found within my own life that we can learn as much if not more from death as we can from life itself. Many times life-threatening illnesses or our death itself can actually be used to change the direction of the lives of others, and through it leave behind a beautiful legacy.

Psalm 23 (A psalm of David - NIV)

¹ The LORD is my shepherd, I lack nothing. ² He makes me lie down in green pastures, he leads me beside quiet waters, ³ he refreshes my soul. He guides me along the right paths for his name's sake. ⁴ Even though I walk through the valley of the shadow of death, I will fear no evil, for you are with me; your rod and your staff, they comfort me . ⁵ You prepare a table before me in the presence of my enemies. You anoint my head with oil; my cup overflows. ⁶ Surely your goodness and love will follow me all the days of my life, and I will dwell in the house of the LORD forever.

Chapter 31

Sometimes Death Can Teach You More than Life

My father taught me so much about real-life and street-smarts. Though I am very different from him in many ways, so much of the best of him made me the man I am today.

Death is a painful experience for all of us, even those who can rest assured of their eternal destination because of the faith they place in Jesus Christ. We tend to all go through the stages of grieving, and rightfully so. However, I have learned that the death of loved ones can many times teach you more about life and the pursuit of your dreams. My prayer today is that through some of my personal stories, you might be able to own that principle as you are reminded of your own mortality. I also hope you can apply it to your life as well as the dreams you are running down!

So Much More than the Other Half of My Cross

My father represents the other half of the cross that I wear. So much of my father's life remains a part of the foundation in my life as I walk through the days in his absence.

He taught me so much about real life, street smarts, dedication, and hard work. He grew up in the coal regions of central PA and later in the back streets of Philadelphia. He grew up watching a single mother raise him and his brothers. He was faced with the social stigmas and career rejections because of his limited education and physical disability. However, his resolve and determination was inspiring! His life was also a lot about providing for us rather than going purely after what he never had. Many of his dreams were helping support our foundation and the realization of the dreams of my brother and I.

Seeing my father die in less than one month is something I can't find the right words to describe. It was heart breaking to watch someone realize their life is being predicted to end abruptly. All I could feel was as if the door of life was slammed shut and that was all there was to it. Fortunately, there is more to the story than that.

Though I didn't understand it at the time, I believe God opened another door. It became a window into my father's soul. On the other side of the door was the true essence of what entering into a relationship with God was all about. He presented my father a choice to embrace God's gift of salvation and an eternal life with Him in heaven. Unfortunately, I don't know if he walked through that door because I lacked understanding and perspective at that time. I was blinded by emotions and could not see God at work before us. Looking back, I realize that before my eyes I saw a person's life and mortality confronted. The door was opened by God through how my dad's life came crashing down around him. It gave him an opportunity to reach out to walk through that door to have a relationship with Jesus Christ whose arms were waiting for him wide open. Looking back, I realize this was a definite take-away from my father's life and ultimately his death in terms of how God truly works in our lives.

I can remember the day I gave his eulogy like it was yesterday. At the time, there remained divisions within our family, and broken relationships. I walked to the front of the room that day to share with everyone what was on my heart. At the time, I just tried to do what I could to be the one that kept everything together as I looked into the eyes of others that were so weakened by our loss. I didn't attribute much of anything I said that day to God or the Holy Spirit. I reminded myself of this reality, by re-reading the eulogy message I typed up and read years ago as I write this story for you today.

I did not make my decision to become a Christian and follow Jesus until a few months after my father's death. Looking back, I realize that I spoke with such conviction, power, and truth through the guidance and prompting of the Holy Spirit. I challenged everyone in attendance to not only celebrate his life, but to leverage his death so it could become a catalyst to see broken relationships restored within our family and beyond.

A few months later, I was thankfully reunited with my uncle and aunt who I hadn't spoken with for many years because of a falling out with my father. God used them to lead me to my decision to become a Christian. God continues to bless me with passion and zeal to live my life as a tribute to my father's dreams that were never realized. A goal of mine remains embracing the best of what he taught me both through his life and certainly through his death. Though he is dearly missed, it certainly adds additional meaning and purpose to my life that could not exist without his absence.

Somehow through my father's departure from life, God created a pathway for him to continue to teach me in even more remarkable ways, as I took over in many ways within my family. I was given opportunities to have areas of leadership and responsibility within the family that he used to take care of, including the care of my mother. I was able to grow as a man and leader in profound ways. I learned how much my father actually was responsible for, and how much more capable I could become by God's grace through the transition to these new responsibilities.

Most notably, God clearly used his death to draw me into a personal relationship with Jesus which I am eternally thankful for, because forever my life and dreams have been changed for the better! God has replaced many of my dreams that were focused too much on me with ones that are bolder, richer, and more meaningful because they better align with His work that is focused on bringing His kingdom on Earth as it is in heaven. As you reflect on anyone you have lost that you miss dearly, or those you worry about losing most in the future, perhaps you can seek God in prayer and ask Him to do the same thing within your heart, dreams, and life.

Perseverance Driven by Dedication and Loyalty

My grandfather, Richard Diceley, embodied both dedication and loyalty. He taught me how to live by the way he lived. He was a man of few words, yet his traits of consistency, loyalty, dedication as well as his willingness to serve, unconditional love, and hard work spoke for themselves. He was a selfless man that put aside dreams of his own to support the dreams of those around him. He was a mechanic and in the military for most of his career. He mostly did automotive, engineering, and mechanical work. One summer growing up, we produced hand-crafted magnets within his workshop and I painted them and sold them at a retail store. He empowered my young passions and dreams in areas I knew nothing about.

I believe much of what kept him going to eighty-eight was perseverance. His love, loyalty, and dedication to my grandmother was amazing. He wanted to make sure that she was taken care of well, despite the frailty of his body. It was in those moments that his dedication and loyalty to his family drove him to persevere from day to day.

My grandfather might have taught me abundantly throughout his life; however, much like my father, his wisdom continues to echo in his absence. He lived in a simple, beautiful, unique way that is rarely seen today, and I'm still inspired to live my dreams because of it. Now that he's gone, I find I am challenged to live my life with the perseverance and dedication I saw in him.

The Depths of Groaning

First, I should start out by saying that I cannot be sure that either my father or grandfather truly accepted Jesus Christ as their personal Lord and Savior. Today, as I live my life as a believer and follower of Jesus, I know that this is the most important decision one can make in life.

In many ways, my spirit groans because I didn't understand this truth when my father was alive. Neither did I ever make the efforts I should have to confirm what my grandfather's spiritual commitments and decisions in life were. He faithfully attended church throughout most of his life, yet I know now that going to any building of worship isn't a ticket to heaven or the be-all-end-all when it comes to having a personal relationship with God through His Son. I do pray, and would like to believe, that my father and grandfather did make that decision. For the most part, I found it easier to bring up this discussion with total strangers as I traveled the globe, than the men I knew and loved dearly. For my grandfather, I let fear of offending him or getting an answer I didn't want to hear keep me from having that conversation. The groaning within me lingers on.

Now I strive to ensure that everyone else I love knows of God's love for them. Furthermore, I resolve to walk forward with God's help to deliver his message of love to the world around me. My prayer is the same for your loved ones, that they would take hold of this free gift from God, which offers ultimate hope and peace.

My grandmother has been a woman who was always full of zeal and moxie. As expected, losing her husband and continuing on in life solo through her 90s was a step that required deep faith and trust in our Creator (both for her and myself). She felt lost: the purpose she had for living was gone. I remembered the groaning within me during the days after she lost her husband and I lost my grandpa. It was hard to see what it did to her. She wouldn't answer the phone. I was always worried, even driving over to check on her sometimes to make sure she was still alive. As I continue to chase my dreams, I often wonder when our last time together will come.

She, like my father and grandfather, continues to teach me so much as God continues to use her. For now, I cherish the sweet moments God continues to bless us with. I intently seek to not only love and serve her with all my heart, I seek to have ears to hear, eyes to see, and a heart open to continue learning from her. I am confident that her spirit remains here to teach the world around her, and I am so fortunate to get so much quality time with her. I believe we both now realize that when your back is up against the wall and you face the reality of your own mortality, your perspective on life and the pursuit of your dreams can change. God has opened her eyes, so she now sees a new purpose for her life without her husband.

The Best Teachers Follow Your Dreams Beyond Life

We need to put aside our pride, and ask God to show us to how to be humble and harvest the best of what He has taught others in their lives. The best teachers in our lives continue teaching even when they're gone. God is good. His ways are not our ways, they are far greater! All you need to do is to open your heart and trust in His love. You can trust Him with your dreams.

Point of Reflection or Action for Today:

Who do you love dearly, that you should reach out to today and discuss your dreams with, while they are still alive to be a teacher?

Chapter 32

What are You Going to do with the Lemons in Your life?

Dreams Profile with Trace Balin

Internationally recognized musician, songwriter, and screenplay writer

As you run down your dreams in life, will you turn your lemons into sweet lemonade or permit them to become bitter roadblocks that sour your entire life? As a child, Trace Balin recounts that she wasn't the popular kid in school; however, she recognized a strong musical gifting. Determined to hone that gift, she saved up profits from babysitting to purchase a guitar and taught herself how to play. Discovering this gift set her on the path to chase down her God-given dreams, come what may.

An Appointed Encounter in Alaska

My chance encounter with Trace and her husband, Joel, on that Alaskan cruise became a special confirmation that her story is an important chapter in the tales that I've been appointed to tell. The simple sincerity in her story remains a daily encouragement to me. May it be the same for you as you or a loved one face dark hours of adversity or epic encounters with major illness or death itself.

Real Fruit Borne from Life's Adversity

Facing even a single one of the circumstances that she's walked through would be life-altering. I love her response to each: allowing God to use each of them to beautifully mature and ripen on the vine of her life. Let's be challenged by her intent to run down her dreams. As a young adult, Trace fought and won a battle with cancer, however, the course of treatment included a full hysterectomy. God provided the children Trace and her husband desired through the adoption of two beautiful Korean children.

After her singing career took off, she struggled with a major bout of pneumonia. With a "the show must go on" attitude, she performed while ill. Performing that night led to an onset of laryngitis that tore up her vocal chords. A bronchoscopy, the procedure intended to fix the problem, rendered her unable to speak for six weeks. Imagine a singer unable to utter a sound!

Trace pressed on, but a few years later she was gripped with a very rare autoimmune disease, dermatomyositis, that attacked her muscles and overall strength. Still, Trace didn't give up.

She boldly proclaims that more growth has come out of adversity than prosperity in her life. She believes our personal responses to life's trials is what defines character. Though she admits that "maybe it was a bit of stubbornness" on her part, she never allowed anything to stop her from finding a way to pursue her life passions and dreams. In the midst of her trials, God's providence was paving the way for her. Following her bout with cancer, Trace landed her first record deal with Word's Dayspring Label from a blind tape she recorded locally. They called her and wanted to sign her on their contemporary Christian label even though she was a fairly new believer. Trace told me that almost never happens in the music industry. Her distinctive, raspy voice that emerged after the pneumonia and the ensuing medical procedure was actually what the record execs and listeners were drawn to!

She recorded three albums that generated eight top ten singles on the contemporary Christian charts. Doors also opened for hit producing projects abroad including cross-over blues albums through a Netherlands-based record label that listeners still clamor for.

Change is a consuming part of Trace Balin's life. Like the willow tree she sings about in her song "Changes," she has had to adapt and bend in the storms of life, or otherwise break. As Trace has persevered through those changes, her music and ministry have spanned nearly two decades, impacting people's lives throughout the world. Since her days on Word's Dayspring label, her artistry has continued to ebb and flow, evolve and expand from the concert stage to ministry as a dynamic motivational speaker, writer, author, recording artist, actress, and playwright.

Maybe the demand for her music lies in the vulnerability and utter dependency on God it shows. Maybe people can hear the hope in her voice that's been carved out of loss... such as when her mother died unexpectedly. Maybe people feel the faith that resonates in the songs... the kind of faith that sustained her after a second throat illness left her with a partially paralyzed vocal cord. She remembers, "I stopped touring when doctors told me surgery wasn't an option. I went to speech therapists and did exercises that brought no improvement. I went through what some people call a dark night of the soul."

Determined not to wallow in self-pity, she asked God to give her direction. His answer? A new stage for Trace to minister joy out of sorrow and weakness. She says, "I taught myself to sing all over again using different techniques to overcome the handicap. It was very hard. At one point I thought I might not be able to do it so I got a real estate license. It was my back-up plan." She laughs, "I figured if I could be so enthusiastic about our eternal home, I could be just as enthusiastic about our homes on earth. It turned out to be a wonderful blessing to me because I've been able to truly help people." During that time, God kept reminding Trace that a merry heart is good medicine and told her to bring good medicine to others who have been broken in spirit. She began to write and produce musical comedies, eight in all, and she developed a passion for speaking encouragement into the lives of women. One listen to the hilarious and compelling production of "Adam's Rib" and you know her joy runs deep.

Coming to Terms with Your True Gifting

So as you look at the dreams you are pursuing in life, or desperately seek inspiration to have new dreams birthed, I pray some of the struggles that Trace has lived through will inspire you. She believes that true gifts can go under-developed when people pursue something they love to do, but are not good at, instead of truly pursuing what they are uniquely gifted in. She believes that following what you are truly gifted in brings forth deep meaning in the person. Consistently developing new and additional skills leads to a creative, productive life of purpose and dreams that can weather each storm in life's changing seasons.

Trace added that "the more you study the field you are passionate about and uniquely gifted in, the more you grow and thrive in it." Resting on talent and gifting alone makes you complacent and ill-prepared to face the trials of your future. Attitude is everything! To achieve your dreams, you need to stay positive, no matter how much adversity you face. "A mountain is simply a massive object. There are many ways you can strategize to climb it, go around it, or perhaps even fly over it," Trace says with joy. When illnesses brought setbacks to her musical career, Trace expanded her talent to coach people on how to do choreography and musical presentations on stage, as well as produced theatrical productions. These new opportunities and dreams would most likely never have been born unless she faced the life-changing trials she did. Trace consistently allowed God to stir what many would see as "life lemons" into sweet lemonade, rather than settling for living with a sour pucker.

When doors open and close, how do we make our dreams fit? How can we mold our dreams to fit God's pathways? Are we willing to reshape our character? These are good questions that we can each ask ourselves and lift up to God in prayer!

A Musician's Memoirs

Undoubtedly, despair and hopelessness abound in today's world. Trace points to much of it being caused by people seeking things that will never truly fulfill their inner most being. She told me when you go after a dream, it should be one that fulfills you and that you have a true talent for, but it should also represent God well. Character really counts. We can't afford to make choices that result in a divergence of our personal and professional lives. Our victories can become a voice of hope and encouragement to others' life paths. Whatever you do or face in life, you should do it with integrity, character, and a good sense of humor. Trace prays when she stands before God at the end of her life that He will say, "Well done, good and faithful servant" like the song "Well Done" (written by Ashley Cleveland) that she sings so beautifully. Her life purpose is to represent God the best way she knows how, and to live a life that brings Him glory.

Let's take Trace's encouragement to seek for God to provide the courage we need to press through fears and trials that come from pursuing a dream. My prayer for you, my friend, is that you seek fulfillment—and press through obstacles—by seeking God's purpose for your life. Don't waste time and effort running after dreams, careers, or a life that dishonors God. Instead, respond boldly with courage when faced with illness or other trials.

*For more information on Trace's ministry, visit www.tracebalin.com.

Point of Reflection or Action for Today:

1 Corinthians 1:27 (NIV)

[27] But God chose the foolish things of the world to shame the wise; God chose the weak things of the world to shame the strong.

Chapter 33

Why Does God Allow Massive Destruction on Earth?

My goal today, as you reflect your dreams and purpose in life, is to share some perspectives that could help you better decide what you believe about the evil we see in this world and God. Furthermore, my prayer is that you would be challenged to truly take your beliefs and measure them against what God has told us through His Word. I have seen too many people develop beliefs in life (including what they believe about God) through the voices of media and the peers around them instead of seeking God personally to find what they truly believe. I think He is certainly a credible enough litmus test to apply our dreams, complaints, worries, and uncertainties in life against.

Personally, I am encouraged that God uses all things, including destruction, for the good of those who love Him. I believe God uses major world tragedies to bring nations together in love in a way like nothing else could. He does so while showcasing His love for us all through the creation of new shared dreams within the hearts of men and women throughout the world.

A Commonly Asked Question

When we turn on the television or radio, open a newspaper, or pull up various online media sources, we would have to be blind to miss the daily tragedies in this world. Hurricane Katrina, the earthquake in Haiti, Japan's tsunami and 9/11 are just a few. *Why does God allow bad things to happen if He is a loving God?*

So many people have struggled to understand God's heart in such matters. There is a difference in God permitting tragedy to happen and Him bringing it upon the world. His love is able to bring good from all bad in our lives (see Rom. 8:28). God doesn't make mistakes, but the mistakes of mankind can be transformed by its Creator for a greater purpose.

Responses from the Heart to Ponder

Like so many people, I have struggled with this question as it pertains to my own life. Only by coming to terms with something terribly sad in my life have I come to understand the role God plays when human tragedies occur. I now feel confident that God does not send tragedies to punish us or test us. In fact, God does not send them at all. Rather, I sense that there are powerful forces loose in the world (forces like evil, disease, and death).

So what is God's role in all the turmoil of the world? If God is not sending the diseases, the accidents, and the tragedies, then why doesn't He step in and prevent them? There is a bigger question to answer. Each person cries out for divine intervention, for healing, for salvation, and freedom from emotional or physical pain. Although miraculous healings do occur at times, it is my experience that there are many times without His physical intervention. However, the "intervention" many have experienced has been as powerful as anything physical He could do. I have grown certain that God actually mourns these horrible events with us. I have seen Him stand by me, protect me, comfort me, and restore my soul.

Why do bad things happen to good people? God's clear answer is there are no "good" people. The Bible makes it abundantly clear that all of us are tainted by and infected with sin (see Eccles. 7:20; Rom. 6:23; 1 John 1:8). Furthermore, Romans 3:10-18 could not be clearer about the non-existence of "good" people: "There is no one righteous, not even one; there is no one who understands, no one who seeks God. All have turned away, they have together become worthless; there is no one who does good, not even one."

A better question would be the reverse: "*Why does God allow good things to happen to bad people*"? Romans 5:8 declares, "But God demonstrates his own love for us in this: While we were still sinners, Christ died for us." Despite the evil, wicked, sinful nature of the people of this world, God still loves them. He loved us enough to die to take the penalty for our sins

(Rom. 6:23). If we receive Jesus Christ as our personal Savior (John 3:16; Rom.10:9), we will be forgiven and promised an eternal home in heaven (Rom. 8:1). What we truly deserve is hell, and that is a harsh reality. What we are given is eternal life in heaven if we come to Jesus Christ in faith. I for one am thankful for God's unconditional love and sacrifice, and I am trying to live a life that reflects my gratitude as I run down my dreams.

Above all, however, we must remember that God is good, just, loving, and merciful. Often things happen to us that we simply cannot understand. However, instead of doubting God's goodness, our reaction should be to trust Him. "Trust in the LORD with all your heart and lean not on your own understanding; in all your ways acknowledge Him, and He will make your paths straight." (Prov. 3:5-6)

Many people believe, on some level, that when something bad happens, it's a form of punishment. Call it karma, bad luck or "making your own bed and lying in it." As a result of my growing understanding of the grace of God, He shifted my beliefs to realize He is always beside me, loves me, and wishes me to know His love without limits. No matter what, He never wishes any harm to visit me. God loves me as though I am the only child in the world for God to love. First, I have to know the unlimited and unconditional nature of God's love for myself. I now know, without a doubt, that my God never wishes bad in the world. Not for me. Not for anyone. He simply allows it to occur, and uses it for our good.

What Does God Have to do with Bad Weather?

Weathermen predictions are many times fallible, despite immense technological advancements in forecasting. How is God involved with Mother Nature? How should we understand God's plan and power in relation to destructive displays of nature? Should those who love God expect to be protected from harm? Examples are recorded in Scripture of God's interventions for his people. Yet there are examples of those whom God did not deliver from physical danger (Heb. 11:35-38). What should we expect? Does God offer any guarantees concerning physical safety in this fallen world?

Each day, dangers affect all areas of life: physical, intellectual, moral, spiritual, social, and ecological. We live in a world full of unsafe people, places, and things. We have good reasons to be concerned about our personal, local, national, and international security. But God does not guarantee safety from harm in this life. Sometimes He chooses to intervene and sometimes He does not. When God allows suffering, it is an opportunity for us to trust Him and to turn our focus toward an eternal perspective in life that goes beyond simply what we can see today.

When our fellow humans suffer, it offers an occasion for helping those in need. Major life disasters can bring a nation or world together in ways that nothing else could. I have seen this firsthand in my missionary work after the Earthquakes in Haiti. When thousands suffer from homelessness, disease, and death as a result of hurricanes and other disasters, we can't just say, "Oh well, that's life in the world we live in." Compassion requires more from us. Whatever we conclude about God's involvement in the bad weather, Scripture never depicts God as helplessly watching events beyond His control like we do when we take in the news stories!

Hope In the Midst of Tragedy

There is so much devastation and tragedy in the world that it is easy to reach a point of great despair. It is easy to feel that dreams are dashed in the face of death or illness. However, there is great hope for each of us. First, we must understand some core concepts, so we can prepare our heart to be softened so we can truly hear from God. It will help us to understand the events and circumstances within our lives better as we run down our dreams. Here are a few that I would like to share that speak of the hope He offers us all in the face of tragedy:

- Perhaps the realities of violent weather are simply part of life in a world turned against its Creator, not the other way around. God is absolutely sovereign. Yet God's control is never presented in a way that diminishes human responsibility (Gen. 45:4-8; 50:20).

- Here is a sobering thought: "To demand from God a world where nothing bad happens, is to risk eliminating ourselves." Why is this true? Because we all do bad things as Scripture reveals, "all have sinned and fallen short of God's glory" (Rom. 3:23).

- We are all sinners, there are no exceptions. Sinners deserve death (Rom. 3:23; 6:23); though thankfully living sinners experience undeserved extensions of life from God.

- What can we expect from God? He clearly promises to be with us in our trials sustaining us with grace and comforting us when we turn to Him. More importantly, He promises eternal life to all who trust in Jesus Christ for their salvation. God does not promise heaven on this earth. Many times life on earth mirrors hell more than heaven. But heaven is the place God is preparing for us (John 14:1-3).

- God's willingness to allow a world where bad things continue to happen is actually an amazing demonstration of His mercy. I recognize that this is easier to believe when bad things are not happening to you. Yet this is what God teaches us through Scripture (see Rom. 9:22-23).

Friend, there is so much hope in the midst of any tragedy. The fact that God would show kindness to anyone is sheer mercy. But the truth of Scripture offers far more. In flesh and blood, God entered this bad world in the person of Jesus Christ and allowed bad people to commit evil acts against Him. Did He have power to stop those who opposed him? Yes. Why didn't He use his power? Why didn't He protect himself? Because in His great love, He willingly chose to provide us with salvation by bearing the punishment our sin and evil deeds deserved. Those who freely receive this gift of salvation will one day be delivered from all evil. Our true hope lies beyond life as we know it on this horizontal existence. It is found within the beauty of an eternal destination God gives us access to through a vertical relationship between His creation on earth and Him in heaven.

Please take heart and remember that God uses all things to work for the good of those who love Him (Rom. 8:28). Furthermore, He uses major world tragedies to bring nations together in love in a way like nothing else could. He also showcases His love for us all through the creation of new dreams. I encourage you to embrace that reality with a sense of empowerment and willingness to grow through any tragedy or season of life you face as you run down your dreams!

Point of Reflection or Action for Today:

Matthew 6:34 (NIV)

[34] Therefore do not worry about tomorrow, for tomorrow will worry about itself. Each day has enough trouble of its own.

31. Sometimes Death Can Teach You More than Life

- The death of loved ones can many times teach you more about life and the pursuit of your dreams than even the most impactful lives ever did.

- When your back is up against the wall and you face the reality of your own mortality, your perspective on life and the pursuit of your dreams can change in a unique way.

32. What are You Going to do with the Lemons in Your life? The Trace Balin Story

- Making the choice to respond to our greatest challenges in life with an eternal perspective will spur you on to your greatest dreams, and it is something we do control.

- Not pursuing your dreams in life because of a confrontation with a major illness, stops us from making a contribution to the world that only we can uniquely make.

33. Why does God allow Massive Destruction on Earth?

- God uses all things (including massive destruction) for the good of those who love Him.

- God uses major world tragedies to bring nations together in love in a way like nothing else could. He also showcases His love for us all through the creation of new shared dreams within the world.

Running Down Your Dreams—Taking Action!

- **Do you have a life threatening tragedy that has happened within your life (or the life of someone you love dearly) that you currently struggle with or blame God for?**

- **Who do you know that is alive that you haven't said "I love you" to in a while that you need to?**

- **Is there someone you need to reconcile your relationship with while you still can?**

If so, I encourage you to journal about it today and take it to God in prayer so He can help you to better understand His purposes within that specific situation. Write about it in the space below, assign a goal date in regards to what your next action should be to make progress towards your dreams found or re-born through reflection on mortality, death, or illness.

My Dream's Name: _____

My Go Date: _____

For more free resources to help encourage you in your pursuit of dreams found through death or illness, please visit: www.livewithpurposecoaching.com.

"Life isn't about waiting for the storm to pass... it's about learning to dance in the rain."

– Vivian Greene

JOURNEY #9

Dreams Found Through Pain, Sorrow & Depression

Theme Focus:

I can testify personally to how powerful our emotions can be, and how they can consume our lives. Pain, sorrow, and depression are ones that we can all relate to in one way or another. I believe we give our emotions too much control at times in our life and they become a force that drive us down paths we wish we never went. When faced with rejection, failure, and longing, these emotions surface. They can bubble over and shift our outlook on life so much that we simply are not able to operate at our best. Emotions can even lead you to destinations you never wanted. My prayer is that through insights and resources from a professional counselor and some of the most open, honest, transparent, and vulnerable stories that I can personally share with you, so that you might be able to avoid making similar mistakes. I also desire to help you shift your course towards the straight and narrow path God desires for you as you continue to pursue your dreams.

Chapter 34

No Limits to the Depths of Sin

Sin, vulnerability, pain, and depression relate to running down our dreams in life. I was a guy that had very grand dreams of being an ideal family man early in life, (one full of love and integrity) among other character strengths. I also found out that I enjoyed communicating in a deep and passionate way. My father, God rest his soul, used to say, "You should have been a girl." I know he jokingly was referring to my emotional and communicative sides that were not typical for a male. I wish I could tell you that my dream came true in the timeline I set, but it simply did not. Instead, God took me through a very unexpected journey based upon patience, refinement, pruning, and complete life purpose re-creation. I had plenty of dreams when I was younger. I even had aspirations of living in a way that honored God, but that was before I followed Jesus Christ. Eventually sin caught up to me, sin that even my good intentions couldn't avoid.

As I think about running down my dreams and watch others around me strive for theirs, I find something obvious yet commonly overlooked. I believe that many times the thing that holds us back most in life as we focus on striving for dreams and accomplishments is ourselves. It can be through our negative outlook. It can be through a lack of patience in which we make rushed, unwise, or uncalculated major decisions. It can be the choices we make while surrounded by people that want to project their voices of mental defeat and concern on our dreams because of their own fears and anxieties. Sometimes those voices become so influential that they re-direct our lives. No matter how we slow ourselves down from reaching our dreams instead of striving for constant life progress, there is nothing that will stop us more dead in our tracks than our ability to sin.

Human beings have a sinful nature and the ability to do evil. We do things all the time that counter what God's desires are for each of us. They come in all types, sizes, and levels of severity. Sins could be small lies or stealing something small from work that will not go noticed, or emotional cheating on your spouse. We can see them as being acceptable when compared to larger sins such as physical forms of adultery, robbery, or murder. However, all sin is sin in God's eyes.

If we are honest, I am sure we have all been driven to emotional or reactionary life states that have prompted us to respond in impulsive and unwise ways. The acts of the sinful human include: sexual immorality, impurity, hatred, jealousy, fits of rage, selfish ambition, dissensions, envy, drunkenness, lusts, adultery, and idolatry (worshipping other gods, figures, or other aspects in our life). Sometimes there are things we place above God that become idols, like the pursuit of money, goals, or searching for a spouse). My goal is not to bring you down through judgment. Rather, I look to expose myself personally so I can share with you my story so you can lift out the wisdom God has shown me through my life path and apply it to the next steps you will take towards running down your dreams. I desire for you not only to understand how there truly is not a limit to the depths of sin, yet that there is clearly a narrow road that leads to victory. I desire for you to find and walk that path.

The Eighteen-Year Factor

People that do wrong can easily blame their upbringing and sidestep accountability and truth when they make bad choices. I do agree, however, that it is clear that our childhood does profoundly affect each of our lives as we strive to grow and reach our dreams. My senior pastor, Steve Cornell of Millersville Bible Church, developed a brilliant concept called our eighteen-year factor. If you want to find out more about this concept in great detail please visit resources at: www.thinkpoint.wordpress.com/category/18-year-factor. The early years of life are the most foundational and important to the formation of our identity, character, future health, and stability. If you've experienced a healthy and functionally stable upbringing, you've received a gift that has become increasingly rare.

But if your upbringing was marked by a significant disruption or a serious dysfunction, it will have a definite affect on your identity, security, and relationship skills. If there were significant disruptions—(like a parent who walks in and out of your life or your parents' divorce) or serious dysfunctions (like a domineering father or mother, sexual abuse, abuse of any form from a parent, an alcoholic parent or an emotionally distant one), you had what is seen as a toxic background. The protective mechanisms children practice to shield themselves from hurt do not protect them when carried into adult relationships. The walls and defensive postures later alienate people and hinder true intimacy and progress in adult life. The toxicity must be addressed if you desire to have healthy adult relationships as you run down your dreams in life.

My eighteen-year factor certainly was full of significant disruption and dysfunctions. Various forms of physical, emotional, and sexual abuse became bricks on the path of my journey. Learning to cope with my feelings and outside attacks by peers as it related to my mother's mental illness and father's physical disability cemented yet more bricks along that path. My feet have never forgotten walking on those bricks, yet as I share with you extremely personal life stories today, it is my prayer that you will see how God's love is a redeeming one. He loves to replace our dreams with better dreams that we can run down for His glory.

Honest Stories of Personal Disgust to Learn From

People many times are driven by their emotions and expectations. Both emotions and expectations are such powerful, life-altering forces. Emotions are not all bad of course, however many times they remove our ability to be objective and make solid choices. Instead, we find ourselves making bad decisions that impact our lives and those around us in negative ways. If we can learn from them and apply change to our future decisions and actions, then all is not lost. Sadly, many people allow their emotions to become a driving force that creates a broken road of repetitive sin, vulnerability, pain, and depression.

I admit I am one of them. I prayerfully submit my stories to you in hopes that you can learn from them and grow as a person as you strive to run down your dreams. If that becomes true, then you become in a sense a part of some of my dreams from God in helping others see their lives transformed for His glory through my personal broken road of the past.

I have done many things that I am ashamed of. Jesus said in the Bible that if you even look at a woman lustfully you have committed adultery with her in your heart (see Matt. 5:28). Now God's standards as proclaimed by Jesus, are high ones (and rightly so in my opinion), since He knows what is best for His creation. My focus here is not to try and put you under any lenses of scrutiny as you evaluate your own life and sin in the areas of male-female relationships. Sexual purity, marriage devotion, and refraining from lust are only some areas of sin. You can take any areas of wrong-doing or bad decisions you make and see them similarly for the sin that they are. It just tends to be one that most humans can relate to through their life or the lives of others close to them. It also becomes an area that most people try and hide the most while they many times make personal concessions so they can validate their own choices. Since this category of sin has been my greatest weakness, my desire is now to open myself up so we can speak candidly with one another. I believe then you can see how God redeems His children when they seek Him.

Some of the names of the stories within my sin will not add value, so I will not even try and share them. I will share the meat of the stories and the lessons behind them, so you can apply them to your life. In the category of my greatest weakness and area of most prevalent sin (lustfulness and sexuality), I had chosen to become a victim of pornography of various mediums, pursued fornication, and even adultery. This is the very same guy that left for college as a virgin with high hopes for being a model family man and role model to other men in this area as a pure, devoted husband and father. I wish I could say that all of my sin in this area of life came before I accepted Jesus Christ as my personal Lord and savior, but that isn't true. Though much of it might have happened prior, some of the worst of the story happened after that time as God continued to teach me and refine me through His patience as I fought a rebellious spirit that was driven by my emotions and expectations. My past choices not only were hurtful to me, but they affected the lives of others. I wish I could erase that more than anything, but I can't. Those very same choices not only cost me emotionally, they cost me in some cases considerable money and the most precious gift of all, inordinate amounts of time that I'll never be able to regain.

I honestly still can't believe how many situations I had allowed myself to get into or in some cases pursued. Yes, I had people approach me in inappropriate, alluring or tempting ways, however in each and every case it was because of the decisions I made that I allowed sin to happen. This isn't simply a confession about a man that lost his virginity and had sex before marriage. Sadly, I know many people by today's standards don't even care if you have sex before marriage. Many people embrace this concept as I once did before I knew how God viewed things. Many people also feel it is wise to explore numerous sexual partners and to live with people before you get married so you can test drive the car before buying it.

I have allowed inappropriate bonds (even if short lived) from a married woman to be formed as I blindly followed my desires, emotions, and expectations. It doesn't matter that I didn't initiate the contact or even saw it coming. It didn't matter that she was a woman that I wanted to always be with, nor did it matter that I always felt if we both got a second chance on life together we probably would have been joined in marriage. The decision to follow-through is and will always remain my personal choice. I simply made a bad decision. I wish I could have seen it for what it was going to become upfront. It would have stopped me dead in my tracks. I also met people through various dating forms, including Internet-based dating, who were dishonest or in various stages of relational turmoil, and allowed myself to become inappropriately bonded with them emotionally, intellectually, and physically in different cases. I even found myself so many times trying to care for someone and reach into their broken life to become their hero and rescue them. In doing so, I put myself and others in vulnerable, compromising, and unwise situations. I wish more than anything that I could go back to my high school years and replay life. I know God knows that, and fortunately His ability to forgive is unending and immeasurable. For that I am eternally grateful. It compels me to live differently as I pursue my dreams.

I allowed pornography to become a drug of choice for me before I even realized it. I was the guy that never did drugs, didn't smoke, didn't even drink, and yet I became addicted to pornography. For years, it seemed like something safe I could do in the confines of my home, and it wasn't directly affecting anyone else. At least that was a lie I fed myself. Eventually I realized that it profoundly affected my decisions and convictions, and therefore affected my relationships. It eroded the man that, growing up, believed in fighting for purity. It allowed me to regrettably see women as objects. Looking back, I'm astounded by how many women use their bodies lustfully to tempt a man despite their relationship status, intentions, or his desire to not initiate any impure contact with her.

There truly is no limit or boundary to the human ability to sin. God has told us that our hearts are deceitfully wicked. Though they are capable of love and beauty because of God's love, grace and mercy, we should never attribute our ability to do good to ourselves. I was disgusted by how this ability to sin became a pattern that spiraled out of control even when I, for most of my life, tried to approach women and all relationships with good intentions. Deep down I was still that pure young man that desired to be happily married and to be faithful to that woman for the rest of my life. Though I shared with you earlier in this book how my eighteen-year factor, past engagement, and blind entrepreneurial drive affected me, I can definitely say they propelled me forward into a pattern of sexual sin as I pumped my fist up at God in frustration because I remained single. He knew I yearned for companionship and wanted to lay down my life for the right woman and build a family. However, He had to show me that I needed to lay down my life for Him first. Then from there, He would spend years teaching me what that decision really meant as He stripped away my hard-wired drive to control my life.

Becoming a Plank on the Bridge to God's Heart

God is willing and able to forgive you of your sins, no matter how many or how despicable they seem to you or the world around you. Forgiveness of our sins first starts with our recognition that sin is real in our life and that we need God's help to receive ultimate forgiveness. Jesus says in Matthew 19:26 that all things are possible with God even though they might seem impossible to man. That includes forgiveness of your sins. He can transform your life and give you a renewed spirit if you seek Him. God will claim victory over your life and break the bondage you might have from your sins. He did this for me and that voice now grows louder so I can be a trumpet for the world to share His song of forgiveness through the new dreams God has planted in my heart.

I believe there is a conceptual bridge to God's heart. God uses our lives and everything in this world to draw people to Himself through His sovereign power. Fortunately, we can become a plank on God's bridge to His heart.

I believe this can be seen in the evidence of how we use our lives for the benefit of others and for God's glory. Obviously, a plank is one individual board that is laid down and connected to form the complete solution that is the bridge. It is a mode of transportation that can lead us to our eternal destination.

During the thirty-three year life of Jesus on this planet, He displayed many characteristics we can learn from: love, joy, peace, patience, kindness, goodness, faithfulness, gentleness, self-control, and compassion. I believe if we focus on His compassion for us and learn to emulate it, that He can have a profound impact on not only our lives, but more importantly on the lives of others we touch for God's glory. If you are or become a genuine follower of Jesus Christ we can help proactively lead people to this bridge through all aspects of our lives. We need to recognize that God is the only one that can give the direction and strength to each person to walk across the bridge to find His heart. He desires to share His loving heart with all of His children through a personal relationship with them.

I needed to first understand the wickedness and depravity of my heart and the heart of others, to be ready to be used by God to passionately run down His dreams for me. It all became possible because of my realization one November of how much I needed a savior because of the lack of limitation to the depths of my own personal sin. Fortunately, God promises us that there is no temptation that has seized us that is not common to man. He is faithful, and promises not to let any of us be tempted beyond what we can bear, but that He will instead provide us a way out so we can escape the temptations of the world and stand up under everything we face with the opportunity to respond properly in His eyes (1 Cor. 10:13). Now I can harness the amazing peace found in God's truth that He proclaims to us in the Bible. There is a newfound power in my life path because of that. I am so thankful that God takes everything I have done wrong, and transforms it to be used for good. Even more beautiful, He is now using me to teach others to honestly confront and turn from their sin, bad decisions, and transgressions in life so they can turn to or back to God and be used for His glory. He now uses the pain I can relate to in others' lives, to help me carry out a deeper life of purpose that was a part of His ultimate purpose for me.

Our human struggles against the flesh and sin is something that will always be a present reality, so I am in no way trying to offer any magic potion. My ability to sin is as great; however, the difference is the on-going change that God is doing in me. While I seek to be honest about my ability to do wrong to others, He continues to re-shape my dreams and inspire new ones. He desires to share in the pursuit of all of your dreams and to help show you the life purpose and dreams that He has for your future. If you don't know what His dreams are for you, all you need to do is seek Him in a genuine, heartfelt prayer. My prayer for you is that you might do that for the first time today or perhaps seek Him out again. He desires to be in constant relationship with you, He loves you, and He desires for you to desire to know Him more.

Point of Reflection or Action for Today:

Hebrews 4:15-16 (NIV)

[15] "For we do not have a high priest [God] who is unable to sympathize with our weaknesses, but we have one who has been tempted in every way, just as we are—yet was without sin. [16] Let us then approach the throne of grace with confidence, so that we may receive mercy and find grace to help us in our time of need."

Chapter 35

A Link Between Dreams & Powerful Emotions: Insights from Judd Buckwalter, MA, LPC

Dreams Profile with Judd Buckwalter

Licensed Professional Counselor, and Professor of Professional Counseling

All human beings have encountered the power of emotions as they have pursued their dreams. There is definitely a link between emotions and dreams.

Judd Buckwalter holds a Master of Arts in Marriage and Family Counseling from Lancaster Bible College & Graduate School. He's now a professor in the undergraduate Professional Counseling Program at LBC. As a specialist in marriage and family therapy that includes child therapy, relationship conflicts, depression, and anxiety disorders, he's worked with a broad spectrum of clients who range from small children to the elderly. Judd is married and has four children.

During his years of helping families and individuals, Judd has seen how people often allow their emotions to get the best of them, and how they can take them down paths in life that they later regret. Ultimately, emotions can, and oftentimes do, become the force that dashes the pursuit of our dreams. I pray that my personal story and the smattering of Judd's insights included here will help you learn from others' mistakes or help you to reshape your perspective on life. This particular exploration can be valuable in understanding the ways that emotions might be holding you back.

Judd often encourages his clients to read The Lost Virtue of Happiness by J.P. Moreland. This book focuses on how we are only happy when we pursue a transcendent purpose—something larger than ourselves—through a selfless preoccupation with the spiritual disciplines. This powerful book offers concrete examples of ways we can each make the spiritual disciplines practical and life-transforming, while they help us pursue a deeper relationship with God.

Resources for Our Human Quest for Love, Acceptance, Security, and Significance

Without fail, every human, whether they recognize it or not, is in a consistent quest for love, acceptance, security, and significance. There's really nothing wrong with pursuing any of these things, in and of themselves. However, we have a lot of faulty thinking that affect our emotions and our quest for these four elements. Judd sides with the cognitive theory that defines our negative thinking as the culprit that can typically lead us astray. Many times our beliefs lead to an outworking of our emotions. Furthermore, faulty thinking can lead to a false belief that God will not help them in a certain area of life. Judd is one who challenges our core beliefs and has helped many to realistically look at ways how past experiences have shaped faulty thinking.

We've got to purposefully battle our wrong beliefs. To that end, Judd recommends the book *Telling Yourself the Truth* by William Backus. This book focuses on how most of what happens in your life happens because of the way you think. Wrong thinking produces wrong emotions, wrong reactions, wrong behavior—and unhappiness! Learning to deal with thoughts is the first step on the road to healthy thinking. It explains the life-changing method known as *Misbelief Therapy*. I encourage you to investigate this book and allow its concepts to affect your reactions to your home, your circumstances, your problems, and your own adverse environment. With its biblically-based approach, this book has helped thousands of people to replace faulty thinking with the truth since its first printing many years ago.

In worst-case scenarios, a mental illness can form from faulty thinking and from blockades to finding a life purpose. Judd stresses that, in many cases, forms of depression are a sinful lack of faith that should be confessed to God. It's also important to recognize that some types of depression are based in a physical trauma or an illness. A true examination of physical and sin issues can be key to overcoming battles with wrong thoughts and depression.

A final resource that Judd recommends is *Search for Significance* by Robert McGee. This book focuses on how to be free to enjoy God's love, while no longer basing your self-worth on accomplishments or the opinions of others. You can gain new skills for getting off the performance treadmill, discover how four false beliefs have negatively impacted your life and learn how to overcome obstacles that prevent you from experiencing the truth that your self-worth is found only in the love, acceptance, and forgiveness of God.

Purpose Driven Therapy

Judd shared with me that his purpose in life is to ultimately glorify God in all areas of his life. One dream and passion is to grow in his ability to offer professional help to folks whose marriages or families need practical life applications and solutions. Judd's family is even building a family retreat center where couples can come for specific counseling on how to proceed passed sticking points in relationships and seek God's healing and personal best for their marriages. It's so sad that many couples fail to seek God as a true source for love, acceptance, security, and significance. Because of that, more people are struggling as partners in eroding marriages.

During our interview, Judd and I talked a lot about dreams and powerful emotions. In response to seeing how emotions can paralyze a person's life and their relationships, Judd shared how he has an increased passion for the concept of a "purpose driven therapy." Judd truly loves helping people define their life of purpose and meaning. He does so while empowering them to take practical steps toward reaching their dreams and growing closer to God in the process.

So many lose heart in momentary failures and find themselves becoming emotionally crippled. To that end, a question Judd regularly asks is, "Where is your ultimate focus?" People tend to live apart from God, even though most believe in a higher being. Furthermore, more and more people define themselves as "spiritual but not religious." It certainly seems like this is related to a pursuit of ultimate control over their own lives.

"The truth is many people believe spiritual faith in God doesn't 'work hard enough' for them to resolve their personal issues, and that it's necessary to have spirituality... plus something else," Judd says. Judd helps people to process their emotions and faith to shift their focus towards true joy, and peace that comes from God alone (see Heb. 12:2-3). Judd has helped so many realize you don't seek true joy in life. It's actually a byproduct of pursuing a relationship with God.

Factoring Out Failure—A Personal Story

I spent a couple years working with Judd personally through powerful emotions that held me back (mainly in the pursuit of my wife and a marriage.) I've had several experiences in my life with professional counselors, but I am confident that one that brings the truth of spiritual faith into therapy is most effective. I know firsthand that my faith in God has truly helped me to deal with the deeply rooted, very real issues. It's so much more powerful than simply looking at surface issues.

If we're dealing with powerful emotions that stop us dead in the tracks of our pursuit of dreams, there's typically an underlying core issue that may not be initially evident. My example was how the concept of factoring out failure in my world was something that drove me emotionally and certainly made the pursuit of my dreams more difficult than necessary. Judd definitely helped me to realize there is always something underneath the powerful emotions that drive us in life.

To give some specific examples: I was afraid of marrying the wrong person, and always trying to be ten steps ahead of any potential failure at my businesses in the seemingly noble pursuit of providing for my team and not allowing failure to be an option. Judd encouraged me to ask myself if I was managing anxiety well or if I was simply wasting my efforts in attempting to factor out failure.

I was lonely at times because of my desire for companionship. I saw the connection between how my wants linked to my needs, while my needs led to powerful expectations and an easy rationalization for being angry with people who didn't meet them. It also seemed like a great justification for waving my little fist at God for my belief that He could be holding me back from my dream of marriage. As a result of my continued time with Judd, I realized how much of a gift it was to truly receive God's forgiveness in regards to anything we struggle with emotionally, versus trying simply to "forgive oneself," as if we have ultimate authority and power over our lives and emotions.

Giving Up Your Dreams for Bigger Dreams

As people pursue their dreams, they many times try and hold on to what they would like most, like a big house, spouse, success, or security. People need to be willing to give up their dreams to welcome God's bigger dreams for their lives. "Our emotions tend to flow out of our agendas and thoughts." We need to abandon the god who is seen as the genie in the sky to run hard after God's purpose for our lives. There might not always be obvious blessing toward us, nor an immediate shift to a better life. In doing so we can bring glory to God while successfully running down dreams. The best dreams are those which help you live a life full of the greatest purpose.

*For additional information, visit www.new-life-counseling.com.

Point of Reflection or Action for Today:

Philippians 4:6-8 (NIV)

[6] Do not be anxious about anything, but in every situation, by prayer and petition, with thanksgiving, present your requests to God. [7] And the peace of God, which transcends all understanding, will guard your hearts and your minds in Christ Jesus. [8] Finally, brothers and sisters, whatever is true, whatever is noble, whatever is right, whatever is pure, whatever is lovely, whatever is admirable—if anything is excellent or praiseworthy—think about such things.

Chapter 36

A Response to a Life Turned Upside Down

Have you ever felt your life was flipped upside down? Perhaps you know someone right now who is so gripped by the power of their emotions that they can't see right. They are devastated, confused and act as if they are unsure how to take their next step in life. There is certainly nothing sweet about that slice of reality cake.

Perhaps you feel pulverized by your emotions, and the thought of your dreams leaves you numb. No matter how positive, upbeat, and encouraging of a person you are, we all hit those low points where our emotions get the best of us. Undoubtedly, it is true for some people more than others. For me, it many times has come through the most unexpected of events. I have been floored by the entrance of a woman I always deeply wanted to be in a romantic relationship with coming back into my life; unfortunately she waited until she was married. I have seen a best friend of a decade with a rich history together simply walk out of my life twice because of my spiritual beliefs and my passionate pursuit of a woman to share my life with. I also have been faced on multiple occasions with a fiancé or girlfriend I believed I'd marry leave without providing any coherent explanation why. My prayer for you during today's journey is that you might be able to see dreams of the past, present, and future in a whole new way.

Strength Found in Letting Go

Unexpected loss, unexpected change, and lack of closure certainly turned my life upside down. I had to re-learn throughout how my response to my circumstances and emotions in life are of paramount importance. We can have eyes to finally see what God has been showing us when we face unexpected, violent storms in life that truly test our faith in Him. Moreover, we can truly be ready to run down a dream that has been waiting for a long time when we are able to let go of relationships. If we are unwilling to let go, it can sometimes delay the inevitable and many times give us a false sense of security where we hold on to relationships that are toxic or have run their course. It can be painful when you have to make that choice, and many times even more difficult when the other person makes that choice for the both of you without any discussion.

There is clearly strength found in the process of letting go, so God can fully work in each of your lives. Sometimes He desires to do a life-changing work in the other person's life, and we just get in the way if we resist the process of letting go. In some cases, reconciliation and restoration become the fruit of that process. Even if that isn't true, doing the right thing is something we need to remember is key as we run down our dreams.

Do the Right Thing, Come What May...

In a practical sense, you could be going through some really tough stuff right now, and I don't want to slight you if that is a true statement. Perhaps you are unemployed or your business is struggling and it is affecting your family. Perhaps your marriage is on the rocks or you are faced with healing from a broken heart. Maybe you or your family have many illnesses they are battling or you are just feeling weighed down by the pace and pressures of the holidays in today's post-modern culture.

Let's be honest, life is tough. God never promised that our lives would be smooth sailing (check out John 16:33). Many times when we are going through seasons of difficulty, our emotions drive our responses. It's been a common reaction of mine. However, over the past few years, I have been able to realize much of what God has taught me, and what the true remedy is to a life full of accelerating pressures and emotions.

Simply put, you need to do the right thing, come what may. What that means for each person could be different. You could also easily raise opposition and state things like, "Who's standard of 'right' are we going to use"? Great question! You can freely choose your own standard, but for me I'm going with God's. Let me give you a personal example from my life right now.

It's safe to say that the last two years of life since writing this chapter have been full of days where the heat in the kitchen was turned way up to a scorching temperature. I felt the heat and at times it hurts, but it has been enlightening to see how God has helped me to weather the storm. During this season, I was faced with difficult family circumstances, notable business challenges on multiple levels, unexpected staffing issues, and a broken heart. My world clearly felt turned upside down!

So faced with all of that, what was my *do the right thing* solution?

- Well first of all, I needed to lean on God, not my own understanding. I needed to ask Him to help me grow in faith through these storms. I was able to do that by focusing on thanking Him daily for so many blessings that were still evident in my life, and for so many past storms He saw me through over the years. He is a God that is unchangeable and unshakable. He is a fortress of strength in our times of trouble. He loves for us to come to Him like a young child to their parent.

- Furthermore, God helped me to realize that much of what happens to us in life, we simply can't control. We can only control our response. That's tough medicine to swallow at times, especially for the self-starting, born leaders with an A-type personality like myself.

- My response during the business challenges was to believe that if I focused on protecting my personal confidence each day, that I would do the right thing daily. I focused on reading God's word, praying, and meditating. I realized God was in the midst of doing something in my life through this and it became very exciting to pursue Him and wait for His revelation while being obedient.

- I focused on serving each person in business that I spoke to with passion and vigor, while doing so to the best of my ability. I focused on quality and creativity more than how much I could do each day. If you walk forward with the right attitude and behave each day in the right way, you are doing all you can.

- I focused on praying for others and looked daily for people I could reach out to in an unexpected, outward focused way. Many times if we focus on caring for others, it helps us manage any personal burdens we carry.

- I focused on giving more of my resources than I ever had before to benefit others and be used for God's glory. In return, God gave me a heart full of joy, hope, love, and thankfulness.

- I focused and continue to focus on believing in the God of all hope. The One who loves us deeply, and desires us to be in reconciled vs. broken relationships with each other. He is the God of second chances and beyond. I know that my ex-girlfriend needed space so God could show her what He was trying to reveal to her. I also needed to continue to focus on my faith in God, and my desire was to see God's blessing over her life so she might feel my love for her through His work, regardless of her ever sharing in my sentiment to be in a reconciled relationship with her.

In my case, yet again God brought forth blessing in abundance after these storms came and I was left to bask in the beautiful rain that He brought my way. My business went from slow to busy. I had a renewed sense of determination, drive, and passion through it all because of the trials. As for my broken heart, it was undoubtedly my least favorite trial. But I knew God would reconcile things in due time if it was His will, which would be better than anything I could muster on my own.

That doesn't change anything God is already doing. Perhaps He has work to do in both of our lives as He prepares us for futures apart romantically and of renewed friendship. Only He knows. I remain excited to see what He reveals in time for us both in terms of second chance romance, a restored relationship, or as individuals that treat each other with genuine love and compassion if nothing else. God doesn't make mistakes. Our meeting wasn't one and the next steps of our life together or apart I am sure will not be either. So my focus remains on doing the right thing and trusting the results in all areas to God, come what may. My focus remains on what brought us together in the first place. It was a focus on honoring all women in my life (not just romantic interests) by building relationships with them, and offering the best of myself through openness, honesty, transparency, and vulnerability as I seek to passionately pour into their lives.

Ironically, I bought a movie during my season of heartbreak that I highly recommend. *Come What May* (www.comewhatmaythemovie.com) revolves around what I've been speaking about here: doing the right thing, no matter what the consequences may be. Now, I am not going to tell you that this solution to life's worries is like drinking some magic potion. We are still human beings, and emotional creatures (regardless of how emotional you are). If you focus on doing the right things every day, no matter how small they are, you will bring God glory, and position yourself for the most beautiful responses possible. Take your focus off your problems and focus on being a part of a solution for other people's problems. Stop for a moment to encourage another person in a busy day. Do an unexpected gesture for them. Spend more time with God. Pray more. Love more. Hope more. Life is too short not too!

What Do You Do When Your World is Turned Upside down?

The last couple years have been full of new understanding and wisdom through the experiences in my life that have brought out the deepest flow of emotions. Below is a poem I wrote that God put on my heart that I wanted to share with you. I pray that it resonates in your heart today as you survey the landscape of your dreams!

We wake up each day full of expectations,

Expectations that cry out from the desires of our heart,

From the plans that we have set for our day,

From the unfilled yearnings that we strive after in life,

Many times we live our lives with our eyes closed,

And the worst part about it all is we believe our eyes our open,

Light at the end of any tunnel could be natural or man-made,

The tunnel could be filled with radiant energy from the sun,

It could however be filled with brightness from artificial lighting,

We don't recognize it until we face the tunnel's opening,

Realizing that then we are confronted with a massive question,

Recently I was confronted to decide what to do when my world was turned upside down unexpectedly,

We all have a point in which we can only handle so much and reach a point of feeling overwhelmed,

I pray that the openness from my heart speaks to yours now,

I am sure your life ebbs and flows would differ from mine without a doubt,

I however was challenged in three major areas of passion as the picture in my life's kaleidoscope changed,

A best friend of a decade, uprooted themselves from my life because of the convictions of the faith I stand on,

A woman that I always felt was a kindred spirit sought me out and fell in love with me,

Though we cannot be together because of the sacredness of the marriage covenant that she stands upon,

I could also never overlook the increasing level of leadership responsibility that faces me in my career,

My fatherly heart to provide for my team's well-being and lives goes well beyond their paycheck,

My desire to compassionately show inner strength and love to my clients well beyond a mere service,

My aim to lead with passion can get misconstrued, while being overshadowed as mere salesmanship,

There is only one way I can explain the peace I feel about these emotional losses and storms,

It cannot be explained by mere human understanding,

I for one am confident that it comes from a peace that God has provided to my heart to minister to me,

As I deal with a tidal wave of life-altering change that is rocking my boat and testing my faith,

So my question to you is what will you do when you are facing your giants?

Will you try and slay and conquer them based upon the limitations of your life experience and those around you?

What will you do when your world is turned upside down?

It is bound to happen to us throughout our lives because life is about the journey, not the destination.

We cannot control the events of our day no matter how hard we attempt to,

However, the choice in how we respond to our life is something we will forever control.

God never promised us that life would be free of pain, sorrow, or depression. He does, however, offer wisdom, peace, hope, grace, and mercy as we face the storms in life. My life has continued to validate that some of our Creator's best work comes through the confrontation with our emotions and our response to them. We can truly be ready to run down a dream when we are able to let go of relationships that need us to do so. Furthermore, as you reflect on your dreams this day, please remember we can have eyes to finally see what God has been showing us when we face unexpected storms!

Point of Reflection or Action for Today:

Proverbs 16:9 (NIV)

[9] In their hearts humans plan their course, but the LORD establishes their steps.

34. No Limits to the Depths of Sin

- When we are truly honest about our ability to sin and do wrong to others, God can help us to finally see His purposes and dreams for our life.

- God always gives us a way out from each temptation we face in life and strength to stand up under any challenge if we seek Him first.

35. A Link Between Dreams & Powerful Emotions : Insights from Judd Buckwalter, LPC

- The emotions that tend to flow out of our self-centered focus on our agendas and thoughts towards the wrong things in life can hold us back from reaching our dreams.

- We need to be willing to give up our dreams many times so God can replace them with bigger ones that link to His true desires and will for our lives.

36. A Response to a Life Turned Upside Down

- We can truly be ready to run down a dream that has been waiting for us for a long time when we are able to let go of relationships that ask and need us to do just that.

- Many times, we can have eyes to finally see what God has been showing us when we face unexpected, violent storms in life that truly test our faith in Him.

Running Down Your Dreams—Taking Action!

Are you currently struggling with how to cope with pain, sorrow, or depression in your life? If so, are you currently seeking any professional help? If not, I want to encourage you to take action to seek out professional help. I strongly recommend you making a consultation with a Christian counselor or meeting with a spiritual leader with whom you are comfortable in your local community. Though there are many counselors, I believe faith-based counselors can bring the most holistic input to help you mentally, emotionally, physically, and spiritually and because of that help you have a unique advantage in working with them.

If you are not currently struggling with these powerful emotions, perhaps you know someone dear to your heart that is facing such demons? Perhaps you feel that you are at a loss for words to personally help them? If so, I encourage you to reach out to them to show them love. Love them boldly enough to share the same recommendation that I have made to you above. We all know people who face such emotions. Will you choose to take action in the name of love for another person you care about? Write about it in the space below, assign a go-date for you to take action, and journal about what your next action should be to make progress toward your dreams or helping them to run after theirs in a new way.

My Dream's Name:

My Go Date:

Dreams Journal

For more free resources to help encourage you in your pursuit of dreams found through powerful emotions such as pain, sorrow and depression, please visit: www.livewithpurposecoaching.com.

Special Dream Chaser Journaling Experience

Today, as we reflect on our journey together so far, I'd like to challenge you to answer the following questions. I recommend choosing a location where you can get away from you daily distractions and be inspired.

1. **If you knew today was your last day to live, what dream would you most regret that you never took action on?**

2. **What have you done in life that you loved the most?**

3. **What moments made you feel most alive?**

4. **What is your biggest dream?** What is your top obstacle?

5. **Do you have a dream that scares you?** What is your top obstacle?

Galatians 5:22-23 (NIV)

22 But the fruit of the Spirit is love, joy, peace, forbearance, kindness,
goodness, faithfulness, 23 gentleness and self-control. Against such things
there is no law.

JOURNEY #10

Dreams Found Through the Gift of the Holy Spirit

Theme Focus:

There are a growing number of different religions, spiritual belief systems and thoughts about God (or the lack thereof in regards to an ultimate creator of mankind). People avoid talking about things like religion, politics, and money. Many people are comfortable with anyone believing anything, as long as they keep it to themselves. There is something to be said about unity amongst all people. I understand people who view Christians or people that appear to be religious fanatics as undesirable hypocrites that rub them the wrong way. For me, I spent twenty-six years of my life there. I acknowledge that everyone's life path is different; however, in this last theme of the book I seek to share with you the most significant lessons I have learned in life as they relate to truly living a life of deep meaning and purpose. It has become a call on my life to inspire others to do the same. My prayer is that through these real world stories and insights, you might be better prepared to affirm your own personal spiritual views, or perhaps be challenged to explore some very good questions that are stirred from within your heart. It has been my privilege to go through this forty-day journey with you!

Chapter 37

The Guy that Called People "Bible Chuckers"

Did you ever meet someone that just seemed so outwardly religious or spiritually zealous that you felt like they were from another planet? Those people never seemed to do much more than frustrate and confuse the heck out of me because they represented such challenge to my belief systems. Deserved or not, I was one that was quick to label and call these type of people "Bible chuckers." Today, I am focused on helping you debunk some common beliefs that people hold on to tightly (like I did). I pray that you learn from some of my mistakes and roadblocks that slowed me down from the effective pursuit of my dreams, so you don't need to repeat them.

I think back to my old friend, Dave. He is a brilliant artist. During my days right after college, he became someone that I built a meaningful relationship with. He was very passionate about his faith in God, and lived in such a way that showed his beliefs and sense of freedom through his personality and daily actions. I always tried focusing on the seemingly non-spiritual parts of Dave so I could best enjoy our time together and keep the relationship at a safe distance. A year or two later, I met a woman named Heather who was very much full of faith and had a servant's heart. She was fortunate to have great parents as role models, including a mother who was a dynamic inspirational speaker. We went on a few dates, and I felt like we didn't connect holistically, so I didn't continue to pursue her. At that time, I just chalked it up to a lack of chemistry. I might not have understood all of what she believed spiritually, but she was just different and somehow I didn't believe we fit well together. Then, I run into this skinny, Aussie fellow on a trip in California when I was twenty-five. He spoke about God freely. He challenged me through our conversations as we had journeys around the world together. I found a thirst that continued to rage as I drank up the water he offered me through our spiritual discussions. However, there was one great vice in my life that was holding me back: the desire to control.

A Vice of Many: Wanting Control in Life

All humans struggle at times to seek control in their lives. It is natural for us to have a vision of our future destiny, and to want to have input into the pursuit of that vision.

We strive towards a life driven by a sense of personal control. It creates a false sense of reality. It is like we are driving our car down the highway at an ever-increasing speed with a blindfold on, and we expect somehow to come out unscathed. It doesn't take us long to look at the news or observe the world around us to realize that there is so much we do not control in life. Control is really about freedom if you think about it. We simply want the ability to be free to do what we desire, while being free from doing those things we desire to avoid. However, if we want to live a life full of true freedom, we need to do so motivated by God's Holy Spirit. Consider Galatians 5:16 (The Message) *"Live freely, animated and motivated by God's spirit. Then you won't feed the compulsions of selfishness"*.

I Never Thought Basketball Nets Could Rock Your World

Many people have a certain mental picture about what a church is and what it is not. To many people the church is all about stained glass windows, pews, religious traditions, seeking confession for our wrong doing, and listening to messages that never seem to make any sense or apply to your life. Churches are seen primarily as places for weddings, funerals or to celebrate major holidays with family and friends.

I never experienced a church that was in a multi-purpose facility, nor one that doubled as a basketball court. I asked myself, "Where are the pews?" I was also taken back by the lack of an organ, and the presence of electric guitars, and a big screen projector. Furthermore, I was so engaged by listening to the weekly message that I couldn't help but sit in the front, even though my natural tendency like many new church visitors was to hide in the back. I felt like the pastor was talking directly to me each week in a personal way as if he had my journal. It upset me at times and stirred my emotions, but it also made me want to come back weekly. In many ways, it felt more like a living room to me with people that made me feel very comfortable right way. Church, for the first time, actually became a place I very much looked forward to going to.

If you have never experienced a church that you felt truly at peace and home at, then I encourage you to continue to seek one out. I say this because I believe God will open that door if your heart is willing. My time at my church has truly changed my life. It has helped me to better understand what a life of purpose is all about, and ultimately more of what God's purposes for my life are. It has also helped me to have a place where I can worship God and bring my dreams before Him. His guidance is the greatest anyone can find as they pursue their dreams. Moreover, finding a church that re-shapes your understanding of what a church is can change your life and give birth to amazing new dreams.

Understanding People of Difference Around You Better

Who doesn't want to be understood at the very deepest level? Another very important aspect I have learned about in regards to spiritual growth is gaining understanding and speaking about the realities of absolute truth in life, while growing in your ability to compassionately discuss different spiritual views and beliefs with those who are of different religions or beliefs. Regardless of what you believe about God and His existence, there are some very good questions to ask yourself. As I have spoken to God about my dreams, I have been confronted with questions like the ones below, that have created road backs in my life path and spurred me on to grow as a man of faith.

Have you ever been asked questions about a major world religion that you couldn't answer? Do you really understand the difference between what

Muslims, Hindus, Christians, Jews and Buddhists believe? Have you ever really read the Bible or any major religious book in its entirety? Would you like to be able to better defend your personal spiritual position by better understanding what others believe?

Each of us certainly is entitled to believe anything in any area of life. The decisions we make, the paths we choose to take and the destiny they lead us to will forever be connected. To begin pressing into some answers or to solidify your own personal spiritual beliefs, I encourage you to look at a tool I created called The Major World Religions Cross Comparison that can be found at: www.livewithpurposecoaching.com. Another great place to start is with opening up a major holy book such as the Bible.

God is in the business of helping us become humble. He many times does so by turning our lack of spiritual understanding, doubts, fears, weaknesses, and opposition to spiritual matters into something to be used for His ultimate glory and purposes. I have seen how God can do miracles within a willing heart. He can change you from a person who calls people of strong love and faith in God "Bible chuckers" to someone who is passionate about spiritual unity and understanding people better who are of different religious positions and faiths. What are you going to do next as you ponder the impact of the spiritual realm on the direction of your dreams and your ability to reach them?

Point of Reflection or Action for Today:

Galatians 5:16 (MSG)

[16] "Live freely, animated and motivated by God's spirit. Then you won't feed the compulsions of selfishness."

Chapter 38

When is this God Phase Going to End?

Christians frustrated me because of their seemingly overt projection of superiority that they conveyed to me as I watched or interacted with them. If I am honest now as I look back, I was really just ignorant about anything that had to do with God, the Bible and this Jesus fellow that people talked about. I didn't like people that judged me spiritually, though I didn't even acknowledge that I was doing just that towards people that had a better basis for their spiritual beliefs because of their understanding of God, the Bible, and Jesus. They spent time actually reading the Bible and speaking to God through prayer. On the other hand I did none of that, but I still formed strong judgments about God and them. Hindsight is always twenty-twenty.

I am thankful that I lived my first twenty-six years believing there could be a God. I remember thinking being spiritual was acceptable and that that was more than enough to make me comfortable in that area of life. I view relationships and life in four quadrants: physical, intellectual, emotional, and spiritual. When I ranked their importance back then, I saw spiritual life as the most minor quadrant as I reflected on who to marry, how to run my businesses, and how to make decisions in life. I truly feel like I can relate to many people that might pose this million dollar question to a Christian: "So when is this God phase going to end?"

There are many people that profess to be Christians that live lives of double standards. They don't practice what they preach, and even worse many times they don't even realize it. People notice it though, as they watch their lives. Regardless of what your spiritual views are or which religion you believe in, I am not trying to say that Christians should be some super human role models. We all are capable of bad decisions, evil, and causing others pain. The world around us is full of so many spiritually minded people that seem to allow a relationship with God to become a phase or a box to be checked off. Perhaps the rest of this chapter can provide some insight in regards to what I learned beyond my first twenty-six years on this topic.

Being a Christian is Not Like Being an American

Let's get back to the million dollar question I spoke about earlier: when will the God phase end? It was amazing to see how so many friends and family didn't understand the changes I was going through. Initially, they didn't say much to me because they thought it clearly wasn't something that would become a voice that permeated throughout all areas of my life. It certainly wasn't going to become something that would make them feel uncomfortable or threaten the boundaries of our pre-defined relationship that had deep roots. Sadly, I believe many of these dear loved ones now see me as a local "Bible chucker."

I saw some of my closest relationships with friends and family members change. Many years later, they wanted to know when the old Joe was coming back, and that made me cringe. Not that I ever viewed myself as a horrible person by the world's standards, but I certainly don't ever want to be who I was. God has and continues to change me from the inside out, and that includes my dreams.

The way God changed me when I accepted Jesus Christ as my personal Lord and savior and received God's gift of his Holy Spirit certainly has been profound. Many times I find myself struggling to describe how amazing the changes have been. It has hurt me very much to see such meaningful relationships in my life eroded as they have been because of my relationship with God. I took things personally at times as I found myself inspired to strive for new dreams that I felt were put on my heart by God. I knew I needed to be prepared to lose any relationship that I had before I left for the course that God was leading me on. I continue to be humbled by how much more I need to learn about love and compassion as a Christian. Now, I strive to ensure that no matter how even the closest people in my life view me, that I need to learn to love them more than ever. As I strive for these new passionate dreams, I desire to learn how to love them in a courageous and contagious way, despite any personal attacks they might bring.

Sadly, a lot of people in America see the question "Are you a Christian?" almost like "Are you an American?" and say "yes" without thinking. They do so not realizing they don't even understand what they mean. Perhaps they simply think going to church, growing up in the church or a being in a family that talked about God somehow qualified them to be a Christian. God wants your heart, not just your mind. As you strive to run down your dreams in life, He doesn't want you to simply know of Him. He wants you to want to know Him more, and that starts with allowing Him to enter your heart and change it. For me, He drastically reshaped how I viewed the four corners of relationships in life that I spoke of earlier. The one I saw as least important, spiritual life, exponentially became the most important. It remains so as I run down the new dreams God has given me. I can say it is something that still captivates my heart and mind.

A Purpose Driven Journey to Cancun

It is a funny thing how travel and books can speak to your heart and really shape your outlook and perspective in life. As I reflected on the pursuit of the dreams in my life one November, I found that both traveling and a book worked together to beautifully speak to my inner most being. On a trip to Cancun, I was reading a book called the *Purpose Driven Life*. I received it as an unexpected gift. As I read the book, I realized that the way I was living my life had to change. I reflected and spoke to God as I looked at some of the most amazingly clear waters in the world. I began asking him to forgive me, and teach me how to become the man I knew He had planned me to be. Through the encouragement of what I was learning in the book, I made a decision that changed my life. That November 25th, I made a contract with God to commit myself to living a life that honored Him, and I began my walk of faith. I literally made a contract too, which still hangs in a frame. I suppose it was my strategic, entrepreneurial mindset that had to take what I was learning in the book and apply it in a tangible way. I am glad I did.

During that time, there was an overwhelming voice that wouldn't leave. It was nudging me to explore and connect with a local church. It drove me nuts, but after roughly five months of being pursued by the voice, I listened. I began yet again a very organized, strategic process to do so because of how I am wired. Eventually, I found my home with a great group of people at a church called Millersville Bible Church. I admired, respected, and found inspiration from a group of Christian leaders that knew the word of God very well and live as great examples for us all.

God changed everything and made me realize how little we really can control, how silly it is when we try to do it, and how much more it made sense to trust in Him. I can't say that I really can give one person or event full credit for helping me find Jesus. However, I will do my best to share with you some of what I know now. I believe He used the death of my father about five months prior to teach me how precious life truly is, as well as show me where I was falling short in living my life the best way I could . My father's death became as important as his life was to me. God has continued to use my dad (even after death) as a teacher in my life. His short battle of one month with cancer before he was taken from earth reinforced to me that tomorrow is not a guarantee.

I was very fortunate to be blessed by others in unexpected ways. My father's death brought my uncle Bill and Aunt Gail back into my life, and a trip several years prior introduced me to a great friend, Steve Charman from Australia. My grandmother has also shown me how to "do everything in love" (1 Cor. 16:14). Even in her 90s, she has never been stronger in her faith or a better model of how to live in a way that honors Jesus Christ. They have all become spiritual rocks and teachers that helped guide me to find the master eye doctor that is God. He has allowed me to see dreams of deeper meaning and purpose that have replaced my dreams of old. For that I am very thankful. If it is clear vision that you need as you think of the dreams in your life, He certainly is the optometrist to go to.

A Farmer and His Four Seeds

It is a funny thing how we can learn a lot from our earth; how life grows and is sustained. The power displayed in the mountain ranges, canyons, and oceans might have been altered over the ages, though they remain a voice that we can learn from. Though farmers might not seem like great role models for running down dreams or inspiring people in a visionary way, I think there is one farmer that would beg to differ. This farmer (found in Matt. 13:1-23) went out to sow his seed. As he was scattering the seed, some fell along the path, and the birds came and ate it up. Some fell on rocky places, where it did not have much soil. It sprang up quickly, because the soil was shallow. But when the sun came up, the plants were scorched, and they withered because they had no root. Other seed fell among thorns, which grew up and choked the plants, so that they did not bear grain. Still other seed fell on good soil. It came up, grew and produced a crop, multiplying thirty, sixty, or even a hundred times.

This farmer's story helps us to really understand a person who possesses a growing, active, and living faith. It is a person much like the seed that fell on good soil, that has an active and ongoing desire to serve God with their life. Religion can easily become a life phase for people but a true personal relationship with the living God is when a phase isn't possible. Seasons of growth and challenge will come for each follower of Jesus Christ, but we are called to grow in faith (not just in knowledge). We are to grow by seeing our faith applied within our life through our actions which require change many times. We continue to become changed more into God's image and in doing so further align with His dreams for our lives.

Now for me personally, I find myself extremely passionate about growing in my understanding of the Bible so I can better understand God's purpose for my life. I relish the opportunities to come together and serve others in honor of Jesus Christ. I believe I can understand people that have not found the Lord yet, nor accepted Jesus as their personal savior. I say that because I spent about twenty-six years of my life there. I would like to share a great analogy I heard from a man of wisdom I know. It is about a stream. We find ourselves all walking upstream during life on earth. The water becomes more challenging and dangerous as we continue trying to walk further upstream. However, if you realize that you are not the only one in the water walking, you realize where you are going, who made the stream and why it exists, all you can do is smile that you are still in the water. That sense of inner peace has given me strengthened faith, so I can continue the walk forward every day (even when my legs are weak and life is difficult).

My hope is I will be able to develop the abilities God has blessed me with so I can love all those in my life for His glory. I am excited because I now face temptation and sin with a sense of real hope. I am striving to follow Jesus and simply allow those I meet while on Earth to see His love for them through me, based on how I live my life each day. I desire to inspire and encourage other people to find their faith in Jesus like others have done for me. If I do that, I believe I will realize I did the best I could in my final hour on this planet. My hope is that I can look up and see in some small way that I made God smile. In closing, I pray through these stories that you can further see that a massive part of running down your dreams in life is realizing what it truly means to be a Christian. God can build a passion and righteous fire within you that drives you in life in a profoundly bold, yet peaceful way. This remains true even as people ask you that million dollar question, my friends. I pray for a step forward in boldness, closeness, and deepness in regards to your understanding and personal connection with God. He desires His one and only Son to not just be known, but to be your best friend....

Point of Reflection or Action for Today:

Romans 5:13 (NIV)

[13] May the God of hope fill you with all joy and peace as you trust in him, so that you may overflow with hope by the power of the Holy Spirit.

Chapter 39

Coming to Terms with Your Spiritual Gifting

Each of us is made unique and in God's image. What an exciting notion to reflect on as you look at the purpose for your life and the dreams that are dearest to your heart today! I have always been a student of life and deep believer that one should continue to invest energy throughout their life focused on understanding oneself at a deeper level. I am confident that understanding how God uniquely made you, through grasping an increased understanding of your personal spiritual gifting, will give you greater clarity to pursue your dreams. Looking at my own life, I am confident that approach has become an integral reason why I have been able to reach many dreams in life while getting extremely clear about my purpose in life at an early age. My prayer today is that the insights I have to share might spur you on to begin a beautiful journey full of self-discovery. I believe that journey can help you reach an increasingly brighter light as you continue to walk down the path that God has planned for you.

Embracing a Life of Learning

Our lives are so rich, no matter how much adversity, pain, prosperity, or joy we experience comparative to other people. We have opportunity every day. We can be fortunate enough to continue to embrace a life full of learning instead of simply going through the motions of the day. The principal I seek to share is simply this: *embrace your life as an opportunity for lifelong learning!* If you do this, you can go beyond the glass is half empty analogy. You can transform that concept and have the ability each day to see your life as full and overflowing, no matter what you are facing. God desires us to have life and have it to the full (see John 10:7-11).

I know that losing a loved one, losing a job, having a failing business, facing unexpected illness, dealing with an unexpectedly broken or lost romantic relationship (or a failing marriage) are immensely personal and painful situations. So often, these pains are tough to put into words that could truly measure the profound affect they have had (or continue to have) on our lives. Many times the affect is life-altering and full of opportunity. The opportunity that you can embrace is in truly walking through each of those seasons in life while looking to process life through God's eyes and ears. What does He desire for you to see now? What does He desire for you to hear now that you are missing? What does He desperately desire for you to learn now through this specific season you face as you look at your dreams? Each season of life is a teacher, and it can be truly embraced by those that approach life as a lifelong learner.

God never said life would be easy, but He said He would see us through the storms. His love will comfort you even when all hope seems gone in your life, if you truly seek Him in the depths of your heart. God can offer you all the strength you ever need. I truly believe we are all symbolic rocks or lumps of clay waiting to be perfected. As we face the circumstances in our life, God graciously molds us like a master potter on his wheel. He also masterfully chisels away on the rock that we are, to form us into a beautiful masterpiece in due time. He does this by taking us through the seasons of our lives as He molds, refines, and teaches us. Both blessing and pain are seen by all humans, there are no exceptions. We can choose to embrace each season for all the wisdom and beauty they possess and encourage others to do the same. Don't settle for a life of going through the motions, as you go through each season. Don't let fear hold you back from walking into and embracing each new season in your life! Soak up the wisdom that is found in both the blessings and pain in each season, by applying the lessons you learn to your future actions and decisions. Be open to each new door that is uniquely opened for you. They are the ones that are crying out to you to leave your mark on them. Every season truly has a reason my friend!

Unique Abilities & Spiritual Gifting

As I stated earlier, each of us are uniquely made. We are also all made in God's image. Each of us have unique abilities and gifts that lay waiting to be understood, harnessed, and leveraged for the betterment of the world. Let's now set up a working basis for the difference between unique abilities and spiritual gifting. Unique abilities are those things that you are passionate about and better at doing than most people. They many times show up in your career, however they exist in all areas of our lives. They are the things that make us tick. Spiritual gifts are the aspects of God's character that show up strongest within us. They are the ones that are ready for us to utilize to benefit the world around us and extend His love in all we do.

Many people think about their unique abilities when they consider their dreams and how to pursue them. However, many times people don't understand or reflect equally on their spiritual gifting, and how that could be the fuel needed to reach their dreams. A key to successfully running down your dreams in life is learning how to link your unique abilities and spiritual gifts together so they can help you to embrace a life of ultimate purpose and meaning. A good place to start is to run assessments to understand both your unique abilities and spiritual gifting. A great resource to understand your unique ability is to begin running profiles like the Kolbe Corp. (www.kolbe.com), or by accessing tools on Unique Ability from The Strategic Coach® (www.strategiccoach.com). In regards to spiritual gifts, you want to look at doing a spiritual gifts assessment or spiritual gifts inventory. Resources for doing just that will be at the end of this chapter!

Understanding & Recognizing Spiritual Gifts

Honestly, spiritual gifting tends to confuse many people. Here's the real challenge. Many people are asking the question, "What is *my* spiritual gift?" When in reality they need to be asking, "What is *a* spiritual gift?" They do not understand the *relationship*s of spiritual gifts. That is, they don't understand how a spiritual gift *relates* to their life, how it *relates* to the will of God for their life, and how it *relates* to the lives of those around them. So to demystify spiritual gifting today, we will talk about some of the major areas of spiritual gifting. I encourage you to read the Bible to further understand spiritual gifts from the mouth of the Creator of the universe. It is a great place to start, don't you think? See 1 Corinthians chapter 12 as one of many great places to gain further insight.

Below is a brief summary of some of the main spiritual gifts, and how they could be seen or used in your life as you focus on pursuing your dreams:

- *Teaching* – Most of us would grasp what a teacher does. Spiritually speaking this is God's character that empowers certain people to become clear communicators of information and educators for the benefit of others. It could be seen in school teachers, coaches of various types, pastors, speakers, and other various roles. When this gift is fully leveraged, you see someone that God is empowering to teach people truth through their roles and/or vocation in their life.

- *Exhortation (Encouragement)* – Some people are natural encouragers and encouragement many times is easy to see in everyday life, yet often taken for granted. Exhortation can be most easily understood as encouragement. God is not a stingy old man in the sky that is watching our every mistake. He is a God of love, hope, and encouragement. He is for us. When this gift is fully leveraged, you see someone that God has empowered to be consistently outward-focused. They are pro-active in lifting up the spirits of others, while also helping them better understand how God views them. Then they can walk forward full of hope knowing that God believes in them and loves them just the way they are.

- *Showing Mercy* – Everyone feels pain in life, and is faced with adversity. Many times people can feel as if nobody understands them, or that most people around them are too busy to stop and lend a helping hand or ear. Those who are gifted in showing mercy are able to show love to anyone (even their enemies). They love those less fortunate and have a heart that feels the pain of others in a deep way. It is a natural instinct. When this gift is fully leveraged, you see these individuals bringing forth love and healing into people's lives. They many times are the first to help and the last to stay, to ensure they walk through the pain with the other person (while truly carrying their burdens with them). Many medical professionals, counselors, and social workers are gifted in this area.

- *Serving* – People who love to serve do it naturally. When something needs to be done, they don't wait for people to tell them to do it most times. They see it and simply do it. They are the first to raise their hands when a committee needs to be formed or a task needs attention. When this gift is fully leveraged, you see God empowering an individual to reflect a humble heart and a willingness to do the smallest or most unrecognized duties. They do it with a sense of pride, knowing that God sees them at work and takes pleasure in all acts of service. Vocationally speaking, you would see this show up notably in hospitality roles, community service associations and, many times, church ministry groups.

- *Giving* – This can definitely be more than money; however, tithing and giving of your financial resources to benefit others and God's work within your local church (and other causes or ministries) is the most common understanding of this spiritual gifting. The people God empowers with this spiritual gift many times give until it hurts, giving well beyond 10 percent or the typical tithe. When this gift is fully leveraged, you see these people take great pleasure in freely giving to bless others, because they realize all that they have is a gift from God. The amount isn't as important as where your heart is at when you give. Do you give because you feel you should, or because you take pleasure in helping others with your financial resources? God loves blessing those who are faithful with little. Many times the brings forth increases in a person's life for His glory, because we were first faithful to Him when they had less.

- *Pastoring/Shepherding* – People with leadership and communication gifts many times show evidence of this spiritual gift. You do not need to be a pastor to have this spiritual gift. Many other spiritual or non-spiritual leadership roles (including business owners or managers of people within business) allow people to showcase their spiritual gift of pasturing or shepherding because they are able to direct, lead, and build up others who are in their care. When this gift is fully leveraged, you are witness to groups of people who are being mobilized to constantly grow, be receptive to change, and growing in desire to see their life be transformed for God's purposes. It becomes a life passion to train others and release them to bless others.

- *Evangelism* – People with this spiritual gift are bold and passionate about sharing God's love with the world around them. They find it easy to share God's truth and Scripture with others of various spiritual beliefs or postures. When you see this gift fully leveraged you will see them easily and consistently share God's love and the message of what Jesus Christ has done for the world with people that they have never met or those in remote locations they visit that have never heard of God's good news. They also freely share this message with those local to them who are in need of absolute truth, love, healing, mercy, and compassion (among other things).

- *Prophecy* – Many people seem to lack understanding of this gift, or believe it is something that does not really exist anymore in today's modern times. They see it as a lost art of a couple thousand years ago when the events in the Bible were recorded. However, it is as real a spiritual gift today as any of the others. God empowers certain people more than others who are able to be in tune with God's Holy Spirit. They get supernatural revelations from God through words of knowledge, dreams, and foreshadowing of events that will come. They gain intimate access to the understanding of the pain and brokenness in the lives of others around them. God uses them to bring forth His love, healing, and joy into their lives because of their obedience to utilize this gift, while believing in the work of the Holy Spirit to accomplish anything (no matter how incredible or perplexing it might seem at the surface). When this gift is fully leveraged, these people are in touch with the spirit of God in a powerful way, and they truly become an active agent in being a part of bringing the kingdom of God to Earth. They are used in a mighty way to carry out God's purposes for the world around them.

- *Administration* – Most groups, churches, and other organizations would be lost without people who possessed this spiritual gift. These people are empowered by God to use their special skills (management, financial, operations, physical labor, etc.) to benefit those around them. They many times not only use them in their vocation, they use them in non-profit or charitable service efforts within their community. God brings them to groups that have a desperate need for the very gift of administration that they possess through His sovereignty. In a church or ministry setting, these people many times take on roles as deacons. However, there are a multitude of vocational, non-profit, and community service applications within this gifting. In business, these people tend to be the glue that keeps organizations together administratively, managerially, and operationally. When this gift is fully leveraged, God helps create a passionate and willing heart to help meet the skill needs that exist with the groups around them. Simply put, He matches a person's unique skills with the need of others in a beautiful way.

Please note that people tend to have several of the above spiritual gifts, though in some cases people could have one that clearly is their ultimate spiritual gift. It is most advisable that people spend increased amounts of self-discovery and life energy towards learning about, and leveraging those primary gifts most. I also encourage people to put themselves in situations throughout life where they are asked to use their lesser gifts. It becomes a process in which they can become challenged and stretched. They also learn more about the fullness of God's character, and there is a sweet intimacy found in those moments. I have been fortunate to see it within my life. For example, evangelism is very low for me. However, I have traveled to countries where that gift was a massive need during my journey. I was left asking God to teach me more about that gift as I remained open to being out of my comfort zone in those teachable moments.

A Key to Spiritual Spurring

Before we close today, I wanted to share with you one key that I have found within life. It is essential to growing spiritually (and as a whole person) as you run down your dreams, and face the trials and tribulations of life. You need to understand that God's best for your life will not come from going it alone or feeling like you can reach a place of final spiritual maturity. You need to continue to surround yourself with others that help encourage you to grow spiritually. They many times could be older than you and bring maturity and wisdom. However, that isn't always the case. The bottom line is that surrounding yourself with people that consistently challenge and encourage you to be accountable to your convictions, while truly applying your spiritual faith to your life choices and actions is key.

Furthermore, it is a blessing and honor for me personally to be a part of groups that discourage complacency and are always focused on growing not only spiritually, but as a whole person for God's glory. This has been one of the greatest keys that has created a spiritual spurring for me to walk out what I know are God's purposes for my life (despite any fears or obstacles I am faced with). Friend, never doubt that understanding how God uniquely made you through better understanding your spiritual gifts will help give you greater clarity and pursue your dreams. Beyond that, if you learn how to align your unique abilities, passions, and spiritual gifts together, it will undoubtedly help you embrace a life full of ultimate purpose and meaning!

Point of Reflection or Action for Today:

Today I encourage you if you have not done this within the last two years, to take a *personal spiritual gifts inventory*. I believe it can help you better understand how God made you as a unique individual, made in His image. It can help unlock doors to live with greater clarity, confidence and deeper purpose. There are many that you can do on-line for free or nominal costs. You can also seek a pastor at a local church many times as well to take one and discuss your results. One free one I have recommended to many coaching clients is: http://www.churchgrowth.org/cgi-cg/gifts.cgi?intro=1

Epilogue

Every Season Has a Reason: Living a Life of Deep Purpose & Meaning

Friend, this book was written as an offering from my heart to help inspire you to live a life of deep purpose and meaning, while offering encouragement to run down your dreams in life no matter where you are at today. I not only want you to realize your dreams, I truly want God's best for your life. As we end our time together, I wanted to reinforce how every season in our life has a reason, even when we don't want to realize or believe it. I will leave you with one more aspect of my personal story that I call my Stage 2 Story.

I do so to encourage you to fully embrace a God-centered life mission, one that can truly alter your life path forever. I want to encourage you to remain hopeful and resilient in life, so you never stop dreaming! Each season in our life happens and is connected for a reason. Each one has a God-appointed purpose if we are open to embracing them. I find that embracing each season and our ultimate purposes in life, many times start by giving up your need for a sense of control in life to God. In doing so, you can give birth to a life of spectacular evolution, growing purpose, and meaning. God can take you places you never dreamed possible.

Reinventing Yourself by Planning a Bigger Future for Others, First

I have been blessed to have had the opportunity and courage (not to mention the support of some amazing people around me) to have launched several business ventures in my first dozen or so years as an entrepreneur. Like anyone, I have faced significant personal and professional adversity at times. And each time, I rebuilt my businesses or started a new one in response. However, you don't need to start a business to capture the essence of this message. Each person's dreams, life calling, and destiny are unique.

In dealing with adversity myself, I first look at the people around me and make it about how I can create a bigger future for the greatest number of people first (no matter what adversity I might be facing in life). I believe it important to always see your future and the future of those around you as being bigger than your past. No matter how bad the personal or professional challenge—be it financial struggles, relationship issues, or health issues—it is critical that you focus on how life could be better through your positive response. The proper response could lead you to new perspectives, insights, resources, or skills to be leveraged not only for yourself, but to bring about a better future for the world around you. There can be beauty within difficulties because of our response to these challenges. By focusing on ensuring a brighter future for those you care about most (including those you interact with in a work setting), you have the unique advantage as you go through the seasons of life by operating from an outwardly-focused foundation, instead of the sinking sands of selfishness that so many succumb to.

A Peek into God's Vision: My "Stage 2" Story

Without a doubt, one July 24th became one of the more significant days in my life and career. It was the day I first did a tool from The Strategic Coach® called "Stage 2 You." This simple yet powerful approach to looking at my future challenged me to write down the story of what my life would look like in three years on a specific date. I was given a limited amount of space in which this tool allowed me to write this story, so clarity of thought became precious as I wrote. There was a buzz in the air as roughly forty entrepreneurs from all over the country sat with me and wrote their own "Stage 2" stories.

My story became alive and real as I put pen to paper. I prayed and asked God to review with me what He saw. And as I wrote, it was like I couldn't write the story fast enough. My story was full of passions that laid dormant within me for years, including dreams of becoming a public speaker, author, business/life coach, spiritual ministry leader, and community mentor. However, at age thirty there was much that came to mind that wanted to stop my story dead in its tracks. Was I really old enough and qualified enough to become these very things? Wasn't I lacking additional degrees and certifications? Where was my gray hair to go with a reputation to handle dreams more wired for those perceived to be more seasoned than I? I also was a successful entrepreneur with so much already on my plate, so was the timing really right to step out in faith to run down these dreams?

My business and life coaching career through Live with Purpose Coaching, and this book (among other things), wouldn't exist today if it wasn't for this tool, and my faith to take action towards the dreams God placed within my heart that day. My passion for helping empower people to live a life of purpose through coaching, public speaking, writing, and helping the less fortunate, became crystallized in a tangible way that day. Since then it has truly been an amazing journey full of exciting twists and turns. The unknown future has become full of new dreams that seem to drop into my life like rain drops from heaven. Though I am a planner by nature, it has been great to grow more intimately connected to God through all of this, because I realize that I need to take each step following the leading of the Holy Spirit. True peace is found in following God with every fabric of your being, and asking for Him to guide you through your life. I have become clearer about what path God wants me to walk out, so my life is focused on the purposes and meaning that would align with His best for my life. I want to continue to dedicate my life passions and focus on helping others live a life of deep purpose and meaning. I want to inspire you and to make the unique contribution to the world that only you can make.

Wisdom for Implementing Your "Stage 2" Story

I am big on taking concepts and ideas and trying to distill them down to actionable items. Even though the tool named above is most helpful in taking the steps of planning, here are some additional items to consider if you want to take your first steps towards your own "Stage 2" story!

- Pick a location that stimulates you and unlocks your passion. Don't overlook how critical this is. It could be a secret outdoor location that is significant to you and/or your significant other. It could be an ideal, off-site location where you feel like you can have a personal retreat. It could also be an out of the way café that is simple but effective in its ability to stimulate your thinking.

- Here are some other insights to consider as you take your first steps in crafting your story:

  - Always make sure your contribution to the world is greater than your reward as you pursue your dreams.

  - Always envision your future as bigger than your past. This becomes the fuel for running down dreams.

  - You will live a life of greater purpose and meaning, when you focus first on how your dreams can create a bigger future for others.

- Here is a great quote and a powerful line of Scripture from the word of God that have both challenged and encouraged me as it relates to these processes:

  - "Many of life's failures are people who do not realize how close they were to success when they gave up." —Thomas Edison

  - " 'For I know the plans I have for you,' declares the LORD, 'plans to prosper you and not to harm you, plans to give you hope and a future.' Jeremiah 29:11 (NIV)

Inspiring Dreams Around the Globe: Pay It Forward...

I have enjoyed walking with you through these forty days and sharing from my heart and the hearts of those I interviewed. If you have enjoyed this book, and feel it has helped you better understand your dreams (including the pursuit of them) or your purpose in life, then I want to encourage you to pay it forward! I encourage you to share this book with those you care about. Ten percent of the proceeds from the sale of this book go to fueling the dreams of the less fortunate throughout the world though Hope International (www.hopeinternational.org). The donations will be used to fund micro-financing loans, so people can pursue their dreams within third world nations. They many times need so little to have an opportunity to take action on their dreams, friend. I hope we can partner together in helping spur on others to run after their dreams!

If you ever have any questions or want further information on any of the stories or concepts shared within this book, it would be my privilege to try and help get you more information. I am also available to speak to groups within your community whom might want to explore these themes about pursuing dreams and living a life of deep purpose. Feel free to visit: www.livewithpurposecoaching.com, and www.runningdownyourdreams. com or to e-mail me personally at: joe@livewithpurposecoaching.com.

My Prayer for YOU:

I want to leave you today with a prayer that is focused on your dreams and my prayer for you to live a life full of great meaning and purpose! God gets all of the credit for my story and everything within this book, honestly. I have found that God loves to share His dreams for our lives as we become more willing to receive them. I now understand that He is the ultimate author of all of my current dreams (and those yet realized). He brought me together with amazing people so I could share their stories with you. He has blessed my unique talents and gifted people all around me that have helped this life project become realized now for your benefit. He continues to take me through a life full of trials and unique opportunities, and they have become the foundation for my passion of helping people run down their dreams in life. Dreams are best created, realized, and pursued recognizing that God is your ultimate author of life and by seeking the guidance of the Holy Spirit each day. Ambition in life is great; however, a growing relationship with God and a willingness to follow Him is far greater!

Heavenly father, you know the reader of this book intimately. You know the fullness of each of their dreams and the true desires of their heart. You know any fears, struggles, shortcomings, faulty thinking, and misunderstandings about who you are that they might have. Let us not ever forget how You are the creator of love itself. We thank You because we know that we are your beloved. I praise You for the love that you have for this reader God. You know them better than they will ever know themselves. We were created in Your image God, and you see each of us as precious. We know that Your dreams for the reader of this book are far greater than anything they can ever dream up on their own. We thank you for that.

My prayer for them is that their heart and mind shift in a profound way, so that one dream becomes their greatest dream of all. That dream is: Loving you God with all their heart, soul, mind and strength as you have encouraged us in Matthew 22:37-38. It has the power to unlock their life of deep purpose and meaning like no other.

I pray Jesus that you would help them to understand the depths of what You did on the cross to the pay the penalty for their sins, so they could be made right in the sight of God, and be purified from all unrighteousness in their lives. Help them to know Your desire to be their best friend (one that will be with them through all things and will never leave them). Help them to know the depths of Your love for them. Help them to know how much Your heart breaks when You see any of Your children not accept Your love and Your free gift of salvation through the Holy Spirit. Come Holy Spirit—come! Move through this person like never before and rock their world forever. Shake up their dreams, alter their life path and give them the ability to see what You see for them through Your empowerment!

I pray that you would help them to understand that You groan on their behalf and bring the cries of their heart before the throne room of our heavenly father. Help them to know the intimacy of Your desire to walk with them throughout each of their dreams in life. Show them Your vision for their lives. Show them the fullness of who You are, and who You made them to be before the world began. Show them that You love them unconditionally. Show them that they can come to You just as they are today. Help them to realize You simply desire their love, and desire they know You more in response to the love You have for them. Help them to seek You today like never before. If anything in their heart stands in the way before You this very day Lord, please remove it so they might fall in love with You today. Help them to ask You to be the author of the rest of their dreams and to the guide them through the remaining days within their life that You bless them with. Amen.

Something I always try to be mindful of is that tomorrow is never guaranteed. With the limited time you have left in life, it is essential you understand how a personal relationship with Jesus Christ is the most critical element to living your life with the greatest meaning and purpose. Many people believe that there are many paths that lead to heaven. Unless you believe that the Bible is false and not the word of God, or you believe Jesus Christ was a mad man, then his words speak powerfully like no other in John 14:6: "Jesus answered, I am the way and the truth and the life. No one comes to the Father except through me."

If you have not yet taken that step of faith, perhaps today is your day. Don't let any baggage you have stop you from believing that Jesus would desire to be your best friend. If you never have prayed to Jesus and asked Him to receive you into God's family, I pray that you would go to a secret place today and with whatever words come from your inmost being offer them up to Him. He will accept you, friend! I have no doubt of that. If you have already made this life changing commitment, then my encouragement to you is to ask Jesus to reveal more of Himself, His purpose for your life and His dreams for your life through the leading of the Holy Spirit!

Perhaps today is the day that God shows you His dreams for your life and how they truly are far greater than any you could muster on your own (like He has done for me)? **Only you can choose your #1 dream, so I pray you choose wisely.**

37. The Guy that Called People "Bible Chuckers"

- Finding a church that rocks your previous understanding of what a church is, can change your life and give birth to amazing new dreams.

- God is in the business of helping us become humble, by taking our lack of spiritual understanding, doubts, fears, weaknesses, and opposition to religion and using them for His ultimate glory and purposes.

38. When is this God Phase Going to End?

- If you want to spend your life growing spiritually while growing closer to God, you need to be willing to face a world full of opposition many times from those that know you best.

- A true personal relationship with God is full of growth and intimacy, and something that never has an end.

39. Coming to Terms with Your Spiritual Gifting

- Understanding how God uniquely made you through the understanding of your spiritual gifts, will give you greater clarity to pursue your dreams.

- Learning how to link your unique abilities and spiritual gifts together, will help you embrace a life of ultimate purpose and meaning.

40. Epilogue: Every Season Has a Reason: Living a Life of Purpose

- Each season in our life happens and is connected for a reason. Each one has a God- appointed purpose if we are open to embracing them.

- Giving up your need for a sense of control in life to God can give birth to a life of spectacular evolution, growing purpose, and meaning. God can take you places you never dreamed possible.

- Tomorrow is never guaranteed. With the limited time you have left in life, it is essential you understand how a personal relationship with Jesus Christ is the most critical element to living your life with the greatest meaning and purpose.

(DAY 40) Running Down Your Dreams—Taking Action!

Congratulations for completing the forty day journey with me, friend! I wanted to leave you with some questions. **What are your answers to these questions?** I encourage you to journal your answers below and reflect on them.

1) What will happen to you the moment you take your last breath of life? Are you truly ok with that answer?

2) Why do you believe you are still alive today when others perhaps even younger or more healthy than you are not?

3) Can you explain how the miracle of child birth is possible?

4) Why do you feel young children from birth are capable of showing their parent's disrespect and being selfish even if their parents did not model that for them?

5) Have you ever thought of things, or have taken action on things you know in your heart are wrong, and you have kept them a secret from everyone? Have you ever talked to God about them?

6) Have you visited a church within the last year of your life? If you have never found a place you felt at home at, do you truly believe no place exists that would be a good fit for you?

I welcome hearing from you personally if you want to discuss any of these questions, or have any questions from the 40-day journey of this book that you just read. You can reach me personally at: joe@livewithpurposecoaching.com.

(DAY 40) Running Down Your Dreams—Taking Action!

7) Have you ever read the entire Bible? If not, does it seem fair to judge its validity and standing of 2,000+ years?

8) Do you have questions that you can't find answers to in life? Have you asked God about them?

9) What do you believe your ultimate purpose is in life? Do you have a dream so big it scares you? If so, what is holding you back from taking action?

For more free resources to help encourage you in your pursuit of dreams found through the gift of the Holy Spirit, please visit: www.livewithpurposecoaching.com.

Works Cited

Batterson, Mark. *In a Pit on a Snowy Day*. Colorado Springs: Multnomah, 2006. Print.

Chapman, Gary. *www.5lovelanguages.com*. The 5 Love Languages. n.d. Web. 15 Aug. 2011.

Cornell, Pastor Steve. *www.thinkpoint.wordpress.com*. n.d. Web. 15 Aug. 2011.

Cornell, Pastor Steve. "Bad Things Happen." *www.thinkpoint. wordpress.com*. 27 March 2007. Web. 15 Aug. 2011.

Cornell, Pastor Steve. "Does God Control the Weather?" *www. thinkpoint.wordpress.com*. 1 Sept. 2008. Web. 15 Aug. 2011.

Dermatomyositis. *www.bettermedicine.com*. Better Medicine. n.d. Web. 15 Aug. 2011..

Eggrichs, Dr. Emerson. *www.loveandrespect.com*. Love & Respect. n.d. Web. 15 Aug. 2011.

"Giving and Tithing."*www.emmanuelypsi.org*. Emmanuel Lutheran Church. n.d. Web. 15 Aug. 2011.

Kuo, David. "Rick Warren's Second Reformation." *www.belief.com*. n.d. DATE OF RESOURCE CREATION. Web. 15 Aug. 2011.

"Questions of Faith and Doubt: Why Does God Let Bad Things Happen in the World?". *www.explorefaith.org*. n.d. Web. 15 Aug. 2011.

"Why Does God Allow Bad Things to Happen to Good People?". *www.gotquestions.org*. n.d. Web. 15 Aug. 2011.

The Author's Back-Story

A Glimpse into My Eighteen-Year Factor

I'd like to share some of my back-story with you. Everyone has a unique upbringing. The first eighteen years of my life were no different. Many people have experienced a greatly improved or perhaps worse upbringing than I, there is no doubting that. However, I seek to share my back-story with you today, in hopes that something within it might connect with your inner-self and benefit your future (as you walk forward in life).

I should mention some of the background for my home environment and family unit first. My father was physically disabled. He was what they used to call a "blue baby" back in WWII times. He was partially paralyzed on his one side. He also never passed the tenth grade in regards to education. He was a hard-worker who worked the night shift most of his life. He was arguably a workaholic, who did whatever it took to put food on the table (including utilizing the food stamps program and being a janitor for the last twenty-five years or so of his life). My mother has been affected by her mental illness. She is now classified as someone with the schizo-affective disorder (a bi-polar, multiple personality disorder). She was in and out of mental institutions throughout her life.

Growing up, I faced all sorts of what I call non-typical adversity: poverty, emotional abuse, physical abuse, and sexual abuse, just to name a few. They were certainly massive hurdles for a young man to jump over, while continuing on the track in a straight path. My brother and I should have become drug dealers, criminals, addicts, or some worse combination. However, we both by God's grace and mercy were able to move on living productive adult lives. To get a full picture of my back-story, you truly need to understand my testimony.

My Testimony

BEFORE - I considered myself as one who believed in the existence of God. I considered myself "spiritual." For example, I used to pound my chest and double pump to the sky when good things happened. I found myself thinking about how so many things happened in this amazing planet and how no man or act of science could really explain it all. I didn't go to church frequently because I bought into the "negative stigmas" that our society unfortunately attaches to attending a church. I think I have always been a "rugged individualist" and found myself living my life that fought conformity. In this case, I was fighting conforming to love our God and spend time with people that felt the same way. Looking back now, I see things differently. I was living selfishly, and truly had my back turned away from Him during my day-to-day actions even though He loved me.

Despite the seemingly positive character traits or accolades that I could receive from those that knew me best, I was confident that they could also see some of my struggles with temptation and sin. More importantly, I knew I that I was not living to my fullest potential. I have been blessed with what I think is a high level of success at an early age, and I thought I got there most of all by my determination, commitment, and effort while I tried to continue to build my own deeper purpose for my life path (though I never seemed to get there and feel completely clear about it). I could have been described up until recently as a guy that tried to plan everything and control way too much, without realizing it. We also all have personal battles and struggle with them in our own ways. Though I might have felt capable of much, I knew that I needed help. I felt as if I was walking through life with one bad eye, while remaining too stubborn to stop to get glasses so I could really see the steps I was taking in my life.

CONVERSION - On a trip to Cancun I was reading a book called The Purpose Driven Life. I realized that the way I was living my life had to change. I reflected and spoke to God as I looked at some of the most amazing clear waters in the world. I began asking him to forgive me, and teach me how to become the man I knew He had planned me to be. On November 25, 2004 I made a contract with God to commit myself to living a life that honored Him, I then began "my walk of faith."

For months, I had an overwhelming voice I that wouldn't leave me. It was one that was nudging me to explore and connect with a local church. I began yet again a very planned and organized strategic process to do so because of how I am wired. I eventually found my home with a great group of people. I admired, respected and found inspiration from a group of elders that know the Word of God very well. They live as great examples for us all.

God changed everything and made me realize how little we really can control, how silly it is when we try to do so, and how much more it makes sense to put our trust in our creator. I can't say that I really can give one person or event the full credit for how I found Jesus, and began to walk with Him on his path He had charted for me. However, I will do my best to share with you some of what I do know. I believe He used the death of my father to teach me how precious life truly is, as well as where I was falling short in living my life the best way I could. My father's death became as important to me as his life. God has continued to use my dad as a teacher in my life. His short battle of one month with cancer before he was taken from earth, reinforced to me that we can and should not live our lives as if tomorrow if guaranteed, because it simply is not.

I was very fortunate to be blessed by others in unexpected ways. My father's death brought my Uncle Bill and Aunt Gail back in my life, and a trip several years prior brought me together with my great friend Steve Charman, who lives across the globe in Australia. My grandmother has also shown me how to do what 1st Corinthians 16:14 states: "Do everything in love." Even in her 90s, she has never been stronger in her faith or a better model of how to live for Christ. They have all become spiritual rocks and teachers that helped guide me to find my eye doctor that is God.

AFTER - Now I find myself extremely passionate about growing in my understanding of the Bible so I can better understand God's purpose for my life. I relish the opportunities to come together and serve others in honor of Jesus Christ . I believe I can understand anyone that has not yet found the Lord, nor accepted Jesus as their personal savior, because I spent about twenty-six years of my life there. If you bear with me, I would like to mention a great analogy I heard. We find ourselves all walking upstream through all the days we have on the earth. The water becomes more challenging and dangerous the further upstream we go. However, if you realize that you are not the only one in the water walking, if you realize where you are going, who made the stream and why it exists, all you can do is smile that you are actually in the water. That sense of inner peace is giving me undying strength to live by faith, so I can continue the walk forward every day even when my legs are weak and life is difficult.

My hope is I will be able to develop the abilities God has blessed me with, so I can to love all those in my life for His glory. I am excited because I now face temptation and sin with a sense of real hope. I am striving to follow Jesus and simply allow those I meet while on earth to see His love for them through me, based on how I live my life each day so I might inspire or encourage others to find their faith like others have done for me. If I do that, I believe I will realize I did the best I could in my final hour, and my hope is that I can look up that day and see in some small way that I made God smile.

God's Sovereignty Continuing to Unfold Beyond My Back-Story

I have been blessed to have a dynamic life path and career to date that has included starting and running a multitude of businesses, and traveling around the world for a diverse set of purposes, including global missionary work. My story now continues to evolve through the leading of the Holy Spirit to take me into newer, additional roles as a business/life coach for other entrepreneurs and leaders, as well as roles as an author and speaker. Though I feel extremely clear about God's calling and purposes for my life today, I am confident that there is much about God's plans that are yet to be revealed. I trust He will continue to show me more of His beautiful purposes for my life, as He continues to reveal the powerful reasons beyond my back-story (as God continues to use it for His glory)!

So what is your back-story? Do you feel you have one? If so, I'd love to hear about it. Feel free to contact me at joe@livewithpurposecoaching.com and share it with me...

About the Author: Joseph Sharp

As a twenty-something college student, Joseph Sharp had little idea of the entrepreneurial success he would be blessed with over the next decade, or of the spiritual transformation he would experience. Nor did he have any inkling how this success in business would evolve into a passion for helping others find their purpose in life.

Since founding Sharp Innovations in 1999, Joe has been blessed to work with professionals in a wide range of industries. He has coached clients who own companies of various sizes and specialties since 2008. He is an expert in helping people pursue their dreams, while living a life of deep purpose and meaning as a life/business coach through (www.livewithpurposecoaching.com). This drive to empower others to use their God-given spiritual gifts and unique abilities comes directly from **1 Peter 4:10**: *"Each one should use whatever gift he has received to serve others, faithfully administering God's grace in its various forms."*

As an advocate for the Sandler Sales Process and a Master Graduate of The Strategic Coach, Joe has had access to a wealth of business tools and interaction with dozens upon dozens of successful entrepreneurs from all over the country. This unique combination of real-world experience and extensive business training has allowed Joe to help other entrepreneurs achieve better balance in their personal lives, with their families and with their businesses, as he strives to become the man that he believes God is fashioning him to be.

Much of Joe's business acumen can be traced back to experiences founding and managing his Internet marketing and development firm, Sharp Innovations, Inc. (www.sharpinnovations.com). Not content with a "business as usual" approach, Joe pioneered the creation of a proprietary, multi-step process to guide his clients From Concept to Solution™ .

This program has been integral to the launch of hundreds of websites over more than a decade. Joe's success in helping businesses solve creative, marketing and technology problems is demonstrated every day through the performance of Sharp Innovations.

Joe directs the sales, marketing and overall strategic/project direction for Sharp Innovations, and works closely with all new clients to ensure their communications and business objectives are met. While serving his clients is job #1, Joe strives for a life of balance that allows him to be a source of encouragement and inspiration to all of those with whom he makes contact. His spiritual faith is extremely important to him, and he attributes his strong faith in God as the driving force for his professional and personal achievements.

Over the last decade, Joe has been an owner or partner in numerous other business ventures, ranging from advertising to nutritional products to dating services to real estate. By continually seeking new opportunities and new ways of thinking, Joe is able to bring an open-minded perspective and valuable, real-world experience to the clients with whom he consults. Having demonstrated success in his endeavors, Joe was awarded a Central Penn Business Journal "Forty Under 40" award in 2003, and has contributed to numerous regional television, newspaper and radio programs.

Joe is a graduate of Millersville University, but considers himself a lifelong learner. He currently resides in Lancaster County, PA, and enjoys athletics, coaching, leadership activities, writing, creative projects, outdoor activities, and music. Joe volunteers for various local community service organizations, as well as his local church, Millersville Bible Church. He seeks to continue participating in missions work on a global scale, and encourages others to do the same.

Joseph Sharp

Business and Life Coach – www.livewithpurposecoaching.com
CEO – www.sharpinnovations.com

"It is my passionate desire to help people overcome challenges by developing solutions that inspire continual progress toward a life of deep-seated meaning and purpose."

For more resources on putting your dreams into action, visit:
www.runningdownyourdreams.com

23072792R00176

Made in the USA
Middletown, DE
16 August 2015